Civic Contestation in Global Education

AF066878

ALSO AVAILABLE FROM BLOOMSBURY

Educational Equity in a Global Context: Cases and Conversations in Educational Ethics, edited by Meira Levinson, Tatiana Geron, Sara O'Brien and Ellis Reid

Pedagogy of Hope for Global Social Justice: Sustainable Futures for People and the Planet, edited by Douglas Bourn and Massimiliano Tarozzi

Comparative and International Education, David Phillips and Michele Schweisfurth

Education and International Development, edited by Tristan McCowan and Elaine Unterhalter

Peace Education, edited by Maria Hantzopoulos and Monisha Bajaj

Schooling for Social Change, Monisha Bajaj

Transnational Perspectives on Democracy, Citizenship, Human Rights and Peace Education, edited by Mary Drinkwater, Fazal Rizvi, and Karen Edge

Civic Contestation in Global Education

Cases and Conversations in Educational Ethics

Edited by Meira Levinson,
Ellis Reid, Sara O'Brien, and
Tatiana Geron

BLOOMSBURY ACADEMIC
LONDON • NEW YORK • OXFORD • NEW DELHI • SYDNEY

BLOOMSBURY ACADEMIC
Bloomsbury Publishing Plc
50 Bedford Square, London, WC1B 3DP, UK
1385 Broadway, New York, NY 10018, USA
29 Earlsfort Terrace, Dublin 2, Ireland

BLOOMSBURY, BLOOMSBURY ACADEMIC and the Diana logo
are trademarks of Bloomsbury Publishing Plc

First published in Great Britain 2025

Copyright © Meira Levinson, Ellis Reid, Sara O'Brien, and Tatiana Geron, 2025

Meira Levinson, Ellis Reid, Sara O'Brien, and Tatiana Geron have asserted
their right under the Copyright, Designs and Patents Act, 1988,
to be identified as Editors of this work.

For legal purposes the Acknowledgments on pp. xi–xii constitute
an extension of this copyright page.

Cover design by Grace Ridge
Cover image © by Ruhey / Getty Images

All rights reserved. No part of this publication may be reproduced or
transmitted in any form or by any means, electronic or mechanical,
including photocopying, recording, or any information storage or retrieval
system, without prior permission in writing from the publishers.

Bloomsbury Publishing Plc does not have any control over, or responsibility for,
any third-party websites referred to or in this book. All internet addresses given
in this book were correct at the time of going to press. The author and publisher
regret any inconvenience caused if addresses have changed or sites have
ceased to exist, but can accept no responsibility for any such changes.

A catalogue record for this book is available from the British Library.

A catalog record for this book is available from the Library of Congress.

ISBN: HB: 978-1-3503-9950-1
       PB: 978-1-3503-9949-5
       ePDF: 978-1-3503-9951-8
       eBook: 978-1-3503-9952-5

Typeset by Integra Software Services Pvt. Ltd.
Printed and bound in Great Britain

To find out more about our authors and books visit www.bloomsbury.com
and sign up for our newsletters.

Contents

List of Contributors viii
Acknowledgments xi

1 **Schools as Democratic Spaces in Fragile Democracies** 1
   Author: Ellis Reid, Meira Levinson, Sara O'Brien, and Tatiana Geron

2 **A Parallel Universe: Conspiracy Theories and the Limits of Education** 13
   Case author: Johannes Drerup
   Conversation facilitator: Johannes Drerup and Sara O'Brien
   Conversation participants: Greta Fexer, Kai Horsthemke, Nikki Spencer, and Anna Zentis

3 **Feeling Exposed in Online Class: Student and Teacher Safety in the Online Civics Classroom** 31
   Case author: Isolde de Groot, Yaël Weening, and Sara O'Brien
   Conversation facilitator: Isolde de Groot
   Conversation participants: Belinda Kleijweg, Clemijn Schreuder, Susan Sants, and Bjorn Wansink

4 **High School at the Coal-Face: The Cost of Getting "What We're Owed"** 49
   Case author: Sarah Gurr and Daniella J. Forster
   Conversation facilitator: Daniella J. Forster
   Conversation participants: James Ladwig, Kristy Pascoe, Lawrence Perry, and Anne Marie Ross

5 Photo Bomb: Responding to Online Transgressions 71

Case author: Ana Romero-Iribas and María Almudena Santaella Vallejo
Conversation facilitator: Ana Romero-Iribas
Conversation participants: Consuelo Martínez-Priego, Carlos-María Alcover, Helena Regojo Bacardí, and Carmen Perdices González

6 Taking the Action Out of Civics?: Polarized Debates over Civic Education 91

Case author: Sara O'Brien and Meira Levinson
Conversation facilitator: Meira Levinson
Conversation participants: Debbie Holecko, Robert Pondiscio, Fernando M. Reimers, and Andrew Wilkes

7 Course Correction: Teaching Critical Consciousness in an Anti-CRT State 115

Case author: Yonas Michael, Nicolas Tanchuk, and Sara O'Brien
Conversation facilitator: Sara O'Brien
Conversation participants: Rebecca Horwitz-Willis, Buddy Boren North, Daniel D. Spikes, and Chloé Valdary

8 No Laughing Matter: Can Showing Religiously Sensitive Cartoons in the Classroom Ever Be Justified? 135

Case author: Janet Orchard, Waqar Ahmedi, and Sara O'Brien
Conversation facilitator: Janet Orchard and Sara O'Brien
Conversation participants: Sally Elton-Chalcraft, David Kerr, and Shammi Rahman

9 Faith in Mr. D.: Accommodating Religion in Schools 155

Case author: Lauren Bialystok
Conversation facilitator: Lauren Bialystok
Conversation participants: Philippa Carter, Allysa Khan, Kevin McDonough, Rebecca L. Starkman, and Rizwan Mohammad

10 Conclusion: Expanding the Conversation 175
Author: Sara O'Brien, Meira Levinson, Ellis Reid, and Tatiana Geron

Appendix 189
Bibliography 193
Index 197

Contributors

Waqar Ahmad Ahmedi is Head of Religious Studies and an executive member of the National Association of Teachers of Religious Education (NATRE) in the UK. He is the author of a number of student textbooks and revision guides at GCSE and A-level. Waqar leads training and is a regular speaker at conferences about Islam.

Lauren Bialystok holds a PhD in Philosophy and works at the intersection of philosophy and education. She has published on authenticity and identity, liberalism and education, curriculum policy, high school philosophy, and sex education. She is co-author, with Lisa Andersen, of *Touchy Subject: The History and Philosophy of Sex Education* (2022).

Isolde de Groot, PhD, is Assistant Professor at the Department of Education, University of Humanistic Studies, the Netherlands. Her research interests are in education for democracy and meaningful education. Her current projects examine teacher disclosure, teaching controversial issues discussions, political efficacy of vocational students, civic purpose of higher education students, and rituals in schools.

Johannes Drerup is Professor of Philosophy of Education and Educational Theory at TU Dortmund University, Germany, as well as guest professor at VU Amsterdam, the Netherlands. His research interests include philosophy of education, philosophy of childhood, educational ethics, and moral and democratic education.

Daniella J. Forster (PhD) is an educational ethicist with expertise in codes of conduct and ethics and a background in philosophy. Her research interests include school moral culture, moral development, and teacher professional identity and she has published on controversial issues of policy use in schools, the use of codes of conduct and normative case studies in teacher education, and other ethical dimensions of schooling. She taught secondary school philosophy and English prior to becoming an educational researcher and teacher educator.

Tatiana Geron is the Design Studio Research & Evaluation Postdoctoral Fellow at the Edmond & Lily Safra Center for Ethics at Harvard University, USA. Tatiana holds a PhD in Education from Harvard and studies the ethical complexity of teacher decision-making and how teachers interpret their core values in relation to unjust social contexts. Prior to entering academia, Tatiana taught middle school English Language Arts in Boston and Brooklyn.

Sarah Gurr (PhD) is Lecturer of Literacy and English Education in the School of Education at Charles Sturt University, Australia. Her doctoral research explored ethical, normative, and epistemic tensions in environmental and sustainability education and translates these to Australian educational policy and fossil fuel community contexts. Sarah is a qualified English and History teacher and currently teaches educational philosophy and ethics to teacher education students.

Meira Levinson is the Juliana W. and William Foss Thompson Professor of Education and Society at Harvard University, USA. She has written, coauthored, and co-edited seven books, including *Dilemmas of Educational Ethics*, *Democratic Discord in Schools*, and *No Citizen Left Behind*, and is currently working to start a field of educational ethics.

Yonas Michael is a middle school principal with over fifteen years of service in public education. He is completing his doctoral studies at Iowa State University, USA.

Sara O'Brien is the Director of Curriculum and Pedagogy for the EdEthics initiative, which is housed at the Harvard Graduate School of Education, USA, and the Edmond & Lily Safra Center for Ethics. In this role, she creates pedagogical tools that help educators, school and district leaders, and policy makers think through challenging ethical questions in education. Prior to her work with EdEthics, Sara taught in public and independent secondary schools in Massachusetts and California.

Janet Orchard is the Director of Post-Graduate Research at the School of Education, University of Bristol, UK, and an Associate Professor. Her research seeks to extend opportunities for ethical reflection in teacher education, given their relative absence from current provision. With colleagues, she has promoted alternative provision through a series of related interventions, including Shared Space, Going Global, and P4T or "Philosophy for Teachers."

Ellis Reid holds a PhD in Education from Harvard University, USA, and is currently an Associate Program Officer at The Spencer Foundation. His primary areas of scholarship lie in democratic theory, practical ethics, and education policy. In particular, his work focuses on the normative dimensions of school governance. Ellis has served as an Ethics Pedagogy Fellow at the Edmond and Lily Safra Center for Ethics and as the Co-Chair for the Editorial Board of the Harvard Educational Review. Before coming to Harvard, Ellis was the Associate Director for Next Generation Scholars, a college-access program in Northern California.

Ana Romero-Iribas is Associate Professor at the Universidad Rey Juan Carlos, Madrid, Spain. A philosopher working in educational ethics and friendship studies, she was Fulbright Visiting Scholar at Harvard University in 2022, and previously a Visiting Scholar at Harvard University in 2018 and at the University of Leeds in 2015.

Almudena Santaella Vallejo is Professor of Graduate and Postgraduate Education at the Universidad Rey Juan Carlos, Madrid, Spain. She focuses on teaching at the secondary level in education for citizenship and human rights. She graduated in law from the UCM, Spain and holds a PhD in Philosophy of Law.

Nicolas Tanchuk researches the intersection between educational, political, and ethical values. He is especially interested in how equitable access to education across the lifespan might form a basis for democratic theory and economic life.

Yaël Weening is a PhD candidate at the Amsterdam University of Applied Sciences, the Netherlands, where she studies discussions of controversial issues in the classroom. She is a former citizenship teacher and researcher at the research institute (Practoraat "Research Lab") of mboRijnland.

Acknowledgments

In addition to the many contributors whose work and ideas make up this volume, there are a number of people and organizations who supported this project without whom this book would never have been finished. First, we'd like to thank Jacob Fay for his essential and long-time support not only in helping to create the EdEthics initiative but also for his specific support in conceiving of, developing, and running the workshop that launched this volume—"Ethical Dilemmas of Educating during the COVID Crisis: An International Workshop on Normative Case Study Development." We'd also like to thank the Writing Fellows who helped us to put on this workshop and whose insight was vital to its success—Alysha Banerji and MG Prezioso. And, of course, we'd also like to thank the Harvard Radcliffe Institute and its staff for providing the financial and in-kind support that enabled this workshop in the first place, especially Amy Montilli, Maura Madden, and Sean O'Donnell.

In addition to the many people who helped in developing the "International Workshop on Normative Case Study Development," we'd like to thank the people who helped us to pull this volume together. At Bloomsbury Publishing, we'd like to thank Michael Hand for his support for this work. We'd also like to thank Mark Richardson, who has been a joy to work with and an important advocate. Additionally, we want to acknowledge and thank Maricruz Vargas Ramirez for translation help and Caroline Bossong for editorial support.

Finally, we'd like to thank the many members of the EdEthics community worldwide whose support and consistent enthusiasm have been indispensable. Thank you to Liz Block for her tireless work across the full range of EdEthics projects. Thank you to the participants of the 2022 Association for Moral Education conference in Manchester, UK, for engaging in discussion of some of the cases published in this volume as they were still being developed. Thank you to Russ Cox, our unofficial and often invaluable IT support. Thank you to the team at the Ethical Schools podcast for helping put together and recording our conversation about "Taking the Action Out of Civics?" Thank you to the many regular participants of our monthly normative case study discussions for your willingness to engage in discussions of new and developing case studies and for your incisive feedback about how to make these cases stronger. And, last but not least, thank you to the many discussion participants whose voices and reflections are captured in the conversations represented here—both for freely giving your time and for providing meaningful and important insight into these eight normative case studies.

1

Schools as Democratic Spaces in Fragile Democracies

Ellis Reid, Meira Levinson, Sara O'Brien, and Tatiana Geron

Democracies across the globe face a multitude of threats. Populist movements, intensifying sectarianism, and rising polarization threaten to transform the civic cultures of many countries into an unending battle between "us" and "them."[1] New technologies allow disinformation and conspiracy theories to spread faster and to larger audiences, further challenging the ability of those with opposing views or social positions to ever find common ground. At the same time, both state and private technological surveillance capabilities continue to grow, shifting and threatening traditional norms of privacy, free speech, and even free thought.[2] Refugee crises caused by war, climate change, and other catastrophes test countries' commitments to pluralism, human rights, and to sustaining a thriving, multiethnic democracy.[3] These are not abstract threats. Rather, they find their ways into our daily interactions in those places where we encounter diverse others. Schools are one of those places.

This book brings together eight normative case studies and accompanying conversations exploring these and other challenges at the classroom, school, and district levels. In light of the global reach of these challenges, these eight cases focus on a range of national contexts—the United States, the Netherlands, Germany, Spain, Australia, Canada, and England. Each fictional but empirically based case explores ethical dilemmas that arise in trying to provide robust civic education in a divided democratic society. Because these challenges can themselves be hard for citizens and stakeholders to discuss in a productive way, each case is followed by a model conversation among diverse participants, including scholars, activists, teachers, religious leaders, lawyers, and students from across the political spectrum. Each conversation is facilitated to enable points of both convergence and divergence to come to light and to model how thoughtful, well-intentioned people from a variety of backgrounds can productively discuss ethical and civic dilemmas across lines of difference. Together, these cases and conversations prompt readers to consider how the walls of the school are porous and how the threats facing democracy threaten the critical civic work of educators, too.

Normative Case Studies and Educational Ethics in a Global Context

While we can't shore up our democracies through education alone, we believe that one important way we can protect democratic stability and vitality is by ensuring that young people receive the civic education they need to become full participating members of their society and of our increasingly interconnected global community. Guaranteeing all young people the conditions necessary for robust civic learning demands that we—educators, policymakers, academics, activists, parents, students, citizens—face up to the ethical challenges that make civic education both particularly important and particularly difficult to do well in our divided times.

The normative case studies and accompanying conversations collected here are at the heart of an effort aimed at mapping the complex ethical terrain civic educators must navigate today. Following Meira Levinson—one of the editors of this volume—and Jacob Fay, we define normative case studies as *"richly described, realistic accounts of complex ethical dilemmas that arise within practice or policy contexts, in which protagonists must decide among courses of action, none of which is self-evident as the right one to take."*[4] Normative case studies aim to represent hard ethical choices actually facing education professionals across both practice and policy in order to provide complex but comprehensible starting points for discussion, scholarship, and action from varied perspectives. The accompanying model conversations partly answer this call, pulling together diverse groups of scholars and practitioners to discuss the ethical and practical challenges raised by these normative case studies.

Ultimately, the cases and conversations in this volume are at the heart of an approach to ethical inquiry that is *engaged, interdisciplinary,* and *collaborative. Engaged* ethical inquiry starts from the problems actually facing education professionals and seeks to understand the values, interests, and challenges as they're understood on the ground. Wisdom from the field can help us to understand the possible courses of action available within a particular case study and identify the various constraints that make some courses of action more feasible and others less so. We will also do a better job of identifying and reflecting on the interests and values relevant to a given case if we know how these values and interests are understood by those actually affected by the decision(s) at hand.

Our approach to ethical inquiry is also *interdisciplinary*. Making progress on the ethical dilemmas described in this volume relies not only on careful attention to the actual contexts in which these dilemmas arise but also to insights spanning a range of disciplines both empirical and normative. As is true of wisdom from the field, empirical insights from a variety of disciplinary perspectives can help us to assess the feasibility of different courses of action as well as their possible unintended consequences. Drawing on the insights from scholars from a variety of disciplinary backgrounds can also help us to clarify the ethical stakes of a particular situation.

Finally, our approach to ethical inquiry is *collaborative*. The preceding discussion of interdisciplinarity already contains one aspect of the kind of collaboration we have in mind—our approach demands engaging with a diversity of scholars across traditional disciplinary boundaries. Our approach is collaborative in a second sense, too. While normative case studies are not neutral, neither are they written to settle ethical questions. Rather, we write normative case studies to be discussed and debated because we believe in the importance of shared inquiry among differently situated individuals to moral progress. While discussion and debate don't lead in a straight line to progress on ethical questions, we do believe that collaboration across the borders between theory and practice and between the various disciplines is vital to realizing educational justice.

Collaboration is particularly critical to this volume, building on previous efforts to grow the field of educational ethics internationally. In *Democratic Discord in Schools*, the last collection of normative case studies edited and partly written by members of our editorial team, we intentionally solicited case commentaries from scholars and practitioners outside of the United States in order to explore how the ethical issues raised in our US-based cases resonate across political borders. Hailing from a wide range of national contexts—including Mexico, South Korea, Singapore, Australia, Germany, the Netherlands, and the UK—the assembled commentators surfaced both differences and similarities in the ethical challenges facing educators under conditions of democratic discord.

To build on these international collaborations, we convened a workshop in 2021 through the Harvard Radcliffe Institute that brought together fifteen scholars from around the world interested in producing normative case studies. Our primary aim was to pair our expertise in producing case studies with other international scholars' knowledge of their own contexts and the dilemmas facing civic educators. The discussions that began in that workshop formed the basis for this volume. In our work together, we found the ethical issues that came up revolved around two main themes—the meanings of educational (in)equity and the challenges of civic education in divided times. Ultimately, our group created sixteen cases, which we have decided to publish in two volumes centered on equity and civic education respectively.

Civic Contestation in Global Education: Cases and Conversations in Educational Ethics represents the first of these two volumes. It draws together fourteen case authors and forty-seven discussants from around the world. The breadth of our collaborations has not only been invaluable for our ability to explore the challenges of civic education today but is also reflective of our approach to ethical inquiry more generally. We believe that the global diversity of case authors and discussants is critical to our effort to begin to make headway on the ethical challenges facing civic educators globally. While each case centers on a particular national context, and the discussants either hail from or work in that context, our hope is that these cases and conversations can lead to ethical insights not possible from a more narrow perspective, helping to identify unnamed assumptions and presuppositions, suggesting ideas that may work well across contexts, and possibly even pointing out democratic threats that haven't yet, but may still, cross national borders.

Cases and Conversations about Civic Education in Divided Times

Normative Case Studies

The normative case studies collected here cover a wide range of contexts and tackle a host of ethical dilemmas challenging the capacity of educators across the globe to promote meaningful civic learning. While steeped in the particularities of their national contexts, we believe these cases have something to offer readers across backgrounds.

The first two cases, from Germany and the Netherlands, respectively, direct our attention toward the evolving significance of new technologies for civic education. Set in a German comprehensive school committed to democratic deliberation, "A Parallel Universe: Conspiracy Theories and the Limits of Education" (Chapter 2) follows a social studies teacher whose pedagogical skill and relationship-building are tested by a student actively engaged in the anti-vaccination Querdenker movement. After being publicly challenged by this student during a class on the history of pandemics, she must decide whether shutting this student down, ignoring his statements, or engaging publicly with him is the best course of action for the student, his classmates, and their school ethos. While conspiracy theories are not new, "A Parallel Universe" shows how new social media platforms leveraging increasingly powerful information and communications technologies allow misinformation to pass through classroom walls in novel ways that can threaten civic—and civil—discourse.

"Feeling Exposed in Online Class: Student and Teacher Safety in the Online Civics Classroom" (Chapter 3) takes readers to a vocational school in the Netherlands where educators grapple with the challenge of supporting controversial issues discussions in online civics courses. After being confronted by an angry parent during a debate over healthcare in her online civics class, a Dutch vocational high school teacher considers the risks inherent to controversial issues discussions in the remote classroom. She and her colleagues value educational access for their students, civic engagement, and teacher autonomy, and weigh whether these and other values are compatible in an increasingly politicized online world. With respect to online learning in particular, this case asks: does the need for engagement in civic discourse outweigh the safety risks when anyone might be listening just off camera?

Two additional case studies, from Australia and Spain, center on questions about the civic culture of schools themselves. "High School at the Coal-Face: The Cost of Getting 'What We're Owed'" (Chapter 4) discusses the trade-offs to civic and economic life created by a contested, tight partnership between an Australian high school and its local coal mining operation. The case centers on one principal's decision whether to endorse renewing an agreement between his public high school and a multinational mining company with significant operations in the small Australian mining town where the high school is located. While the partnership has secured much-needed funds, which have been used for a range of vital services including laptops for at-home learning during the pandemic and funding for academic scholarships, the school community is divided on whether these financial benefits are worth the costs of the partnership, given the immense cost of mining on the land and the students' lives. Is the school limiting its students' vision of their future careers by showcasing the mining industry, or do these industry connections better prepare students for future opportunities? How should school leaders weigh different perspectives, especially those of Aboriginal students and their families who have often suffered the most significant harms?

"Photo Bomb: Responding to Online Transgressions" (Chapter 5) picks up on the theme of technological change, shifting the emphasis to questions related to digital citizenship. Set in a private K-12 school in Madrid, this case revolves around a school crisis set off by two twelve-year-old students who impersonate an older boy on social media and ask a female classmate for a revealing photo, which they go on to forward to their classmates over the course of a weekend. Beyond any potential legal consequences, the case asks readers to deliberate over whether the school should respond, what values and principles should guide a response, and whether the school should prioritize the individual needs of students or collective responsibility in the community. Although bullying has long been a part of schooling, new technologies ensure that local transgressions—even those that take place off-campus and outside school hours—can have ripple effects across an entire school, even an entire community. Moreover, these technologies demand educators grapple with what exactly digital citizenship involves and how they should go about teaching it. How should educators respond to online bullying in a way that meets the needs of all students and promotes a school culture conducive to good digital citizenship?

Two case studies set in the United States explore current disputes over whether civic education is empowering or indoctrinating students.

"Taking the Action out of Civics?: Polarized Debates over Civic Education" (Chapter 6) examines the American debate over a form of project-based civics education called action civics, in which students research a topic of their choosing and then take action to create change. In this case study, a parent's crusade to end the action civics project prompts a high school to examine the purpose of civic education, the rights of young people to influence their community, and the ways that polarized discourse influences schools. Should young people be recipients of civic knowledge rather than agents of change? How should input from the community influence school decisions about curriculum? In a polarized community, is it better to make waves or smooth tensions?

Our other US-based case, "Course Correction: Teaching Critical Consciousness in an Anti-CRT State" (Chapter 7), is set in the wake of new state legislation targeting the teaching of critical race theory—an academic framework that originated in critical legal studies. The case follows the Black principal of a predominantly White middle school as he weighs whether or not to renew a course centered on the development of critical consciousness. Caught between belief in the importance of such courses to the civic mission of schooling, the imperative of protecting his staff, and the chilling effect of the new legislation on educators who believe learning about power and hierarchy is critical to the civic mission of schooling, the principal must consider: How much must educators risk—both personally and professionally—to support the civic education of students? And how, if at all, should community preferences inform how educators teach about issues related to identity and power?

The final two cases center on perennial questions about how to balance respect for and accommodation of religious diversity with other key democratic commitments. "No Laughing Matter: Can Showing Religiously Sensitive Cartoons in the Classroom Ever Be Justified?" (Chapter 8) is set in England and explores the ethical challenges created by schools' legal duty to prevent radicalization among their students, commonly referred to as "Prevent." In this case, one Multi-Academy Trust has developed a new lesson to help students build their critical thinking skills and learn to challenge radical, Islamophobic ideology percolating in the school. However, because this lesson uses *Charlie Hebdo* cartoons satirizing the Prophet Mohammed—cartoons that have been condemned by many Muslims as blasphemous—the CEO of the Trust is unsure how to respond. While copycat graffiti on the school walls suggest that students have already seen the cartoons and need a structured space to talk about them, are they ever appropriate to use in a classroom setting? How can educators take seriously their legal obligation to Prevent while also being sensitive to their religious students?

"Faith in Mr. D.: Accommodating Religion in Schools" (Chapter 9) shifts the conversation on religious equality, democratic inclusion, and academic learning from England to Canada. In the context of Canada's policy of religious accommodation in schools, a principal at a majority-Muslim public middle school in Ontario must figure out how to respond to the large number of students missing Friday classes to pray at a nearby mosque. While the principal believes he's found a strategy to accommodate the diverse demands of his students and his professional responsibilities, teachers raise questions about the ways that religious equality might hinder gender equality, and, suddenly, the decisions about school prayer become even more complicated. In the public school system of a multicultural democracy, where is the line between accommodating diversity and endorsing religion? What happens when the rights of different groups, or a school's educational commitments, seem to conflict with one another?

Together, these normative case studies cover a broad range of dilemmas concerning our ability to provide all young people the civic education they deserve and that is critical to supporting democracy globally. While none of these eight cases are neutral and each—in naming and describing a decision as a *dilemma*—represents a particular ethical point of view, they're offered in the hopes of stimulating further dialogue. Such dialogue may prove indispensable to making progress on the ethical challenges facing civic educators today.

Model Conversations

The conversations paired with each case are designed both to provide additional substantive insights into case studies themselves, and to model and stimulate further civic dialogue. Each conversation features a group of four to five people engaged in a facilitated discussion of the ethical, political, and practical challenges raised by that case. The discussion groups are intentionally diverse. Discussants vary by: professional, experiential, and disciplinary background; by race, religion, or ethnicity; and by political ideology, among other lines of difference. The groups are united, however, in their willingness to discuss challenging, value-laden questions across lines of difference and in their deep familiarity with the particular context of the case under discussion.

As a result, each conversation opens up new lines of inquiry and insight that have the potential to expand readers' ethical and pragmatic imaginations. For example, "Faith in Mr. D." revolves in part around troubling practices of gender segregation—boys in front, girls in back—in the Friday prayers being led in a public school cafeteria. Educators in the case understandably raise concerns about the school's apparent endorsement of gender inequality by accommodating these practices. In the conversation about the case, however, Allysa Khan draws on her experiences studying the religious practices of Muslim girls to show how accommodation can actually provide spaces for the empowerment of girls not broadly accessible outside of the school context. She explains that some girls have taken charge of leading female-only Friday prayers, and in other schools girls have been able to take on religious leadership positions that would not be open to them in their mosques. The conversation doesn't *resolve* concerns about how schools should balance ideals of gender equity and religious accommodation, but it does expand readers' imaginative universe beyond assuming there is a simple, binary trade-off between ideals. It also provides concrete insights into novel practices that may help case readers wrestling with similar challenges in their own contexts. When readers encounter Khan's account of the practices of Muslim girls in Canadian high schools, for instance, we hope they see possibilities for further exploration within their own settings, if not exact models for what will work.

Other case conversations introduce new perspectives, values, and ways of knowing that may unsettle the premises of the case itself. In the conversation of "Regional High School at the Coal-Face," for instance, Laurie Perry and his fellow discussants bring Aboriginal environmental ethics into their interpretation of the case. Discussing the long-term ethical considerations of transitional climate justice, Perry introduces a new time scale to the question of how schools should work with local communities "at the coal-face." As schools around the world confront the challenges of climate change and wrestle with their own obligations to act—often pressed hardest by their own students leading Fridays for Future school strikes or other actions—these questions of scale, time, and the sources of ethical insight will become only more pressing. Each of the eight case conversations makes a similar substantive contribution to our understanding of the issues and avenues for action at stake.

These conversations can also serve as models for how to engage in ethical reflection through normative case study discussions. As we discuss above, normative case studies can play an important role in advancing our understanding of complex issues in educational ethics—about the values and interests at stake, about the courses of action available, and about the most salient ethical principles (including new principles that must be theorized). Normative case studies can also play a key role in helping education professionals develop good ethical judgment to address dilemmas that arise in their work. Here, we understand judgment as a kind of practical wisdom that is brought to bear on specific questions of action. A moral agent who exercises good judgment not only has an understanding of the ethical and practical issues in front of them but ensures this understanding is practically engaged and effective in their actions. Normative case studies support the development of good ethical judgment by providing readers the space to slow down and think deeply about the ethically salient features of particular real-world decisions. This sort of slow, careful attention to authentic dilemmas of educational policy and practice allows readers to think more broadly about which considerations are relevant to the case at hand and how these considerations ought to be weighed against one another in contexts mirroring what they're likely to experience in the course of their professional life.[5] These model conversations offer one lens on how normative case study discussions can help education professionals develop good ethical judgment.

Those who are interested in facilitating case discussions may also find the conversations useful for modeling case facilitation techniques. The conversations in this volume all use the facilitation guide developed by the EdEthics initiative at the Harvard Graduate School of Education, which you can find in the appendix. The most distinctive feature of this approach to facilitation is that it encourages discussants to push back the moment of decision, focusing first on the ethical dilemmas in play and the different values, interests, and practical constraints that constitute these dilemmas. It isn't until the end that the discussion transitions into what should be done and by whom. This insistence on carefully attending to the particulars of the decision in question and the context of that decision is designed to encourage the kind of slow thinking critical to the development of ethical sensitivity and ultimately practical wisdom.

Facilitators play a key role here. In a number of conversations, we can see facilitators directing the attention of their group to potentially relevant issues that hadn't yet been addressed. In "Taking the Action Out of Civics," for instance, Levinson directs her group's attention to the previously unmentioned issue of parents' rights. Might parental interests bear on the kind of civic education that can be permissibly taught? In "A Parallel

Universe," Johannes Drerup ensures that his group engages with the possibility that reasoning with a student caught in the grip of conspiracy may be ineffective in encouraging critical thinking. If this were the case, how can a civics teacher handle the misinformation that is increasingly prevalent in the classroom? While all of these conversations are edited and streamlined, we believe they offer—in addition to substantive ethical insights—valuable models for how to teach with normative case studies. For more suggestions about how to engage with this volume, refer to our conclusion. There, we offer more fine-grained teaching ideas and suggestions for how to use both the normative case studies and model conversations as teaching tools.

Finally, we hope that these conversations can serve as civic models, showing readers what it looks like to disagree well. Especially given significant polarization and entrenched disagreement globally, civil discourse on difficult ethical questions can be hard to come by. However, dialogue plays an essential role in supporting the educational aims of normative case studies. We believe that ethical dialogue among differently situated individuals is critical to developing the judgment education professionals need to navigate the ethical dilemmas they face. Readers inevitably bring a diversity of perspectives and lived experiences into any case discussion. These differences in perspective and experience partly shape how they understand a case, affecting which details appear most salient, which values stand out, and which courses of action seem most appropriate. In discussing normative case studies, we're forced to compare these initial judgments with other people. This encourages us to think more deeply about how we've come to form our own judgments and whether we have missed any ethically salient considerations. Especially when a good facilitator helps to ensure respect for group discussion norms conducive to critical thinking and respectful exchange, this kind of "epistemic friction" provided by encountering perspectives different from our own can support the development of good ethical judgment.[6]

The normative case studies in this volume tackle authentically challenging ethical issues. Consistently across the conversations, we see real disagreement—about the meaning of civic education, about what we owe students, about how to promote the civic culture of a school. The diverse interlocutors brought together through these conversations, however, display vital norms of civic discourse we hope can serve as a valuable model. Ultimately, we hope that these conversations further the important ethical inquiry necessary to dealing with the challenges of our time.

Conclusion

Today, the challenges we face span borders and so must our responses. We sincerely hope that the normative case studies and conversations collected here, representing the work and thought of scholars and practitioners from across the globe, can help support ongoing efforts to address the threats facing democracy. In particular, we hope that this volume can help readers better understand the complex ethical dilemmas that seep into classrooms dedicated to civic education under conditions of division and develop the judgment needed to respond to these challenges well.

Notes

1. Jennifer McCoy, Tahmina Rahman, and Murat Somer, "Polarization and the Global Crisis of Democracy: Common Patterns, Dynamics, and Pernicious Consequences for Democratic Polities," *American Behavioral Scientist* 62, no. 1 (January 1, 2018): 16–42, https://doi.org/10.1177/0002764218759576.
2. Shoshana Zuboff, *The Age of Surveillance Capitalism: The Fight for a Human Future at the New Frontier of Power*, First Trade Paperback Edition (New York: Public Affairs, 2020).
3. Martin A. Schain, "Shifting Tides: Radical-Right Populism and Immigration Policy in Europe and the United States" (Migration Policy Institute, August 2018).
4. Meira Levinson and Jacob Fay, eds., *Dilemmas of Educational Ethics: Cases and Commentaries* (Cambridge, Massachusetts: Harvard Education Press, 2016), 3–4.
5. Ellis Reid and Meira Levinson, "Normative Case Studies as Democratic Education," in *The Cambridge Handbook of Democratic Education* (Cambridge, UK: Cambridge University Press, 2023), 133–7.
6. Reid and Levinson, "Normative Case Studies as Democratic Education," 137.

2

A Parallel Universe: Conspiracy Theories and the Limits of Education

Johannes Drerup

After the fourth grade, children in Germany may—depending on their abilities, grades, the wishes of their parents, and the recommendations of their teachers—attend one of four different kinds of secondary schools: Hauptschule, Realschule, Gymnasium, *or* Gesamtschule. *While some types of schools focus on a vocational or university track, the* Gesamtschule *(comprehensive school) combines all educational tracks in one school. The* Gesamtschule *brings together students of all ability levels and socioeconomic backgrounds and is typically less selective with a more heterogeneous student population than, for instance, a* Gymnasium. *The* Gesamtschule *in this case is grappling with the role of conspiracy theories in the classroom. The public debate about conspiracy theories in Germany was partly triggered by the election of Donald Trump in the United States and also by the rise of right-wing movements and parties within Germany as well as Europe more generally. The debate intensified after the outbreak of the Covid-19 pandemic and the ensuing formation of political protest movements like the "Querdenker" movement, whose political views draw heavily from various conspiracy theories. The Querdenker movement consists of a mixture of individuals with varying political leanings, including right-wing extremists, and has become increasingly visible in Germany through the public protests of its members.*

--

Peter raised his hand, and Mrs. Faulkner instinctively held her breath.

As the country continued to grapple with the changes Covid-19 had brought to schools, Mrs. Faulkner had chosen to cover the history of pandemics in her social studies class today. She had begun with a primary source document: a newspaper article from 1918, detailing the impact of the Spanish flu on society. Then she had asked her students to compare the societal reactions from 1918 to those from 2020 and into the present.

"Of course, the situation in 1918 was different; they didn't understand the disease well and had no vaccines like we do today. But what sounds familiar in this article?" She had scanned the room for responses.

Peter's hand had shot up instantly—of course. Mrs. Faulkner had searched for other volunteers, but many students were eyeing Peter warily, reluctant to raise their hands. While she had managed to catch two students' eyes, they just shrugged and looked away. After a minute, she exhaled and said: "Ok, Peter, what's on your mind?"

"It's pretty clear to me that the so-called Spanish Flu was part of a big plan. Pandemics are powerful tools to control the population—our bodies and our minds. Isn't it a rather strange 'coincidence' that almost exactly 100 years after the Spanish Flu, we allegedly face this global pandemic? It's all about who controls the information. The 'official' history here," he announced, brandishing the course textbook, "leaves out a lot of relevant sources. History is written by those in power, you know."

Mrs. Faulkner sighed. At one time, she had loved Peter's contributions to class. He was intelligent, insightful, and sometimes critical. Unlike many of his classmates, he had a passion for history and current events. He read the newspaper every day and had devoured the many books she had lent him about topics ranging from the French Revolution to the Vietnam War. But something had changed in him. He'd become isolated, socially withdrawn. Rather than borrowing books written by historians, he spent more and more time reading online, pulled into conspiracy websites making inflammatory claims using questionable evidence.

Mrs. Faulkner gathered her patience; she had been through too many conversations like this with Peter, and she worried that this one would again take up valuable class time. But she couldn't just let that point stand.

"Although those in power do sometimes manipulate official accounts," she conceded, "we shouldn't infer that all official history, written by experts, is a big hoax. There are certain things that we can know are objectively, historically incorrect. For example, Germany was not invaded by Poland in 1939, as some people claim; Germany was the invader. You're right to be skeptical in principle, Peter, since there was indeed a conspiracy going on during that time. Germany claimed that Poland was attacking, but this was a straightforward lie. Throughout history you do find networks of powerful people who engaged in conspiracies to further their political interests—like the Nazi regime did. But this doesn't mean that we can't distinguish between historical facts and fiction."

"Exactly, I think we're finally on the same page," Peter interjected. "As I said, official sources can't be trusted. If people had been more critical back then, Hitler would have never risen to power in the first place. And yet we've learned nothing. People still believe the propaganda the state gives them: they all wear masks and get vaccinated, just like the mainstream media tells them to."

"Peter," Mrs. Faulker retorted, "people wear masks because they're critically evaluating a serious situation. But I'd like to hear what other—"

"This has nothing to do with critical thinking," Peter interrupted, visibly frustrated. "Most people behave like sheep. And skeptical people who use their brains are stigmatized as 'conspiracy theorists.' You should always ask yourself: in whose interest it is that people believe a particular version of history? We need to seek out alternative sources and alternative perspectives."

As Peter spoke, Mrs. Faulkner watched the other students. As in previous discussions, some rolled their eyes, while others simply looked uncomfortable. But several of Peter's classmates nodded eagerly and leaned toward him, ready to hear more. Concerned for those students, Mrs. Faulker attempted to find common ground while debunking Peter's more radical claims.

"Ok, that's a good point, Peter," she began. "But the comparison you make between our current liberal and democratic government and the Nazi government is problematic and just wrong. People are free to voice their opinions in our society today. We all have equal rights here, which obviously wasn't true in Nazi Germany. Now, I do want to hear what others think about this article."

"A liberal democracy?" Peter countered. "A country that even considers vaccine mandates hardly qualifies as liberal. Don't I have the right to decide for myself what I want to do with my body? And quite a few people believe that the vaccines are much more dangerous than any virus could ever be. As I said, you should check your sources. To get closer to the truth, we need more than one perspective, especially the official perspective of so-called 'experts.'"

"Damn straight," one boy said to his neighbor. Meanwhile, a girl across the room was on the verge of tears; Mrs. Faulkner knew that she had lost multiple family members to Covid-19, before the vaccine had been developed.

"I'm glad you brought up expertise, Peter, since the people who propagate the views you're promoting generally do not have the relevant expertise to make the claims they do. But we'll have to leave it at that." Mrs. Faulkner looked at her watch. With only a few minutes left in class, she explained the homework and silently berated herself for allowing Peter's perspectives to dominate the discursive space once again.

After class, Mrs. Faulkner reflected on Peter's development over the last few years. Peter had been one of the more promising students at Sophie Scholl School in Dortmund, an upper secondary comprehensive school in a district known for its socioeconomic problems. Although most students came from low-income families, the school was highly culturally diverse, with a sizable percentage of students whose first language was not German. While these factors had at times created difficult working conditions, she believed that the teachers fostered a stimulating educational environment for all students. The ethos of the school was both inclusive and dialogical, with a strong egalitarian and democratic orientation toward "respecting differences," openly discussing controversial issues, and promoting critical thinking. Teachers were expected to nurture an atmosphere of charitable debate and not to shy away from addressing conflicts and controversies in their classes, which Mrs. Faulkner really appreciated.

Peter's educational achievements and personal development in his early years at the school had been generally positive. And he had always been a favorite of Mrs. Faulkner. By the time he turned sixteen, however, something changed in him. In the beginning, the teachers just chalked it up to puberty. Peter began to isolate himself more and more from his classmates, though he and Mrs. Faulkner remained close.

When the pandemic hit Germany and schools closed down for a couple of weeks, Peter became a committed member of the so-called Querdenker movement. The longer the pandemic lasted, the more extremist Peter became. As it turned out, Covid-related conspiracies were just the beginning: the deeper he immersed himself in the world of conspiracy theories, the more he questioned his old worldview. He told Mrs. Faulkner that he felt like a secret agent who had finally begun to understand the true nature of world history.

Thinking back to today's class period, Mrs. Faulkner couldn't believe how much her relationship with Peter had deteriorated. She no longer knew how to handle the way he questioned her authority and refused to engage in rational dialogue. She had made no progress today—she had simply given him a stage for his views yet again. But she still cared deeply for him, and she wanted to help him. She simply didn't know how to help when he was so closed-minded. He seemed to live in a parallel universe.

Entering the teachers' room, Mrs. Faulkner saw her colleagues Mr. Berger and Mrs. Schmitz. They had discussed Peter's worrisome development many times before. Today they read her distress on her face.

"What is it?" Mr. Berger asked.

"I just had another debate with Peter about his conspiracies. I'm really worried about that kid," sighed Mrs. Faulkner.

"I'm starting to worry more about his classmates," Mr. Berger replied. "Misinformation is spreading like a virus in my classes. The more time we use to discuss this stuff, the more we legitimize his 'theories.' I worry that other students are starting to believe these are normal political views."

"Yes, several of my students were agreeing with him today," Mrs. Faulkner admitted.

"Ok, that is a problem. But when it comes to Peter himself, I'm not so pessimistic—I think it's only a phase," Mrs. Schmitz explained. "We just need to keep questioning his views and over time he'll see he's on the wrong track."

"Yes, but time is exactly the point," Mr. Berger responded. "We are spending so much time on this boy and his ideas that we're neglecting the other students' needs. I cannot keep having these debates about unreasonable and frankly crazy views, while most of my students are struggling with the real effects of the pandemic. Think about Susanne—she barely can write a single proper German sentence. But I'm supposed to engage with Peter´s fantasy world? No, the next time Peter starts with this stuff, I'm going to tell him to focus on Goethe's Faust, instead of the Illuminati."

"Yes, and he'll probably tell you that Goethe was a member of the Illuminati and that you should check your sources," Mrs. Faulkner chuckled ruefully, shaking her head.

"Exactly, this has to stop!" Mr. Berger emphasized. "I agree that Peter is a very intelligent and promising student, and I care about him, too. But we need to think about the other students. Some of his 'theories' have clear antisemitic undertones—like when he says that all 'official' history books were written by the Rothschilds. Did you know that Anton in your class is Jewish? We have to protect Peter's classmates. These 'theories' do not belong in the classroom, not in this school and not in this country with our history. It's simply not acceptable."

"Agreed," Mrs. Schmitz said. "But Peter's just a kid. We can't leave him alone to deal with this."

"I also don't want to give up on him," Mr. Berger clarified, "but I cannot see what else we can do. I never thought I would say it, but I really think it is hopeless. We can't convince conspiracy theorists by rational means. I mean, my family couldn't celebrate Christmas together this year for the first time in three decades because my brother fell in with conspiracy theorists. He now refuses to get vaccinated even to protect our mother, who is high risk, as you know. I tried everything to persuade him, and everything failed. If I can't even reach my own brother, what can we do as teachers? Seriously, if not even scientific experts and professional politicians know how to handle these issues, what can we do?"

"I'm so sorry. What a terrible thing to happen to your family," Mrs. Schmitz sympathized. "But as teachers, we can't give up on a kid, whatever his beliefs and wherever they may come from. And giving up is certainly not in line with the ethos of our school. We can't preach dialogue and critical thinking and then shut students down every time they say things out of line with our expectations."

"True," Mrs. Faulkner agreed, "but I doubt that what's going on with Peter counts as 'critical thinking,' and we certainly don't want to foster just any type of debate in our school. There are limits to what counts as a reasonable controversy, and his views are irrational."

"Yes, sure, but we have seen harder cases," Mrs. Schmitz reminded them. "Remember Andre Jacobi? He was truly addicted to computer games, but we didn't give up on him, and now he's studying to be a neurosurgeon. I've seen it many times: with constant effort and care, many obstacles can be overcome."

"You worked so hard with Andre. You really have worked wonders before." Mrs. Faulkner smiled fondly at her colleague. "But Andre was receptive to our help. Peter doesn't seem to hear a word we say."

"What about his parents? Did you talk to them?" Mrs. Schmitz inquired.

"Not yet," Mrs. Faulkner responded, "but I assume that they play an important role in this mess. I've heard that they actively engage in the Querdenker-scene."

"Given how deeply Peter is immersed in his conspiracy world, I'm not surprised," Mrs. Schmitz nodded.

"I'm pretty sure all we'll get from them is another round of fairy tales," Mr. Berger warned. "Besides, you don't want trouble with these Querdenker guys. The papers report that many of them are becoming increasingly radical. Some even are considering violence as a response to current policies."

"I still have to try. I'll talk to them next week at parents' day," Mrs. Faulkner replied. "It may not be my business what they think about politics. But it is my business what happens here. Their son is drifting into this conspiracy world and spreading his ideas in our school. I need to talk to them even if nothing comes of it. I don't think we should fear these Querdenker guys, but then again, they definitely mean trouble … What crazy times we live in." She sighed.

Mrs. Faulkner left the meeting even more uncertain about how she should position herself in the classroom. Should she engage in more discussion to publicly deconstruct Peter's views? Would this help Peter—or his classmates? Should she just shut Peter down next time and write him off as a lost cause? Or should she simply ignore his statements and not engage in a debate in order to keep the peace? But wouldn't it be irresponsible not to take a clear stand here—despite political pressure from outside the school—especially around safety issues like vaccination? And what about the dialogical ethos of the school? What was the right thing to do?

Conversation

Johannes Drerup: What are the dilemmas in this case and for whom? What do you think?

Kai Horsthemke: You've got a situation where the discussion centers around Covid-19, but you've got Peter who has been dabbling in conspiracy theories. The dilemma is the following—should you take him and his views seriously? Should you shut him out? He obviously demands attention in the class, and he obviously has some charisma because some kids do agree with him. How do you as a teacher respond to that?

Greta Fexer: I think the question of how to handle dilemmas like this one is not easy to answer because the young people are in an age in which they are easily influenced. It's not easy to handle as a teacher.

Nikki Spencer: Everybody knows of somebody who follows certain conspiracy theories, but you don't usually engage, whereas in a school context the dilemma is we actually need to encourage debate. You can't just say, "Okay, I don't agree with this." You can't silence students. The dilemma is—what's my responsibility? And how far am I facilitating conspiracy theories by letting Peter have quite a big platform? In the family context, it tends to be, "Okay, we're just not going to agree with someone, not meet up with them." Everyone has their bubble.

Greta Fexer: Conspiracy theories spread mostly via social media or other platforms pupils use. It is highly probable that pupils will be confronted with such ideologies and that these ideologies will remain even when you discourage them. For teachers, this dilemma is an opportunity and challenge at the same time. Handling this challenge is highly individual and dependent on the study group. I think it is the wrong strategy to ignore what the pupils think about and what they want to say. Maybe it's a chance to speak together?

Johannes Drerup: So you think shutting him up is not an option, then?

Greta Fexer: In my opinion, banning or restricting students' freedom of expression and ignoring their opinions is the wrong strategy because their points of view will still remain and may become more dangerous if not discussed. It is better to use the opportunity in the classroom to change their ideas. This is not just a challenge but also a chance to change.

Kai Horsthemke: We do have these problems in our families. The difference is that you don't need to treat a family reunion as a discursive space. You can go around certain issues and not address them at all. You can decide to just talk about the cake or some television program. This is obviously different from situations where—what Greta said is really important—you, as an educator, have an obligation to nurture discussion.

I'm wondering what could be done to nurture discussion and combat misinformation in the classroom. One thing is to talk about the rules of discourse. What are the rules of argumentation? What space do we allow for various arguments? Perhaps one of the rules the teacher might mention is to point out that if you advance an argument, you have to make sure that it's—what's the word?—falsifiable.

Sara O'Brien: I'm going to interrupt briefly. We will have the chance to talk at the end about what should be done in the case. As you're seeing, people often want to jump to what should be done, but we're going to spend the first part of our discussion just surfacing the dilemmas. I think you are all pointing to really important dilemmas around the discursive nature of schools and the idea that there are responsibilities that come from knowing that students are going to encounter conspiracy theories throughout their lives. We can also talk beyond the central dilemma to look at dilemmas for other characters. Have you seen any dilemmas for students in the classroom or for the other teachers?

Anna Zentis: One point that is missing is how students consume media. We have to discuss how the students use media and how they can reflect on this consumption.

Johannes Drerup: This is certainly an important dimension of the problem.

Nikki Spencer: It's similar to the dilemma Anna mentioned. Teachers are going to constantly come up against the fact that their students are living in an age where they are quick to adapt to using new media. So teachers are actually on a shaky footing in some ways. I tend to stick to the media that I know—Radio4 from the UK and not many others. Students are quicker ahead in that sense but at the same time not necessarily ahead in other ways. They are young and inexperienced, and they might not be able to channel what they see online as well.

Greta Fexer: Another dilemma I thought of in this moment—the balance of power in the classroom. Who can say anything? Who can say nothing?

Anna Zentis: And this is an emotional topic. Corona damaged the social development of many young people, who couldn't go out and meet friends. This makes this topic a particularly emotional debate in the school, in this lesson.

One more problem is that sometimes these theories have some truth inside in the beginning, so it's really hard for me as a teacher to say, "Wow, this is all wrong and stupid." We have to discuss the theory to find the problems. That's a problem. I need a long time to do this, and I don't always have the time in my lessons to go deeply into one topic.

Nikki Spencer: Anna just touched on another aspect of the dilemma, which is how attractive conspiracy theories are. They've got the word "*Querdenker*," which is to think alternatively to the system. I think for young people it's incredibly attractive to say, "You know what, this is what the system thinks, but I'm going to do it differently." Generations of teenagers have wanted to do things differently. The challenge is to figure out how to counteract that without them feeling like you're saying as a teacher, "No, you follow my system. I know better."

Kai Horsthemke: Can I just add something? I think one thing we haven't talked about yet, which I think is also at the core of these issues, is the notion of expertise. What counts as expertise and what should our attitude be toward expertise? And coupled with that is the notion of skepticism. And here we might distinguish between a kind of healthy skepticism and a kind of toxic skepticism.

Johannes Drerup: I totally agree. This is a super difficult issue—the thin line between reasonable skepticism on the one side and on the other side certain forms of conspiratorial thinking. Now we're moving to the next issue. We've piled up quite a few dilemmas, and now the question is, why are these dilemmas? What values or principles are at stake here? And how do they relate or how do they clash?

Nikki Spencer: How free and open do you allow a discussion to be? And where do we draw the frameworks of the rules? And where does allowing somebody's freedom of expressing their views come up against a limit of possible damage to other people?

Greta Fexer: Why are these dilemmas? Because there isn't a right way to answer how to handle it. Maybe this is also the answer to why these are dilemmas. Because there are so many individual things you have to think about before you can handle these situations. It's about your learning group, it's about your students, it's about your personality. There's not one answer.

Sara O'Brien: Could you elaborate on the different values or the different considerations you see Ms. Faulkner having to take into account in the case? What are some of the values or considerations you see her running up against as she tries to figure out how to respond to Peter?

Kai Horsthemke: Perhaps, if I can come in there because it might have a bearing on what I wanted to say. There's a dilemma between letting Peter talk and being sensitive to the emotional states of some of the other kids. One girl is on the verge of tears because she's lost a couple of family members. What Peter says or what Peter denies has direct bearing on her own family. To establish some kind of balance between what can be said or what shouldn't be said is a huge problem.

Greta Fexer: My answer would be: be transparent for your class with your decisions as a teacher. Vagueness may increase distrust. Teaching decisions should be based on key educational objectives of education—maturity and social participation and learning to discuss within democratic limits and learning to argue. Pupils need safe space to discuss controversy. Of course, it needs a framework—yeah, this is a challenge for the teacher, but be open and transparent. When you say, "Okay, I will shut him down because I can't handle it," be transparent with your decision because I think vagueness may really increase distrust.

Anna Zentis: I also think it's a good way to put the discussion in the next lesson. You can give homework, and say, "Please search for the sources. Where have you got your information?" Maybe it will be more clever not to judge that in the first moment—to prepare so all the students are able to discuss on the same level. For me as a teacher, I should prepare some information about the danger of such theories so that we all develop sensitivity to the theories and the spreading problems associated with them.

Kai Horsthemke: That's a really interesting point, Anna. It bears on something you said earlier. It all goes back to digital literacy. How do we nurture digital literacy? On the one hand, we've got our kids that can tell us anything. They really know how to work these new technologies. I mean they're extremely ahead of us. On the other hand, there's also a kind of ignorance or a kind of lack of critical engagement with the information.

Johannes Drerup: I will just press one point. What about the perspective of Mrs. Schmitz, who always tries to keep on engaging with Peter? What if it just doesn't work? My personal experience with conspiracy theorists is that it's pretty much impossible to reach them. This is a huge challenge because it's very much at odds with core aspects of educational thinking. Any thoughts on this one?

Nikki Spencer: I basically agree. From personal experience, there's just a limit... It's very, very hard—or impossible—to change the views of people who believe these conspiracy theories. It goes back to what are the values of the teacher, the value of giving everybody a platform in the class and respecting everybody in the class's need to be listened to or have their experiences respected. If you look at the dialogue, Peter does dominate the discussion, and that's kind of allowed. I think the teacher feels, "I need to contradict, I need to somehow counteract this," but she just doesn't really manage that very successfully. I don't know about a solution, but maybe looking at a new framework for where to let opinions stand and not necessarily contradict them to give everybody else the space to be heard.

Greta Fexer: I just think about Andreas Petrik. He has another way to encourage critical thinking in the classroom. He describes how to deal with it in practical ways. He says that the pupils have to falsify the conspiracy theories for themselves with the help of scientific knowledge. Maybe they can hear the arguments of *Querdenker*, of Peter, and falsify the arguments. Here we can discuss, what is true scientific knowledge? Or is scientific knowledge just an interim result of scientific work? I think the pupils need to understand the difference between conspiracy ideologies and scientific theories. This must be clear for pupils. Okay, scientific concepts use the scientific method, and ideology is more feeling or attitude-based. Maybe this is a practical framework to handle this?

Kai Horsthemke: Perhaps a central issue concerns the value of deliberation. Public deliberation. The value of critical thinking but also the limits—are there limits to public deliberation?

Johannes Drerup: Greta said it's better to have a deliberative space where students can voice—if they believe conspiracy theories, that they can voice them. At the same time, one may also argue that these kinds of theories don't have a legitimate place in the classroom in the first place. What's your take on this one? What are the limits of controversiality?

Nikki Spencer: I find it very difficult because it's hard to go down any line where you'd say, "This shouldn't come into the classroom." We choose our curriculum according to what we agree with. Like we've already said, people live in their bubbles, mostly friendship groups or family groups, of people who agree with them. There is no other platform I can think of other than schools where you might create a forum where these views might be challenged.

Greta Fexer: What are controversial topics? You said controversial topics are suitable for classes when they're based on human rights and discussions about what is necessary for a good private life and society. And you use a combination of criteria—from the politically authentic criterion to the epistemic criterion—because there isn't just one way to answer or handle it. I think you need as a teacher more than our Beutelsbacher Konsens [consensus of Beutelsbach], which is more an overall consensus than a practical framework for teachers. You need a very individual combination of criteria. This goes beyond the Beutelsbacher Konsens.

When you see radical or inhuman statements, then you have to shut up the students. These are not arguments, so you have to set limits. But it's really hard to give an answer.

Kai Horsthemke: I'd be quite interested in hearing a little more from Anna because, Anna, you're working at a *Gesamtschule* [comprehensive school]. How do you deal with controversial issues that arise in the classroom?

I'm thinking of my wife who is also teaching at a *Gesamtschule* in Lübeck, Geschwister-Prenski-Gesamtschule, which is exactly like the school that you describe here, Johannes. The Geschwister Prenski were siblings that were sent to a concentration camp and died there, and the school is committed to maintaining that memory. Now, back to my initial question, how do you deal with controversy in the classroom? One of the issues now—especially when you've got kids with various kinds of cognitive ability or disability, you've got kids with a migrant background, especially with this wave of Ukrainian children—what is the common ground? How do you distill what is important here? Perhaps the issue is respect. Trying to get the learners to arrive at a kind of shared notion of respect. What constitutes respect? How do we practice it?

Johannes Drerup: Anna, what's your experience?

Anna Zentis: I think I'm a lucky teacher because I didn't have someone who said, "Oh, Corona, I don't know …" Right-wing stuff didn't exist in my classes. During the Ukraine war, I had a discussion with a student with a Russian background. I think Russian, I'm not sure. In the first days of the war, he said that Putin had come over to Ukraine because the Ukrainian people are right wing, and they fight for their country, and they kill some Russian people. I didn't have any information. So, it's not a really big conspiracy theory. I think he was living in a bubble. I confronted him in the next lesson with my information, and the discussion ended and that was all. I don't have a really hard case of stuff like that.

When the student mentioned the Ukraine right-wingers who killed the Russian people, I decided to check at home. It was at the end of the lesson when he came to me, so not many people were listening to us. There was not big pressure to answer.

Greta Fexer: But maybe this is an answer to the question, why are these dilemmas? Because the challenges you faced are transferable to other ones. We're discussing conspiracy theories, but you also can say, "Okay, now we discuss not about conspiracy theories but about the Russian war." Maybe this answers the question before, why are these dilemmas?

Sara O'Brien: I find it interesting to think about Peter's family—because the idea is that Peter's getting a lot of this from family. I know that in the United States right now we have lots of parents complaining about schools teaching values that really belong in the family. There's a lot of tension about what schools should be teaching and what is actually the purview of families to teach. I'm curious to know how people think about the role of Peter's parents and whether that plays into the dilemma at all?

Nikki Spencer: In England, parents can home-school, and we actually know someone who home-schools. In Germany, it's not allowed. Part of it, I understand, is to protect children from being stuck at home under the tyranny, you could say, of parents. You have *Schulpflicht* [compulsory schooling] to allow them to be in a school environment where they can have something that counteracts the home environment. I think England is *Unterrichtspflicht* [compulsory education], and Germany is *Schulpflicht*.

I think it's the role of school or the school authorities to protect the child and say, "You need to be in school." I don't know where the line goes where you could sort of enforce it and have someone pick up the child and bring them into school. In the UK, you've got the authorities who can pick up kids and bring them in. I would say there is a duty that teachers have to ensure that children are able to attend school.

Johannes Drerup: The legal dimension is quite clear in Germany. The *Schulpflicht* is super strict, and I think there are fewer options for parents to move out of the public school system compared to the States or to the Netherlands. Greta?

Greta Fexer: But I think the problem is that the responsibility lies with Peter or the other students. On the one hand, there are the family and the peer group, and on the other hand there are the school and the teachers. I think Peter also began to isolate himself and lost friends and lost his standing. Either Peter is the victim or the other students are victims, and this is the problem I think.

Sara O'Brien: That's so fascinating. So, on the one hand Peter bears responsibility, and on the other hand Peter is a victim, which to me is a really interesting tension. We've talked a lot about the school's responsibility, so I'm really curious to hear more about Peter's and students' responsibilities and also how that runs up against him as a victim of parental influence.

Johannes Drerup: Anna?

Anna Zentis: I want to know: what is Peter's motivation to discuss in that way? Is it only because he's living in a bubble, and he gets the wrong information? Or is the motivation to destroy the system? Or is it only a rebellious act because he's sixteen? "Yes, I'm the class clown." I don't know. For me, it would be clear to go talk only with Peter and to reflect with him on, "What's your motivation?" I think we have lost him really if he says, "Yeah, I don't like Germany. I don't like the system. You are all wrong. You are speaking bullshit." But if he is only living in a bubble, we have a chance to get him back—to reflect on his media consumption and show him ways where he can get information that has been checked or teach him to consume more reliable news.

Greta Fexer: I want to ask how we can protect our students. I think they need knowledge, and we have to think about, as I said before, the key objectives of education. We want critical thinking and reflection, and students need a safe space to discuss. Yes, within limits. The teachers have to set limits. But the students need a safe space to discuss controversy and to train critical thinking and reflection. So, yeah, maybe the students are victims or suffering, so we have to protect them as a teacher.

Anna Zentis: I think in this case it will be really productive to show him what will happen if all the people trust in those theories. What will happen with our society? I think in this case it will be really important to sensitize the students to the problems of those theories. That's a normal way where the *Beutelsbacher Konsens* works, but not in this case.

Johannes Drerup: We can now turn to the third question. But before I ask the third question, I want you to take into account the possibility that it's really perhaps impossible to reach him. As I said, in my personal experience with conspiracy theorists, it was always impossible to reach people who believe conspiracy theories via rational argumentation. So, what do you think should be done in this case by whom and why?

Nikki Spencer: I agree with what Greta said a while ago. I wouldn't choose the option of not allowing him to express these views. From reading the case, it seems like the teacher's floundering, and he is dominating this discussion. She needs a few more tools or a framework so that the discussion is a bit more fixed. You only have so much time to speak, or you can put your hand up only so many times. I don't know how you'd do it ideally. In most classrooms, there are lots of students who don't really want to participate—the shyer ones, the people who are not so sure of their opinion, et cetera. He is by default given a very large platform. I wouldn't say these views need to be completely denied a platform because they are dangerous, but maybe a look at how much space they're given.

The other thing I would say from personal experience is that I would go with the premise that it's not likely that his views will be changed. It's going to be very hard or possibly impossible. The family context is quite interesting. The main conspiracy theorist in our family is a professor of mathematics and cancer research statistics who travels the world as a professor. It's impossible to change his views, so I'm not sure how easy it would be to change a sixteen-year-olds.

Kai Horsthemke: I don't know how successful this would be in this case, but one idea is to point out certain contradictions. I was intrigued by Peter, in the conversation with Mrs. Faulkner, assuming a kind of anti-Hitler stance. You know, he says, "Well, if this had happened, Hitler wouldn't have come to power." He seems to think that is a good thing. But later we learn from Mr. Berger that some of Peter's theories have a strongly antisemitic orientation. There's a kind of possibility to point out certain contradictions.

Johannes Drerup: Yeah. That's a good point. I mean one problem according to my experience is that with the epistemic disorientation of conspiracy theorists also comes an ethical and political disorientation. The person doesn't really feel or he doesn't really see the contradiction anymore. In some cases, I've seen that at least.

Nikki Spencer: Maybe instead of saying, "Yes, but" and trying to give an opposite point of view, she can say, "Here is another point of view, I'll just let that stand." Rather than being adversarial, create a place where you say other things that contradict it without saying, "This is my view, this is what I want you to believe." Just say, "One could also look at it from this point of view."

Greta Fexer: And maybe she needs the help of another teacher. Peter should have a safe space to discuss his ideas, but I think he needs a counterweight. She needs the help of another teacher to be clear, and maybe she can help balance the conversation.

Johannes Drerup: She needs someone with authority then.

Greta Fexer: Yeah.

Johannes Drerup: As a counter authority, perhaps. So giving up on him is not an option then?

Kai Horsthemke: I think that's part of the dilemma. That's what makes it a dilemma. As committed educators, that's really not an option—unless he comes to school the next day with a gun, intent on blowing everyone away, you know.

Sara O'Brien: I'm curious—how did thinking about these issues about conspiracy theories with this fictional case study compare to the other ways that you have thought about or written about the issues and dilemmas brought up here?

Greta Fexer: I think we have to strengthen connections between research and practical work in school. For all these dilemmas and situations and case studies, the practical workers like Anna need theories or practical frameworks to handle those situations.

Kai Horsthemke: Perhaps a task for the students in the case would be to take this debate outside of the classroom and to treat it as homework, as Anna suggested before. For each one to go home and to reflect on what constitutes evidence for their views, whatever their views are. What constitutes evidence? Why does it constitute evidence? And why do they think this evidence is good? That would be a possibility for everyone to do some reflection at home without any kind of threat of being side-lined or of being shut up.

Johannes Drerup: I think this is quite interesting. You just could make it part of children's homework and see what happens. You've brought the factor of time into the discussion. As a teacher, you do not just focus on one hour or one week, but you take into account that there's a development over time. You don't need to deal with everything in one hour or in one week. You have a broader temporal horizon, so to speak. That's quite an important issue. You have quite a bit of time to engage with these issues.

Sara O'Brien: What do you hope that people reading this conversation will continue thinking about?

Greta Fexer: I hope that they see that students are thinking humans. They're not just young people. They are thinking humans, and we need to provide a good education for them. It's important to hear them, to see them, and to give them a space to discuss. To learn how to discuss and to learn how to argue. They have to train for it. We are not just born as critical thinking humans.

Nikki Spencer: What I'd like people to take away from our discussion is that critical thinking per se is actually missing from the education system. We have lots of subjects where it's basically, "Here is lots of information you need to learn," but there's very little about our current education that I think teaches critical thinking—even just asking the question, "Why do you think such and such?" and getting pupils to back up and say, "This is why I think such and such" or "That's why I had this idea." Changing the education system so there's more focus on people thinking about why they think what they think, rather than learning questions and answers.

Johannes Drerup: As Kai said in the beginning, there's no easy solution to a dilemma, perhaps no solution at all. In Germany, we have this saying, "Du sitzt wie ein Ochs vor'm Berg": "You're sitting like an ox in front of a mountain." If you confront a real dilemma, this is how you may feel. In some cases at least, you just have to accept that there is perhaps no solution at all. I mean, there are different ways to tackle the issue, different ways to interpret the challenge. But on a really practical level, there is no way to make everybody happy. I think this is a quite common educational experience that your educational and pedagogical ambitions fail.

Greta Fexer is a research assistant at the University of Cologne, Germany. She focuses on teacher training in the social sciences, working particularly closely with students training to teach politics and economics. Her doctoral thesis deals with, among other things, controversy in the classroom.

Kai Horsthemke is a professor of philosophy at the University of the Witwatersrand, South Africa and KU Eichstätt-ingolstadt, Germany. He teaches philosophy of education, and his research interests include animal ethics, social epistemology, and environmental education.

Nikki Spencer teaches primary school in Münster, Germany, and is originally from the North of England. She spent almost two years working as a bilingual assistant in Kindergarten in Germany before returning to the UK for her teacher training and qualification, which was recognized for the German education system in 2016.

Anna Zentis studied German language and political science from 2010 to 2017 at the University of Trier. Since successfully completing her teacher training at the Sankt Michael Gymnasium in Monschau, she has been working since 2019 at the Europaschule Herzogenrath Comprehensive School as a teacher.

Character Guide

Setting	
Sophie Scholl School, a *Gesamtschule* (comprehensive secondary school) in Dortmund, Germany	
Primary Characters	
Peter: 16-year-old student **Mrs. Faulkner:** history teacher at Sophie Scholl School	**Mr. Berger:** literature teacher at Sophie Scholl School **Mrs. Schmidt:** teacher at Sophie Scholl School

Discussion Questions

1 How should the school's inclusive and dialogical mission impact the teacher's decision-making?

2 As Mrs. Faulkner points out in the case, recent German history does include examples of conspiracies covered up by the Nazi regime. How should a country's history impact the way that its educators approach conspiracy theories in the classroom today?
3 While this case is rooted in the German context, conspiracy theories are flourishing in countries around the world. Which elements of this case seem context-specific to Germany? Which elements feel more universal? What are some conspiracy theories that teachers might encounter in the classroom in your context?
4 How should teachers draw the line between reasonable controversy and conspiracy theory in their classrooms?
5 How does Mrs. Faulkner's close relationship with Peter—"a favorite" student—impact the dilemmas she faces?
6 The teachers in the case debate whether they should be more concerned about Peter or the impact of Peter's views on his classmates. How should the teachers balance the needs of the students in the case?
7 In the case, the teachers speculate that Peter's parents share the views he's propagating at school. How does this case help us think about the rights of parents to direct their children's upbringing and the responsibility of schools to provide new viewpoints that children might not receive at home?
8 This case centers on three teachers. What responsibilities (if any) does the school leadership have to Peter, his classmates, and his teachers?
9 How do the teachers' past experiences, both personal and professional, influence the ways they approach Peter and the dilemmas raised by his beliefs?

3

Feeling Exposed in Online Class: Student and Teacher Safety in the Online Civics Classroom

Isolde de Groot, Yaël Weening,

and Sara O'Brien

The Netherlands can be characterized as a democratic and pluralist society: 25 percent of the Dutch population has an immigrant background.[1] *Among Dutch young people, many attend* Middelbaar Beroepsonderwijs *(vocational education institute), or MBO institutes. At MBO institutes, students who completed pre-vocational education can obtain a starter qualification that facilitates entry into industry. Civics is a mandatory course at MBO institutes and is mostly offered in years 1 and 2. There are relatively few legal requirements for Civics at MBO institutes, so teachers have a lot of autonomy. During the Covid-19 pandemic, classroom instruction across the world moved online, exposing both the promises and the challenges of civic education for teachers who must educate their students without significant state guidance. This case examines the particular challenges that arise when civics educators organize discussions of controversial issues in the online classroom.*

--

Linda Fraser's heart pounded as she closed her computer and shut down the microphone and camera set-up she had jerry-rigged for online teaching.

"How on earth could class have gone so far off the rails?" she wondered. "And with such a simple prompt, too? What if this becomes a thing on social media?" Her mind flashed to the teacher from Rotterdam who had been forced into hiding because of threats from parents and others on social media. She shook her head to clear the frightening thoughts. "What am I going to do?"

In retrospect, Linda couldn't believe how naive she had been. She had been slightly nervous about running a controversial issues discussion with her group of seventeen-year-olds online, since it was hard for her to track how they were reacting to the conversation over Zoom the way she did in person. But she had intentionally chosen a topic that she thought wouldn't be particularly sensitive for her students to discuss: "Should people who drink or smoke a lot pay more for their health insurance?" She had also been careful to set expectations for online discussions with her students. It just hadn't occurred to her to worry about students' parents, too.

The discussion had started well. Students had shared a variety of viewpoints, citing freedom of choice, privacy concerns, and public health, among other arguments. But before Linda could follow up with her next question, Jeffrey's mother had popped onto his screen, her face twisted in anger. "What?" she demanded. "Now you're telling my son that I don't deserve health care just because I smoke? I'm not worthy?"

Black boxes appeared across the Zoom room as several of the students clicked to turn their cameras off. Taken aback, Linda sputtered as Jeffrey's mother continued: "I've heard about the ways that leftist teachers try to indoctrinate our kids, but I never thought it would happen to my family. You can be sure I'll be calling Dean Doozer to let her know what you're up to!"

Jeffrey's mother disappeared as his camera feed went dark. The class was silent. Her head spinning, Linda quickly moved to the next part of the lesson. Consulting her lesson plan, she popped several articles into the chat and asked her students to spend the rest of class time reading through them to find the key arguments for or against charging different rates for health insurance based on lifestyle. Though she told her students she would remain online if any of them wanted to speak with her, she was soon the only person left in the Zoom room. Was it a mistake to have even tried this?

After reaching out to Jeffrey's mom via email, explaining that she was sorry about her feeling disrespected and inviting her to sit down together, Linda got up from her desk. Wandering unsteadily into the kitchen to make herself a cup of tea, she reflected on her Civic Education class at MBO-Holland, a vocational school serving 30,000 students. She had taught civics there for eight years, and felt good about her teaching—or at least she had when she was teaching in person.

Ironically, before Covid-19 hit, she had been known in her department for her ability to deftly lead discussions about controversial issues. But during Covid—and now post-Covid, as the MBO-Holland school administration had figured out they could serve a more diverse and expansive student body, with a smaller budget, by offering online courses—she had been teaching half of her civics lessons online. It had taken her a while to adjust to the new set-up, but she now felt she was finding her feet again. Or at least she had felt that way until Jeffrey's mother had reamed her out in front of the entire class during their first controversial issues discussion of the semester. The experience left her wondering whether she should even have tried the discussion—and whether she should try anything like it again.

When she arrived for her next in-person teaching day, Linda was relieved to discover that Jeffrey's mother hadn't followed up on her threat to contact the administration. But her questions about the experience remained. The episode had made her see that she just couldn't control who was present at these online discussions or guarantee a confidential space for her students. However, civic discussions had long been a key part of her teaching, and she was reluctant to minimize the role they played in her curriculum. Linda was glad to have a chance to discuss her concerns at her department's weekly team meeting. She knew many of her colleagues were also unsettled by the school's newfound commitment to online and hybrid teaching, particularly when it came to discussions of controversial issues, which could be challenging even under ideal circumstances. She hoped that their views would give her some clarity.

"So, here's the challenge," Linda began, after recounting the encounter with Jeffrey's mother to her colleagues Stan, Latifa, and Claire. "How can we prepare our students for respectful participation in civic discourse, both online and in person, if they cannot even practice this skill in school? But at the same time, is it fair to ask teachers and students to share their views in an unprotected space? I just don't know."

Stan, a longtime teacher at MBO-Holland, replied immediately: "Well, you kind of give the answer yourself already. The main question is: can we organize online discussions, whether spontaneous or prepared, in a way that protects us and our students? The answer is simple: there is no way to be 100% sure that classes are not recorded or witnessed by other parties without prior notice. Hence, we cannot fully protect students—or ourselves—so we shouldn't organize online discussions of civic issues."

"Although," Linda interjected, "making and sharing videos from class without permission is prohibited by law."

"Illegal things happen all the time," Stan argued. "We don't know what students are doing at home."

"I agree that we cannot completely guarantee that our students, and we ourselves, are safe in class," Latifa began. Before beginning her career at MBO-Holland, she had worked for several years at a nonprofit organization that helped migrant workers find jobs. She and Linda had joined the faculty in the same year and had become friends as well as colleagues. "However, we can do a lot to increase our safety. There's MBO Holland's online education protocol, for example, the one that we adopted from 'SocialmediaIMPACT.' At the start of a new module I always remind my students about these guidelines and about our own protocol for online discussions of civic issues. Having these guidelines has made online discussions run smoothly in my class."

"But I wonder how many parents know about the protocol?" Linda asked. "I went over guidelines with my students, too, but I still ran into trouble. Maybe it would help if we provided more information at the institution level? Have parents and students sign a form, for example?"

"What would they agree to do?" Stan asked. "Keep their objections to themselves? Don't get me wrong: I do think it's a good thing that we offer online education guidelines at the institute level. I just don't see how the signatory stuff would work. Some parents may feel like they are being asked to shut up, which might create a lot of unrest."

"Yeah, before we know it, this could be framed in the media as a leftish-teaching thing," Latifa chuckled.

"At least Jeffrey's mother didn't threaten to go to the press—only the administration," Linda said, grimacing.

"And there's a practical problem," Stan continued. "We cannot force parents and students to sign. What if they refuse to? Will we have to develop alternative civics classes for them? I'd rather stick to teaching facts and concrete skills in my online classes. Saves us a lot of trouble, and extra work."

"It's a complicated question," Latifa mused. "But just because we can't prevent problems from arising, that doesn't mean we shouldn't organize online discussions at all. After all, students engage with each other on social media all the time. Online, family and even strangers can listen in and comment on their contributions. As civics teachers, we are well positioned to raise students' awareness of their vulnerability online, and to help them learn to cope with negative consequences of their engagement online or in real life."

"True," Stan agreed. "Our students are vulnerable outside of school as well. But in their private lives, students can choose whether or not to join online civic discussions. In school we would be forcing them to participate."

"But we all agree that teaching discussion is part and parcel of civic education, right?" Latifa asked. Her colleagues nodded. "Then why make an exception for online discussion? Our students are not made of sugar: every one of them has experienced or witnessed online conflict by now. Our migrant students, for instance, have received hateful messages on social media just because of the color of their skin. They know how to deal with conflict. Most of our students have also had social media education in primary and secondary education. Maybe we are making this too big a thing."

"But it is a big thing," Linda protested, "*especially* for our students from migrant backgrounds. Latifa, you know the discrimination they face when looking for an internship, and I've heard your horror stories from your last job. I've seen what my students here face! By explicitly addressing experiences with harmful speech in our classes and giving them skills to confront this harmful speech, we let our students know that we care about them, that their school cares."

"I disagree," Stan objected. "We can show them that we care by not exposing them to yet more potentially unsafe online spaces. Our migrant students, and students from other groups that often experience marginalization, they are the students we most need to protect."

"What about us teachers?" Claire, who had been silent thus far, burst out. She was a second-year teacher who often turned to this group for support. "We are on the line 24/7. What protection do we have? Dealing with conflicts in the regular classroom is enough of a challenge for me. I would feel very uncomfortable adding another layer of complexity with the online element."

"Moderating discussions can be extremely difficult, especially online," Latifa affirmed. "I can definitely understand wanting to reserve discussions for on-site classes, especially when you're still a relatively new teacher."

"On-site classes are not completely safe, either," Claire went on, visibly upset. "When I was teaching intercultural competencies before the last election, several students threatened to put me on the hotlist for leftist teachers. And don't forget about Samuel Paty; the anniversary of his death just passed. I haven't organized any discussions for a while now. I just don't want to risk my safety—or my family's."

"I didn't know about that hotlist threat; I'm sorry. I totally understand your reticence," Linda reassured her. "In that sense, we are lucky that there are no formal requirements concerning classroom debates in Citizenship Education legislation for vocational institutes. Each of us can pretty much decide for ourselves what we want to do."

"Thus maintaining inequality in education," Latifa sighed. "I bet that students from our pre-university institutes have not put their debating classes on hold during the pandemic. Our vocational students deserve the same attention to be paid to their civic development."

"I wonder," Linda mused, "whether the school can do more to actively encourage the development of online and offline safe spaces for discussion, and encourage students and parents to share their views in a respectful manner. My class might have gone very differently if we had that kind of support."

"I can help you out on that one," Stan replied. "When Claire had the hotlist incident, I went to Dean Doozer to discuss how to handle the situation. She expressed her sympathy, but that was about it. She basically told me: it's not a criminal offense, so there's little that she can do."

"Leaving it to the individual teacher to restore relations and deal with incidents," Linda sighed. "I see. So chances are low that Miss Doozer will invest in additional measures to further students' and teachers' sense of safety in online classrooms. We seem to be on our own."

"Of course, there is another option," Stan pointed out. "What if we returned to in-person education full time? Then we wouldn't need to worry about these online discussions."

"The question of teaching students to engage in civic discourse online wouldn't go away," Linda responded, "but being able to teach those skills in the onsite classroom would remove some of the challenges. Plus, having our students here in person would have other benefits. I'm worried that we'll see more kids drop out with this blended model; it's hard to build strong connections over Zoom."

"I know there's been pushback to this new blended model," Latifa said. "But it does allow students more flexibility; we're able to enroll some students who might not be able to come to campus all day, every day. Besides, they'll only be living more of their lives online as time goes on. We need to prepare them."

"Plus, these discussions of controversial issues don't automatically become safe just because we're back in person," Claire pointed out. "I personally won't be running them at all, but I do see how being back onsite could make them easier for you, Linda."

"Any chance that our board would reconsider their decision to make civics a hybrid course?" Linda asked.

"Maybe, if enough of us got together. At our next meeting we should start working on a petition asking for citizenship courses like ours to be offered only onsite," Stan suggested.

"I'm not fully convinced that's the right course, but that's a question for another day," Linda said. "It's time for the next period."

Walking to her next class, Linda still felt undecided. While her colleagues had brought up insightful points, she felt like she had more questions than she started with. Should she play it safe and stop organizing classroom discussions until she was teaching all of her classes onsite? Or should she embrace the risk, together with her students, and help them build the public discourse skills they would need as digital citizens? Could she resume organizing online discussions with some extra precautions, and try to view any bumpy moments as learning opportunities?

And considering Stan's final suggestion: should she and her team petition for citizenship courses to be offered 100 percent on-site, to facilitate both spontaneous and structured conversations on civic issues that students grapple with? Or should she embrace the blended model, as a way for students to prepare for hybrid civic participation in their adult lives? How would she engage students in discussion, now and in the future?

Conversation

Translated by Isolde de Groot

Isolde de Groot: The idea of NCS discussions is that every time you sit down with new people, you learn new things about a case. This conversation thus offers another step in the eternal process of exploring new perspectives and knowledge. So my first question is: what are the central dilemmas in this case?

Bjorn Wansink: For me, the core dilemma is whether or not to have online discussions. Specifically, the dilemma is about organizing online controversial discussions in Citizenship. There are Citizenship themes that lend themselves better for online teaching than controversial discussions do.

Susan Sants: This is also the central dilemma that I identified—we've seen this dilemma at our school in the context of safety. During Covid-19, some of the classes that were considered suitable for online teaching turned out not to be. Particular subjects (religion, sexual preferences, politics, etc.) where students have different points of view are difficult to address online. Going online was not always the right and safe choice.

Belinda Kleijweg: Indeed, some of the choices made during the pandemic were not safe at all. As citizenship educators, we were opposed to the decision to make Citizenship an online course. This decision whether to hold controversial discussions online or not is also the main dilemma for me.

Clemijn Schreuder: Can you offer a safe learning climate online or physically? And apart from the possibility of having a safe online learning climate: Do you think it's desirable to have these kinds of challenging conversations online in the first place?

Bjorn Wansink: I was thinking of an initiative called "Ter Info" (FYI). For FYI, we make lesson plans to teach about socially destructive moments. We did this, for example, about the war in Ukraine. During Corona, we also made a lesson plan for an online lesson about the curfew riots in the pandemic era. When developing the lesson, we were very conscious about the fact that parents might listen in …. And I'm still undecided about whether or not it is desirable to organize controversial issues discussions, on-site as well as online. It's desirable under the right conditions, which aren't always there, especially online. I find it very difficult: what is the purpose of having such discussions? I am cautious about having controversial conversations in class in general—it's not necessarily a positive thing. And with parents in the online classroom, it even becomes more complicated. So my big question reading the case was: What was Linda's learning goal? What did she want students to learn from engaging in the controversial conversation in this case? And if the learning objective was to teach them how to engage in controversial issues discussions: were there safer ways in which Linda could have organized this conversation? Safer for herself, safer for her students, especially for Jeffrey?

Isolde de Groot: You mentioned that one shouldn't always discuss controversial topics. How do you decide which learning goals are appropriate for student discussions?

Bjorn Wansink: I think it's context dependent. Sometimes, teachers have weeks to prepare for a classroom conversation about a sensitive issue. When they plan to talk about the Holocaust, for example, they tell students, "In six weeks we will be discussing the Holocaust, and this may be sensitive or difficult for you." They then have a long time to prepare. But this is much more difficult in the online environment. What you simply miss online is that *fingerspitzen*-feeling [context sensitivity]. In an in-person lesson, you can take account of student responses: "Hey, that student isn't saying anything, but there's definitely something going on." You lose all that in the online environment, even without a parent bumping in, which is an extreme case.

And there's something else about online discussions that gives me pause. Education must happen in a safe environment that you co-construct with your students throughout the year. Lecturers will not organize difficult conversations until after eight or ten weeks of class, once they have established a relationship with students. But online, all kinds of other actors enter the field, over whom you have no influence at all. In this case, it's a parent that Linda has no control over. What does this mean for education? This has not been thought through yet. Especially during Covid-19, when teachers have been thrown into online teaching, school leaders haven't yet thought through what online education means for the teacher and for students. I myself am not even sure about what it means exactly, but the online environment definitely changes the context of a lesson: It influences your role as a teacher, and it influences the responsibilities you have, because apparently you are not only teaching your students. You are also teaching parents. But that was not the agreement that was made beforehand. Those parents have never been in your classroom before. It requires us to look at education differently.

Clemijn Schreuder: Many people also experienced this at the start of Covid-19: How am I going to teach online? This was a whole new task. I wonder to what extent it was a very conscious choice for Linda to organize an online classroom discussion. In general, I noticed that teachers continued doing what they always did in person in the new online setting and then ended up being surprised that their usual teaching methods were not working anymore. This was what I received most questions about an I-coach at the beginning of Covid-19.

Belinda Kleijweg: As a citizenship teacher, I know that students sometimes enter the classroom preoccupied with something that happened outside school or in another class. Take for example the 2019 shooting in Utrecht city [in which a man shot people in the subway, leaving four dead and six injured]. Students came to my class talking about this. For many discussions, you simply don't have the time to prepare, which can be complicated. I am grateful, Bjorn, for the lessons that your team has been making. Yet you can't always prepare properly, either online or in the physical classroom. And sometimes I get the most out of discussions that emerge spontaneously, discussions that arise from student emotions. I find them very valuable, but I find it difficult to have such spontaneous discussions online, as I have no control in the online classroom. In the physical classroom you have your position in front of the class and you can use your whole body to direct a conversation. In the online classroom, everyone has an equal slice of the screen.

Susan Sants: It's interesting what you say, about being more equal online than in person. I never thought about that.

Clemijn Schreuder: This was also a problem in the beginning of the pandemic: That all rights were equal. The user rights were not set correctly, and students could, for example, mute each other or throw each other out of class. In the physical classroom, it's impossible to throw the teacher out. No one would consider it.

Susan Sants: Or the students could call in their friends!

Clemijn Schreuder: It's conquering the monkey rock [dismantling the hierarchy] all over.

Bjorn Wansink: With all the technological developments, many of the technological issues will be solved in a couple of years. But teacher professionalization is another matter. There are promising developments in online instruction. But this does not yet mean that teachers are able to organize online discussions in a pedagogically sound and safe manner. We also don't have many good practices. How do other teachers hold these discussions online; what do scholars propose? During Covid-19, teachers had to figure it out by themselves. But they have to learn it somehow, to be able to discuss how to organize online discussions on sensitive or controversial issues before they do it. And it does happen. In Israel, for example, there are teachers who organize well prepared controversial issues discussions online or collaborative inquiry with Jewish and Palestinian students together. The knowledge exists, but you need the right context and good preparation.

Clemijn Schreuder: Organizations need to give teachers the opportunity to prepare and discuss these kinds of lessons. At our school the online support team developed a vision document for online education. Our main message was: teachers need assistance, not only on a technical level, but also on a pedagogical and didactic level. You can't expect people to do it alone.

Bjorn Wansink: In this case, that ship has already sailed. Linda does not feel supported by the school management, which is fatal. Of course, school leaders also find this very difficult, but Linda should not have been on her own. The teaching profession is a very isolated one, which makes proper organizational support very important.

Susan Sants: As a teacher, you need to respond to things that happen in society, but it's hard to capture what to respond to and how to respond in a policy document. I think that teacher support is very important here but also complicated. Think for example about a violent incident that happened close to one of our locations. One student was injured, and there were many police present. As a teacher you cannot ignore the incident, but students have very different ideas about whether or not it is legitimate to use violence when one's involved in a rival youth group. Some said that the victim deserved it. Classmates were crying. As a teacher you need to decide in the moment how you will attend to what happened only minutes before the start of your lesson, and how you will attend to the different perspectives and emotions that students bring to class.

Belinda Kleijweg: Some teachers are trained to organize conversations about controversial issues, but a large proportion of educators are not. Shouldn't everyone attend such a training? You shouldn't leave all discussions about what happens in school or society to the citizenship teacher, but this is often what happens. In the case of the school shooting, for example, somebody from victim-support needs to be around the next day. The discussions should not be left to the teachers.

Susan Sants: Those trainings are being offered at our institute. However, I noticed that teachers only realize the need for such training when something happens. Some teachers find it easier to handle such things than others, but support should certainly be provided to all teachers. Colleagues and management must support teachers and talk with students, to let them know that they are there for them. We know people really value this kind of support.

Isolde de Groot: Do I understand you correctly, Belinda—you feel that it is often left to individual teachers to take up a controversial issue, particularly civics teachers?

Belinda Kleijweg: Both teachers and school leaders must be aware of what is involved in guiding such improvised conversations. Some scholars argue that one needs to be as neutral as possible, but this underestimates the impact an event can have on teachers themselves. It's crucial that teachers learn what it means to have this kind of conversation, from the techniques that one can use to the emotions it can evoke.

Bjorn Wansink: That is so true. When I speak at conferences, I sometimes have an audience of only ten people. Yet, as soon as something happens in society, I have a full room. Attention for discussing controversial issues easily drops. Citizenship teachers are more aware of it and engage in more permanent reflections. But other teachers often ignore or postpone learning how to facilitate these discussions. They don't feel the urgency. And then, when something happens, they do not know what to do.

Clemijn Schreuder: I've had a lot of conversations with students about personal issues. Students who tell me that they are forced to marry someone or get beaten, for example. Then you think: "I never learned to handle this situation in teacher training. How do I deal with this?" At that point, it's difficult to say: "Hold on, I'm going to figure out how to respond, and then I'll be right back." You then have to make the best of it.

Bjorn Wansink: What are your responsibilities as a teacher? How far will you go? These questions are also at stake in this case. Do you have responsibility for that parent? I don't think so. And how far does your responsibility for the kids go? Thinking in terms of responsibilities, things become very diffuse. How far does your responsibility as a teacher go, for example, in the case of radicalization? When do you alert others? Are we becoming a society that criminalizes kids? How do you interpret what is happening when a sixteen-year-old girl suddenly starts wearing a headscarf? Is it a sign of radicalization or simply a sign of identity development? It is important to consult others on such questions. And how do schools position themselves in this? Conversations about these questions are important, and external expertise is needed. There is no right and wrong. It's just important to look at such questions from different perspectives.

Isolde de Groot: So far we have talked about whether or not controversial discussions can be organized safely, and what it takes to organize them. You also raised many questions. How is Linda's learning objective important? What are a teacher's responsibilities, and where do they end? How should teachers prepare to lead these conversations? What is the role of school leaders and the school policy in this preparation? Let's move on to an underlying question: Are we talking about the same values? Many of you mentioned safety as a key value, for example.

Clemijn Schreuder: The dilemma is a trade-off between two values: safety and social responsibility. It's important to have conversations about controversial issues, because people should be able to do this in real life as well as in school. But you don't want to organize them at the expense of your own safety. You have to balance these two interests against each other.

Bjorn Wansink: I didn't get the impression that we agreed on the values that we deem most important. Everyone thought it was important to have conversations about controversial issues in schools. But we think differently about how you organize them.

Belinda Kleijweg: In my view, the central theme is safety, with its multiple angles.

Susan Sants: Everyone experiences safety differently—it has a different meaning for everyone. It's always easy to categorize something as a safety issue. Sometimes it refers to people's feelings. Other times it refers to people's sense of security in a given situation. It all depends on what prior experiences you've had.

Isolde de Groot: We talked about the sense of security of teachers, from several perspectives. What about the perspective of the parent?

Bjorn Wansink: There is little information about Jeffrey's mother in this case. It seems that she misunderstood the aim of the discussion and the status of the perspective shared. I think Linda could have fixed this misunderstanding by starting a conversation with the parent and explaining that the goal of the discussion was to raise different perspectives about the initial statement. I don't see Linda as an activist trying to convince everyone to quit smoking, so with adequate intervention, her conflict with Jeffrey's mother could easily be solved in my view.

Clemijn Schreuder: Well, we don't know how much of the lesson Jeffrey's mother overheard. The whole lesson? How many weeks had Linda been working on it? Maybe they had already read an article beforehand? Maybe they already put things in the chat that the mother didn't know? I fully understand how Linda got stuck.

Bjorn Wansink: Communication helps. I often have phone conversations with parents because of my research. For example, students have taken pictures of pieces of a questionnaire, showing a question totally out of context. In such instances you have to do a lot of repair work. I'm not saying that these conversations always succeed in clearing the air. When parents are radicalized, for example, it's very difficult. But Jeffrey's mother doesn't seem radicalized. Maybe she smokes, or has just been to the hospital, or has recently lost someone to smoking. You don't know what's going on in her life. It's important here to keep an open attitude and to think about how to interpret and act in this situation as a teacher. In case of a misunderstanding, it is important to solve the issue right away, maybe in tandem with the school leader, and not let it simmer. Now it's left unresolved, which is very annoying for Linda.

Clemijn Schreuder: And for Jeffrey.

Bjorn Wansink: You also don't know if the values are different. Linda might have said, "We live in a democracy and we are allowed to disagree. You may disagree with me. My point is that we learn to disagree within the framework of democracy. You can smoke, that's fine." If she's lucky, Jeffrey's mother would have understood. It is important that you say this with respect for the mother and for her vision. And Linda shouldn't be alone—she needs other people to take the load off. This should be the job of the school board.

Clemijn Schreuder: Things like this happen. Yes. You sometimes get an email from a parent saying, "I hear that you have discussed this, but …" Then you can quietly think about how to answer—that makes a big difference. You can even think together with your school management, for example, before you send an email back.

Bjorn Wansink: I think Linda couldn't have done much because Jeffrey's mother was very emotional. There should have been a period of cooling down. Linda should have just accepted that the parent was going overboard for a while. And above all, she needed to keep herself and her students safe. The conversation with the mother was not possible just then, certainly not with the children present.

Belinda Kleijweg: Prior to the next lesson she should have spoken with Jeffrey, and during this next lesson she should discuss it with the whole class.

Isolde de Groot: What should be done in this case?

Bjorn Wansink: Linda must look at different perspectives. What should she do with Jeffrey's mother? With Jeffrey? With the other students? With the school board? You always have conflicting interests. There is no solution that satisfies everyone, so you make a conscious choice within all these opposing interests. It's difficult to know what is right or wrong. There are too many interests.

Clemijn Schreuder: I don't have a solution, but Linda must have someone she can talk to about this. She cannot and should not be alone in this. The team leader has to step in to help her. At mboRijnland, we have I-coaches you can work with. We have an education service center. But when talking to a parent you have to work with the team leader. For the educational part Linda needs to talk to the education service center, and for the online piece she needs an I-coach. She needs help.

Susan Sants: I agree with that. If she's struggling emotionally, she should also talk to a counselor.

Belinda Kleijweg: The team leader must be aware and stand behind Linda, in case Jeffrey's mother makes a complaint. And maybe for the sake of confidence she should avoid online discussions and start in the physical classroom, talking about how to have conversations, rather than organizing the discussion online a week later. It is important that there is a conversation. We generally find it difficult to start conversations, but it must be done in the classroom. It would be a waste if teachers would see no other option than to hold back from organizing controversial issues discussions altogether.

Bjorn Wansink: I agree. You also have to see it in perspective. Maybe you have good conversations for ten years and you have this parent once. Or to frame it more radically: Should you refrain from teaching controversial issues discussion because there is always the slightest chance that you will become the next Samuel Paty, the history teacher in France who was killed by a terrorist in 2020? In my opinion, don't be tied down by terrorists. You have to resist and have the conversation. But you have to have faith in it. Self-confidence is important. Then you can deal with a parent more easily.

Susan Sants: Tools are also important—you need to know what to do.

Belinda Kleijweg: Organizing opportunities for teacher reflection and collaboration is also very important. It would be a shame if teachers would refrain from facilitating classroom discussions because they feel that they are the only ones struggling. We would miss out on some beautiful, spontaneous conversations. For example, at our school a student from Wassenaar who has only attended White schools and a student who has only attended Islamic schools can find out that they both came to MBO with the same fear: fear of each other. It's a shame not to have those conversations. Sharing these experiences as teachers is important. And it's important to support these conversations and recognize how challenging they can be to organize so that teachers feel heard.

Clemijn Schreuder: We like to share our good experiences, but it's also important to share bad experiences. That way teachers can learn from each other.

Isolde de Groot: What do you hope people think about after they read this case and this conversation?

Clemijn Schreuder: Linda is not alone. She must feel that she can go anywhere at her school to get help.

Susan Sants: This conversation was very instructive. We leaders may think we are very transparent and that everyone within our organization knows where to go for help, but it is not clear to everyone. Also, the sense of urgency must be there: what happened to Linda could happen to me, too. Sometimes this urgency is lacking. I hope this case will raise that urgency.

Belinda Kleijweg: I think it's very important that controversial issues discussions take place. But we need more collaboration. It's important that teachers learn to share their experiences. I think that this way, teachers would discover that they have similar experiences with these discussions.

Bjorn Wansink: We must put things in perspective: ninety-nine times it goes right. We can't focus on that one time. Teachers should be proud of the work they do. Just know what you stand for and what your goals for civic education are.

Belinda Kleijweg, BSc, has been a Citizenship teacher at mboRijnland in The Netherlands since 2015. She has a special interest in citizenship education development and is currently doing a master's degree in urban pedagogy at the Rotterdam University of Applied Sciences.

Clemijn Schreuder is a teacher and I-coach at mboRijnland in The Netherlands. As I-coach, she supports and inspires her colleagues with their implementation of blended learning, along with the application of digital tools to enhance their (physical) lessons.

Susan Sants is a safety coordinator and program manager for diversity, inclusion, and equality at mboRijnland. She is responsible for concern policy, prevention, and awareness concerning safety and school culture/wellbeing. Besides working with mboRijnland colleagues, she also collaborates with municipalities, law enforcement, and other educational institutes.

Bjorn Wansink is an associate professor at the Faculty of Social Sciences of Utrecht University, The Netherlands. In his research work he deals with themes such as cultural diversity, history, citizenship, critical thinking, multiperspectivity, and controversial issues. He regularly acts as an advisor for organizations such as the Council of Europe and the Radicalisation Awareness Network. Wansink is also a trainer for the European Association of History Educators in countries where political transformation goes hand in hand with inter-ethnic and inter-religious tensions.

Character Guide

Setting	
MBO-Holland, a vocational school for students ages 16–25 in the Netherlands	
Primary Characters	
Linda Fraser: civics teacher at MBO-Holland **Jeffrey:** 17-year-old student in Linda's class **Jeffrey's mother**	**Stan:** civics teacher at MBO-Holland **Latifa:** civics teacher at MBO-Holland **Claire:** civics teacher at MBO-Holland

Discussion Questions

1 In the case, Latifa insists that online controversial issues discussions are crucial for nurturing future citizens of the digital age, while Stan argues that they expose students "to yet more potentially unsafe online spaces" than they already face. How should the broader incivility of civic

discourse online impact teachers' decisions whether and how to run online discussions?

2 How is the online classroom distinct from the in-person classroom? How are they the same? How should educators diving into controversial issues take these similarities and differences into account?

3 How should teachers decide which issues are "controversial"? How should they decide which controversial issues to bring into their classrooms?

4 Stan suggests that teachers should not hold controversial issues discussions if they cannot "be 100% sure that classes are not recorded or witnessed by other parties without prior notice." Do you agree with this assessment? Why/why not?

5 Multiple teachers in the case raise concerns about safety—for both themselves and their students. How would you characterize their views about "safety"? What does "safety" in the classroom mean to you (online and/or in person)?

6 The teachers in this case feel they are "on their own" in this discussion, unable to turn to their administration for answers or support. Why might school leadership be wary to enter this conversation? What kinds of support from leadership might be helpful to teachers?

7 Latifa raises concerns about inequity in civic education between the vocational students at their school and the pre-university students at other schools in the country. How should the school's mission as a vocational institution impact the decisions that the teachers make here?

Note

1. "Bevolking; geslacht, lft, generatie en migr.achtergrond, 1 jan; 1996–2022," StatLine—Statistics Netherlands, May 31, 2022, https://opendata.cbs.nl/statline/#/CBS/nl/dataset/37325/table.

4

High School at the Coal-Face: The Cost of Getting "What We're Owed"

Sarah Gurr and Daniella J. Forster

This case study draws on research and media concerning environmental sustainability, coal mining, and education, as well as our experiences living in the Hunter Valley in New South Wales, Australia. This region is one of Australia's largest coal mining regions and is home to the biggest coal export port in the world. In Australia, where there are growing inequities in public funding of schools, schools are looking to non-government sources, commercial sponsorship arrangements, and private contributions to supplement the government funding they receive. To do so, public schools must report annually to the Department of Education on how private funding arrangements benefit department, school, and community outcomes. Sponsorships are not philanthropic, but involve an exchange between the private company and the school where both parties benefit. Fossil fuels companies are large donors of education initiatives and it is not uncommon for schools in fossil fuels communities to receive funding, resources, or sponsorship from mining companies in exchange for their gaining access to the school community, promotional opportunities, non-tangible benefits such as an enhanced corporate social responsibility reputation and the potential for future workers. However, partnerships with mining companies are controversial, with concerns about the impact of these corporate sponsors on school curriculum and their appropriateness in a climate changed world.

"Let's move onto our next agenda item. Let's see … the Executive is working on their report for the Department of Education on the impact of South Mining's sponsorship on the school community. Nick, what do they need from us?"[1] Regional High School Parents and Community Association (P&C) Chairperson Carol Peters looked across the round table.

Principal Nick Donovan straightened up in his seat to survey the group. It had been a productive meeting with most of the time spent planning the upcoming trivia night to raise funds for the Year 12 Formal, but frustrations had grown when Carol announced that their latest funding request to relawn the school's oval had been unsuccessful. This had been the third time the school had requested funding from the Department to upgrade the school's sporting facilities, and with the oval worsening with each summer the rejection was particularly disappointing.

Nick addressed the group. "As you know, as a condition of our sponsorship agreement with South Mining, the School Executive are required to submit a report to the Department of Education each year. This year, we'd like the P&C to again make comments in our submission as a representative of the school community to support the continuation of South's sponsorship. We've been very lucky to have secured this partnership, particularly given the events of the past year. South's sponsorship was critical to our remote learning plans during the COVID-19 lockdowns.[2] Many of our students needed laptops at home, and we could only provide them with South's funding. Their support has allowed us to continue running the literacy intervention program they sponsored while students were isolating. I think we need to do what we can to continue this sponsorship and would like to find ways to strengthen it. In fact, from my conversation with South's community relations officer, they're open to supporting the development of engineering-based curricular materials for Science and Technology, and funding new robotics equipment, too."[3]

Carol added, "Thanks, Nick. Does anyone have any questions or comments about our sponsorship agreement? I think we should consider how South Mining could support the school community in the future, to add weight to the continuation of the sponsorship."

"Yeah, I've got an idea, Carol." Steve Jones raised his hand. "What if we reached out to South Mine about the oval? My son hurt his knee there last month during training. I don't know if we can afford to wait another year for the Department to consider funding it. South sponsors the boys' rugby team and donated equipment to the club. I reckon they'd be happy to chip in for re-turfing the oval, too."

"Thanks, Steve," Carol replied. "Perhaps they could also fund some shade sails to give the kids somewhere cool to hang out at lunchtime. I think South helped Regional Primary School last year with shading for their playground. And maybe we can work with them to do something about the classrooms without air conditioning. My son has been complaining that the classrooms get so hot he can barely concentrate."

Carol looked across the room. "Helen, did you want to add something? I'm sure you know a few more projects they've sponsored, like, The Healthy Kids, Healthy Food program and the Breakfast Club."

Helen Gordon had raised her hand briefly while Steve was speaking but lowered it, apparently thinking twice about adding to the conversation. Helen had joined the P&C relatively recently, when she and her husband had moved to town on a tree change,[4] filling the vacancy for doctors at the local practice.

After a moment's pause, Helen spoke, "What benefits do the mines get out of this sponsorship agreement, I wonder? I think we should hold off on reaching out to the mines to fund this. They are already involved in so many projects with the school, I—" she hesitated, choosing her words carefully. "I'm worried about the message this is sending our kids. My daughter wanted to be a vet before we moved to town, but ever since that Careers Day earlier this year, she keeps talking about applying for an apprenticeship at one of the mines after Year 10 because she thinks it's the only way to make money in this town. I'm worried we're limiting our kids' dreams of what's possible for their future by spotlighting the mines all the time."

Helen continued. "And then there's the message we're sending to the community when we partner with companies like this. South has done some good for our school, but they're not squeaky clean, what with the botched rehabilitation after that big fish kill in the river. I'm not saying ..." She paused again before continuing. "I just think we should try to fundraise what we can on our own and reach out to some other stakeholders. There's more to this community than those mines."

Helen's comment was greeted with stares. Carol broke the silence, "Thank you, Helen, um, are you saying you don't support a continuing sponsorship agreement?"

Helen responded defensively, "Things are changing and we need to think carefully about where we stand. What if there's another Juukan Gorge tragedy[5] and South is responsible for it? Tens of thousands of years of history crumbled to dust, and we're partnered with the company at fault?"

"Let's not jump to conclusions—there's a strong Aboriginal consultation process in place," interjected Steve. "We can't cut ties with the biggest investors in town just because they're coal miners. The coal mines do a heck of good for all of us. Most of the people in this room are connected to the mines in one way or another."

Steve continued, "If anything, I'm concerned about the message *not* reaching out to the mines to help pay for this sends to *our* kids. At the mine, we've been finding it hard to get properly qualified technicians. We need a stronger partnership to build a specialised mining academy here to meet demand. The mine has a long lease on the land. My kids came home after a Science lesson last week, going on about the negative impacts of mining and barely mentioning just how important coal is to our everyday lives. It's not all truck driving and blowing stuff up! It's like teachers are trying to make my kids feel guilty about what their parents do for a living."[6]

"No, I'm not saying we should be demonising the mines or cutting ties with them, just that we should engage with other businesses first," Helen responded. "Diversify a bit. And spend some time building relationships that will serve us better long after the mines are gone. What about that new wind farm that started up?"

"Thank you, Steve and Helen," Carol started, "I appreciate you sharing your concerns."

Nick stepped in: "I will speak with the Executive. We will try to take these points into consideration in our future planning, but we will need a statement from the Committee on how South's sponsorship has contributed to the broader school community. Perhaps you can connect with the parents of a few of the kids who got the laptops, Carol?"

Helen shifted uncomfortably and began gathering her things as Carol called the meeting to a close.

"Well, that could've gone a lot worse," David Matthews muttered as he joined Nick in reassembling the library furniture in the emptying room. Nick and David were neighbors and their kids often played together, but the two men had gotten to know each other better when David took up the school's Aboriginal Education Officer[7] position a few years ago. As the school had a high proportion of students who identified as Aboriginal and Torres Strait Islander, David played an important role in the community in supporting the learning and wellbeing of Indigenous students.

"I thought it was going to when Helen spoke up," Nick admitted, gesturing for David to grab the end of a table with him. "What do you reckon? Are we focusing on the mines too much for funding and job opportunities?"

"I get where Helen's coming from," David began. "In an ideal world, I don't think we should have sponsors at all. Public schools should be publicly funded."

"Yeah, but we're not in an ideal world," Nick sighed. "Public schools have drawn the short straw of the funding deal between state and federal governments.[8] Until the funding is more equitable, we need to look elsewhere to cover the costs. We're being encouraged to supplement the funding we get through sponsorships like these, and if we don't ..."

David nodded, "My niece just started her teaching degree this year and having a scholarship from East Mine has made things so much easier for her. I know the good that these mines are doing for our kids." David paused. "Honestly, I think they should be doing more. We all see how much coal goes out of here on those trains, and it's not like these mines are getting any smaller, and now with a gas plant opening down the road ... These companies are desecrating Country for profit, they're ignoring the objections of our Mob, and the government is letting them.[9] And it's these kids—our kids—who'll be left with the clean up bill and lost heritage when the mines are gone. If we can't stop them, our kids may as well reap the benefits of the mines and their money in the meantime. It's what we're owed."

***

Heading to the staff meeting the following afternoon, Nick bid goodbye to students as he passed. As he approached the staffroom, Nick walked into a conversation between new science teacher, Jessica Young, and Greg Martin, the science head teacher. Jessica had secured a permanent position at the school at the start of the year as part of a scholarship program for new graduates who would teach in rural or remote communities. The school had had a difficult time attracting new teachers and had been unable to offer physics as a Higher School Certificate subject since the old physics teacher retired four years ago. When Jessica arrived with codes for physics and biology, her appointment was greeted with optimism. But since then, her enthusiasm for climate science and environmental advocacy had rubbed some the wrong way. Not that she was wrong, Nick thought. Sustainability was a Cross Curriculum Priority and science was the right place to integrate it.

Jessica and Greg were discussing the upcoming School Mines Tour for Year 9 students. The tours were part of a long-running program that fostered dialogue between the community and mining industry, serving as an opportunity for students to learn about the impacts and benefits of mining in the region. With a smile, Nick joined their conversation.

"Why do our students tour the mine sites?" Jessica asked. "Are there other options available to students interested in something else? I was talking to my Year 10 class about sustainable ecosystems and balancing human needs last week, and students started talking about the impact of coal mining on the environment and species like the black throated finch and how completely helpless they feel to change any of it. It was really sad. Surely they're not alone in this? And if they're not, shouldn't we be giving them the chance to tour some rehabilitated sites, maybe get involved with Indigenous mining rehabilitation groups? They want to make a difference and to do something that gives them a bit of hope for the future. Some even mentioned organising a protest against the new gas power plant."

"I appreciate that they're passionate about this," said Greg, "but I don't think they should let themselves get upset about something that's outside their control. If they want to do something to make a noticeable difference to the environment, they could get involved in the school's recycling project, or volunteer to plant some trees at the North Mine rehabilitation site one weekend. Some students a few years ago used to clean up the creek every month, maybe these kids could start that up again."

"I'm sure these students would be interested in those projects—I'll pass it on." Jessica continued, "But there's a double standard here. We are encouraging them to be more environmentally conscious while we work with coal mines who have been fined for pollution!"

"We're required by our Code of Conduct to work in partnership with our community," Nick explained.[10] "And really, the mines sponsor so many projects we take for granted here. A lot of the environmental projects we run are supported by the mines. South helped fund the community garden and their staff helped us plant the veggies they donated when it opened. They've donated equipment to your faculty and subsidized the costs of excursions for our students.[11] In the broader scheme of things that might not account for much, but it's more help than some might offer."

"I think we should do better than that." Jessica's voice quietened, deflated. "I never saw myself making concessions for coal companies. It makes me feel complicit for all the things I stand against."

"Jess, I know you mean well," Greg said reassuringly, "but this isn't the time to debate about coal mining and climate change; this is about what our students and our school need. Either we partner with businesses who can help cover the costs of what we need, or our students miss out. We compete with the private school for enrolments every year and then at the end of Year 10, we lose even more students to them because they can offer HSC subjects that we can't. That's all well and good for the families who can afford it, but for the ones who can't, or the ones who choose to stay, we owe it to them to provide the best education we can. Sometimes that comes with compromise."

"And what about our students' futures, or their children's? Don't we owe them those same promises? Or is that part of the compromise?"

***

As Nick returned to his office after the staff meeting, he picked up a torn piece of paper that had fallen out of a bin. In large red letters it read "GAS POWER PLANT." Taped to a window nearby, he found the full poster, "SAVE OUR FUTURE! STOP THE REGIONAL GAS POWER PLANT!," next to a flyer for an upcoming School Strike for Climate protest.[12]

Sighing, Nick mentally added this to his ever-increasing list of concerns as he churned over questions in his mind. The sponsorship agreement with South Mining had been critical in supporting his students' academic and socio-economic needs in recent years, and continuing this sponsorship would ensure ongoing support for these students. Was the school becoming too reliant on the mining industry to supplement the Department's limited funding? What kind of relationship should the school and fossil fuels industry have now that community sentiment is becoming increasingly polarized? How should he lead his school through this sponsorship evaluation process while respecting community stakeholders' fears and responding to students' concerns?

Conversation

Daniella Forster: I just would like to begin by saying how excited I am to see you guys all at once, all together, and I just wanted to say thank you so much for joining me today to talk about "High School at the Coal Face: The Cost of 'Getting What We're Owed.'" We're going to be discussing this normative case study about a high school principal, Nick Donovan, in an area not unlike our wonderful Upper Hunter Region, in which he's seeking community input on a sponsorship arrangement with a local coal mining company. He's faced with the problem of how he should lead his school through the sponsorship evaluation process, while respecting community stakeholders' fears and also responding to students' climate concerns.

What are the dilemmas in this case, and for whom? I'd like to start with Kristy, if I can put you on the spot, as an experienced educator in the Upper Hunter Region.

Kristy Pascoe: The case took me straight back to one of the places where I'd worked for a long time and to dilemmas that I had in exactly the same situation. The whole reason that I became a teacher was to try and address some of the inequities that still exist within our educational system, especially for kids that don't come to school with that cultural capital that they need to achieve success. Caring for the environment and the climate crisis is one of the things that I'm really passionate about and have been for a long time. In this situation, being an Aboriginal person, having ideas of how we need to address the climate catastrophe, I'm trying to marry those together.

I was a part of an enrichment program for quite some time that tried to address the discrepancies between the achievement of Aboriginal students and the other kids at school. The funding came from BHP, a mining company. That didn't sit well with me. But then there's the whole thing where, of course, we should be taking whatever money they're going to give us because look at what they're doing. Drive out of town and look at the disgusting landscape. "Why do these people always get everything? And why should we go without?" So trying to balance that fine line of getting some sort of compensation or recompense with wanting to cry or shut my eyes every time I drove past the mining site. At the same time, I have family members who work in the mines. It's just really tricky. I've been away from that school for a couple of years and I don't know, if I went back, how I'd do it. I'd get backlash from parents about some of the things that I delivered in the classroom in relation to the mining industry. It's always walking a very fine line, but it's to the point now where I wouldn't hold my tongue anymore. It wouldn't sit well with me anymore. I wouldn't be able to take the money. I wouldn't be able to justify it as I'd been able to in the past.

Daniella Forster: So, for you, this has really been a process of thinking these things through, experiencing how you behaved in the past, and then coming to feel quite differently about accepting the money and figuring out what's owed?

Kristy Pascoe: It's tricky. We used to call it a race to the bottom, where kids would get more money leaving school and driving trucks in the mine—even the doctor's daughter who always wanted to be a vet and move away. The careers adviser and I were really good friends, and that was one of the things that we'd come across. He was quite a lot more outspoken and quite militant in his views, and he would not take any funding and wouldn't have any personal interaction with the mining companies. We were always worried that kids sometimes didn't aspire to other things because they equated success with money. We'd get kids coming to school saying, "Why should I have to learn this? My dad didn't do this, and my dad didn't go to Year 12, or my dad didn't do the Higher School Certificate (New South Wales)." And he might be earning almost twice as much money as I was at the time. And then you have kids from the horse industry, and they had quite personal confrontations at sporting games and things like that with people from the mining community. They didn't want to take the money either because of how they'd seen that manifest. And at football games one father's standing there from the thoroughbred industry, one is from the mining industry, and they end up almost coming to blows. So the scholarship might make life easy for kids who might not necessarily have that opportunity, but how well does it sit with you?

Anne Marie Ross: I would like to bring in some of the factors that our environment is dealing with at the moment. Australia is at 1.4 degrees Celsius, and we lose the islands at 1.5. We've got huge biodiversity loss, and land clearing up there with the Amazon. I don't want to catastrophize, but I think we need to put those factors on the table so we can see what we're up against.

If the money's taken from these companies, I think that it needs to be clear that there's a lot of questions to be answered. We need to make changes, but all the students can get involved in that and help. There's the mining history to look at. There's the social, economic, political systems thinking that comes together. Is this company an international company? Is it locally owned? Has it got more coal mines being opened? Or will it finish in a few years' time? Can the students be involved in looking at the future? It's a rich way for students to learn, particularly students in inequitable situations. I think there are possibilities there that are really kind of exciting.

Laurie Perry: I live smack bang in the middle of the mining industry. I understand what goes on here every day. I was involved in the mining industry for ten years of my life, working underground. But I also look at the culture and heritage, the Land Rights Act, and the Native Title Act, and I see how they divide Aboriginal communities and people. Then you're looking at mining companies who contribute donations to Aboriginal organizations and to the Aboriginal community to help with their education or health matters. You're really in a Catch-22 position because the mining companies pay royalties to Government and have the great ability to also divide Aboriginal communities and organizations because of that money factor—like "how come you be giving it to them and not to us?" So, you're back to square one again. Damned if you do it, and if you don't. The kids suffer or the community suffers.

James Ladwig: I am on land that is not far from the context you're talking about, and I drive through it often. I've thought about this kind of stuff a long time. What I'd like to do is tease out some of the ways I think about the ethical dilemma for schools. The public school is in a position where it has to represent the public, but the public in this case is fractured, with a lot of different competing interests and a lot of very open public debate. The other thing that would be helpful to know for readers beyond the Hunter Valley is the scope of the mines we're talking about. It might be worth going on to Google Maps and getting a little picture, because it looks like a moonscape. You can stand on one side of the mines on the south end, and then look out toward the north end and see the towers of the power plant. Between you and them, there's next to nothing left. It's all dug. And that's about eighty kilometers overall. The mining companies do what mining companies do. They live within an ecosystem and a legal structure that allows them to do what they do, which includes all kinds of really dodgy stuff. Like I love the way they keep building up mounds and dirt next to the highway so nobody can look in. This is not accidental. The environmental impact of the mines is unquestionable, and it is unquestionable that the communities have been reliant on the very small economic slice they get from the mines. That's what I try to keep reminding people. These days, most of the money generated by the mines doesn't even stay in the country, much less in the local community. So the school and the principal, they're in a situation where there are going to be some of those kids and some of those families who are very much supportive of and dependent on the mining industry. There are going to be some of those kids, as Kristy pointed out, that are going to be in the thoroughbred industry, which is in direct competition these days, and that's even before you bring in the vintners or the local folks that run retail.

But, for the school there's a simple issue here. I think it would be irresponsible for the principal to turn the money away. The question becomes what is learnt from that money? In the case study, you gave the example of a corporate-generated curriculum. And to me that was obviously leading the bill of indoctrination and propaganda. But using a computer? Well, there's lots of things you can do with that. This is where the schools have an obligation to generate curriculum that gives the students the knowledge, the skills, the dispositions to be critical participants in the democratic decision about what happens to our land. This means you might take money from a corporate sponsor, but then you also have an obligation to make it very clear what the public debates are, what the different perspectives are. Students need to know about what's happening to the environment and the scale of it. By the way, I've written curriculum on this. It is in the national framework now, parts of it. To me, the issue is trying to balance the benefits—in this case, it's straight-up money and technology—and asking what is going to be the impact on the kids. The last thing I would be doing is handing over the curriculum to any kind of corporate sponsor. I do think the ethical demands of providing resources lead to one conclusion, but the next question is: what is the educational impact after? And that depends on what you do with it.

Daniella Forster: It seems to me that we've got some alignment here on issues of: How are we going to provide for the students' needs? How are we going to make mining companies accountable for the damage that is taking place across enormous swathes of land toward some kind of transition to bring the community engagement into real focus? So the next question that I'm posing to you is, what are some of the values that we've just been drawing on here?

James Ladwig: Can I just name one right off the bat, which the principal would have in mind, and probably most parents. That is, public schools have a remit to work with whomever they get, and part of that means there's an ethical obligation on the part of public schools to value the children and their families, whoever they are. As much as I have arguments with my neighbors, and the miners down the road, if I was the principal, I would want to not do absolutely anything to suggest that the school thought less of people because of their work. You can have everybody understand why people make the decisions they make, and you can disagree with them. But that's not the school's job. The school's job first and foremost is to value who is there.

Laurie Perry: Mining, the power industry and the education system are all changing right now. How do the mining industry and the power industry engage with the community? I agree, kids should really know more about the holes in the ground and how they're going to fix them. What's the rehabilitation plan? What's the transitional goal? But we're back in that Catch-22 area again. You're damned if you do, or damned if you don't. At the end of the day, you're fighting a system that brings a lot of money to the government and brings a lot of money to the community. We know that mining exists, and we know the mining dialogue of taking the kids out to the mine and saying, "Have a look at this fantastic big mine!" But what's it doing to the environment? And how do we fix that?

Daniella Forster: And Nick Donovan's in the middle here, trying to figure out how should we negotiate with this partner so that we can provide some opportunities for students to reimagine this future, this transitional future.

Laurie Perry: It's critical. It's critical now that this next generation of kids learn about the future of the new energy phase and what it's going to look like and what's going to happen to the holes in the ground and to the environment.

Anne Marie Ross: With some inquiry learning the kids might come up with solutions to that problem. There's some good STEM education with a really big dose of environmental | sustainability education within it.

Back to the values of Aboriginal education. I hope in this area that there is a lot of voice to Aboriginal culture because there'll be a lot of ways forward in how to look after the land and fix the land that we can mention. But I also think we've got to be really careful not to demonize people who are working in the industry. I think everyone's got to hold hands, look at the problems, and find the solutions. The coal companies can't stop that anymore. They've got to go forward. They can't open up new coal mines, they need to transition, and they have to come to terms with the last IPCC [United Nations Intergovernmental Panel on Climate Change] report and the state of the environment.

Kristy Pascoe: It's difficult when you live in these small communities where you have such a huge divide between the haves and the have-nots. When you teach at a school like the one within the story, there are students who come from ridiculous wealth, and kids who know what day the welfare money goes into their parents' account. We're dealing with these kids all the time. One of the terrible things that makes it really difficult when we're talking about not demonizing people that work in the industry, however, is there is a mentality that sometimes comes with the people when you're living in these towns, a prestige that went with obtaining these jobs within the industry. People take on this over-inflated sense of self-worth in comparison to other people who don't have access to the amount of money they do. It creates a divide within these communities.

My father has worked in the industry for a long time. My ex-husband has worked in the industry. I've got friends and cousins that still work in the industry. Many of them did not cope well with the mentality of some of their work mates, with the way that they treat other people, or their views on the world. I do agree with James that one of the biggest things in this situation is to value those people that are in this school, regardless of wherever they come from within the community. The terrible thing is, though, the people who work in the mining industry value themselves enough where their voice is the one that's always heard, or they're the ones we have to tiptoe around. It's the other kids, the ones that always miss out, whose voices are never heard as much as the ones that have all the money or resources. As much as we do value all students, there's sometimes a need to give those ones a little bit of a lift up. To put the mining industry up on the pedestal, to make it what the kids are aspiring to or seem like that's what you need to do to be to be successful in this area, I think it's something that really needs to be addressed.

Daniella Forster: You're talking about triaging needs here, and it sounds to me you're concerned around the same kinds of issues Helen is concerned about. We need to diversify, to try and offer different opportunities for students.

James Ladwig: Can I point out some implied demands of public education? One of them is this valuing of all voices, no matter their background. If you have a student that thinks they're great because their dad makes a lot of money in mining, you can call him out on that! "No, that is contrary to democratic values, that is not acceptable." The reason we need that is because of the need for creating a society in which all voices are heard.

Recognizing what it is that public education stands for is the first order of business. The second order of business is creating a public that can work together democratically and value each other. That's a tall order. It doesn't help that we have schools that don't do that in all kinds of ways. Laurie was talking about the need for making sure these kids understand the challenges at hand and the need for understanding what the transition is. There's two points that I think are crucial. First, students need to understand our impact on the planet. The reality is kids in suburban schools need to understand what their life has done to the land on which they are living, and the only way you're going to do that for any kid is to get them connected to the environment outside them in a serious way, as first-order business. The second thing I'll point out is the demands we are facing these days. One of the criticisms of attempts by schools to create environmentally useful curriculum is that it's "watered down." The reality is in this situation that we need exactly the opposite. These students need to understand the chemistry and the physics and the engineering and the high-level mathematics needed to model what's going on in the environment more than ever before. STEM is not about just introducing kids to scientific stuff. It's about a level of science that the general public doesn't have. We need more, much more, not less.

Daniella Forster: That comes back to Jessica's point in the case. As a science teacher, she feels compromised about providing scientific knowledge that may be watered down, may be inaccessible to some students, and perhaps even inaccessible to herself at some point. But how does she then balance that desire to provide a deep understanding with the knowledge that her Year 9s are going out on mining tours, and the school's technology is funded by South Mining? Can she hold those two complicated positions at once?

Kristy Pascoe: In one of the schools that I was at in the Upper Hunter, I did a Year 9 unit about having a voice, and in one of them I was teaching about the really militant climate activists, Extinction Rebellion. We watched something about them on SBS, and I had this big kid in my class. He was a fantastic, lovely boy; he'd always been so nice and so engaged. So we had the Extinction Rebellion, and we contrasted that with Greta Thunberg, and all of these other people like putting their opinions across. There was an article from the *Guardian*, lots of different things, and talking about the different language that was used and the way that these activists went about their work.

From that time on, I completely lost that student. He refused to acknowledge that there was any climate change, any climate catastrophe, that there was anything going on in the world. He just thought they were all basically a pack of idiots, and he must have gone home and chatted to his parents, who were dairy farmers. It didn't matter what I said to this student after that. I could not get him back. When you try and call climate change out in the classroom—the backlash that this poor young teacher would have had—sometimes it really hurts. I don't know if there's any real way to address it.

Anne Marie Ross: There's a website, Regeneration Australia, that's actually really positive. They've got a movie at the moment where they actually come from the angle of 2029 and how far we've come along. It goes through everything that we've done. It's really positive. It's excellent for students. I think climate change can be too much for people sometimes, and it can freeze people. They can push it away because it's pretty scary stuff.

Daniella Forster: I'm going to move us on to the next question. We've had a look at the principles at stake. We've thought about some of the practical considerations, different personalities, how students can cope with the climate crisis psychologically. Now, what do you think should be done in this case, and really home in on by whom and why?

James Ladwig: For all of these issues—for the big lad who went home to talk to his dairy farmers—the selection of material as a teacher becomes crucial. I think it is crucial for all teachers to take whatever resources are exciting and interrogate them seriously. That would include, in this this case, taking the mining literature and seeing their arguments and trying to understand how they've come to the view they have.

There's an argument about how much money the mines bring to the community or how many miners there are. And, lo and behold, when you look at the detail … some politicians are saying there are 14,000 miners there, and in reality there aren't even 14,000 miners in the whole state. He is literally using false information. You have the opportunity as a teacher to say, "Okay, let's take this view seriously. How could we check this? How could we verify this?" And it's actually quite easy. You go to the ABS [Australian Bureau of Statistics] right now. "So why would he be using this data to make that argument?" You take the different views seriously, and you interrogate them. That includes bringing in views that are really distorted, ones you don't have any kind of real faith in. But, pedagogically, you have got to go with it. I mean, there are people that honestly believe that economic class has no impact on education. Well, I'm not going to persuade them until I take their models seriously and understand how it is they've come to the conclusion they've come to.

Daniella Forster: Principal Nick Donovan, at the end of the case study, has heard the views of Jessica, the young teacher concerned about these curriculum questions that that we've been discussing. He's heard the mentor teacher give her solutions about how to avoid annoying or upsetting the mining companies. We've heard Helen bring in her concerns about needing to diversify sponsorship and Steve saying, "Actually, we need to strengthen the partnerships because there's not enough miners." They're struggling to find technical support. Then he sees "School Strike for Climate" posters around. Even though some of the students want to go to work for the mines, others are mobilizing against those mines. Then there are David's concerns about the impact on Country due to the impact of mining and fossil fuels on the climate, which he must balance with his awareness, as Laurie brings in, of the benefits to Aboriginal students and the educational opportunities the sponsorship could provide.

So what should Principal Nick Donovan do with this sponsorship agreement? What are some solutions for him?

James Ladwig: The first order of businesses is do not give away any rights on curriculum. Yeah, you could agree to having the corporate logo on the machine and leave it at that, but I'd be very restrictive about what the influence of a corporation would be beyond the physical material.

Daniella Forster: Because it's not a philanthropic relationship, is it? It's an exchange for both parties.

Laurie Perry: People have got to understand—the schools and principals—that none of us went to school to become a coal miner. It's only because the mines were here, and they're a resource. The education system has to change to look at what's really needed. From an Aboriginal point of view, the education system is quite clear. Fund the things that are going to be supportive for those five hundred Aboriginal people who live in that community. Fix their needs. Get the parents into a positive parenting class. Work with the community, find the gaps, and close them. That's what they should be developing.

How do you engage with the mining industry from an education point of view? Well, look at the figures, you know. Look at the statistics that are happening within the school system because, like Kristy said, you can get a job in the mining industry like getting something out of a cardboard box. It's not that hard. You don't have to be highly educated to get into the mining industry. It's about what's going to be left when they go? What will they be doing before they go? That's what the education system should be looking at. Don't be afraid to get some money out of a mining company as long as it's going to improve the community. Get as much as you can out of the mining industry to improve the community but have a strategic vision when you do that.

Kristy Pascoe: I totally agree with what Laurie just said. They need to pay, and we need to fix the gaps, and we need to sort out what's going wrong in this country. But it's bigger than just taking money from the mining industry. The education system is broken, and it needs to be fixed. The system has never been structured in a way where everyone had the opportunity to have a fair go or everyone was equal. Education in this country hasn't changed for so long now, but the kids that are sitting in our classrooms are completely different than when they first set it up. Society is different.

But like James and Anne Marie were saying, maybe it's all about greater transparency. "This is where the money's come from. This is what these people are doing." Take the money, help the kids that need the help or the people that most need it, but make the mining companies accountable for the things that they've done. Have greater transparency with what this money is doing, where it's coming from.

Take what you can, help the kids that need it the most, but maybe start diversifying as well and looking for the places outside of that organization.

James Ladwig: I would add something that will be quite alien to New South Wales, but not to many school districts in the United States. These issues, this question, this topic, and the knowledge behind it should be part of the local curriculum. It should be the local curriculum. The centralization of curriculum in Australia has become a strait jacket to the point where relevant deep knowledge cannot be done. In the United States, there is a lot more flexibility at the local level in curriculum development. It has to be done well. Why schools are not incorporating local knowledge of all stakeholders is astounding to me. When it comes to the mines, the first people I would be talking to are the people who were around before the mines existed. There are truckers that'll tell you what happened to the water in the Hunter River. There are Aboriginal folks who will tell you what life was like on the rivers before the White folks came. The knowledge exists, but it is local knowledge that will be most relevant, most important, and most needed for these kids who are going to have to figure out what are they going to do with their life after school. They're going to have to make a choice. Our job, as far as I can tell, is to make them prepared sufficiently so that they can be reflective and know the pluses and minuses of the choices they're making. They may well surprise you.

Daniella Forster: It sounds to me that we've come around as an alignment. We're recommending to Nick Donovan to take as much sponsorship funding from the mine and the fossil fuels companies in his area as possible, minimize the exchange in terms of promotional material and indoctrination so that we can have these critical conversations about where this money has come from, what it's cost us to have, and then to use this money to create a whole bunch of transitional opportunities and triage for those students who need it the most. My last question to you—what do you hope others who will listen to our conversation today take away and keep thinking about when they're trying to address similar issues in their areas?

Laurie Perry: From my point of view, the whole education system needs to have a complete turnaround. It needs to start now. Everybody that is involved in the education system needs to engage First Nations groups because First Nations people have a connection to wind, fire, land, rivers, rain, sea, and sun.

James Ladwig: Just the phrase—nobody owns the sun, nobody owns the land. Humans don't own this place. We're a small part of it, and that itself is a radically different ethic than our cultures have been built on. Keep that in mind. If we continue using Western culture to—everybody cites Francis Bacon on this one—control Mother Nature, we're creating our own destruction. We can't keep doing it.

Laurie Perry: That's right. No one owns the sun, no one owns the rain, no one owns the skies. We didn't own the land here. We managed and cared for it. We looked after it. We never had a piece of paper that said we owned it. That's not how we do business, not how we've ever done business. Our signatures are in the caves, mountains, creeks, rivers, and trees. The way we cared for the land was with all the tribal groups trading and working together to manage it. We can transition to a healthy community and society if we plan properly and listen to people.

James Ladwig is an associate professor of Education at the University of Newcastle, Australia. He is recognized nationally and internationally as an authority in sociocultural understandings of education, with specific expertise in school reform and the restructuring of systems of schooling and on issues of educational equity. His work draws from disciplinary backgrounds outside of education itself, primarily sociology, philosophy, and social and political theory, and has been published around the world.

Kristy Pascoe is a book lover; music fanatic; feminist; proud Aboriginal woman; environmentalist; doting mother and grandmother; supporter of social justice and facilitator of learning for teenage people, and the Leader of Learning in the English program at San Clemente High School in New South Wales, Australia.

Lawrence (Laurie) Perry is the CEO of the Wonnarua Nation Aboriginal Corporation, which represents the Wonnarua people, the Traditional Land Owners of the Hunter Valley in New South Wales. Laurie's work explores ways to help members of the Wonnarua Nation access educational funds to improve their educational achievements. The Wonnarua National Aboriginal Corporation works with all mining companies in the area as a Registered Aboriginal Party. Laurie is a former Rugby League player and spent a former career working at Coal and Allied Liddell Underground Colliery.

Dr. Anne Marie (Anni) Ross teaches at the University of Newcastle, Australia. She has a background in environmental analysis, environmental/sustainability education and research, and teaching and education research. At the moment writing a global iteration of her PhD based on a history of environmental education centers, Anni is also involved in a fledgling research group focused on environmental/sustainability education and volunteering with a local Landcare and community environment organization.

Character Guide

Setting
Regional High School located in the Hunter Valley, New South Wales, Australia (Years 7–12, ages 12–18)

Primary Characters	
Nick Donovan: principal of Regional High School **Carol Peters:** Chairperson of the school's Parents and Community Association (P&C) **Steve Jones:** parent on the P&C, employed by South Mining, a multinational mining company	**Helen Gordon:** parent on the P&C, doctor **David Matthews:** Aboriginal Education Officer at Regional High School **Jessica Young:** science teacher **Greg Martin:** head science teacher

Discussion Questions

1 The subtitle for this case references "what we're owed." What do fossil fuel companies owe local communities and organizations like schools? What do schools owe local communities and employers? How far do the responsibilities of each extend?

2 The case mentions a variety of student needs, ranging from concrete needs like laptops and athletic equipment to abstract ones like agency and hope for the future. How should Nick weigh those different needs as he considers extending South Mining's sponsorship?

3 Nick's, teachers', parents', and students' own assessments of students' needs often conflict with one another. Whose perspectives should have priority, or are there ways to bring them into conversation and consensus?

4 Nick mentions that the school must "work in partnership with [the] community." How do different characters in the case view that responsibility?

5   A number of characters bring up the Aboriginal community's objections to not only the environmental damage caused by mining but also the destruction of lands held sacred by Aboriginal people. How should these objections impact the dilemmas in this case?
6   The characters who raise the strongest objections to the influence of South Mining at the Regional High School are newcomers to the community: parent Helen and science teacher Jessica. How might their status as newcomers impact their views on the sponsorship—and how those views are received?

Notes

1. The NSW Department of Education Commercial Arrangements, Sponsorship and Donations implementation policy requires that schools report annually on how commercial arrangements, including sponsorships, benefit the department, school, and community outcomes. Sponsorships are not philanthropic, but involve the provision of "money and value-in-kind contributions to support a particular program, event or initiative in return for certain specified benefits." Value in kind may include acknowledgment of the sponsor through promotional materials relevant to the program, opportunities to address the school, and/or the right to distribute sponsor advertising "to staff, teachers and participants over 18 years." In the annual report, the principal must demonstrate that the sponsorship agreement is in the school's interests and that their association with the mining company will not bring the Department of Education into disrepute. "Commercial Arrangements, Sponsorship and Donations," Implementation document for the Commercial Arrangements, Sponsorship and Donations Policy (New South Wales Department of Education, November 16, 2022), https://education.nsw.gov.au/content/dam/main-education/policy-library/associated-documents/pd-2009-0399-01.pdf.
2. South32 Illawarra Metallurgical Coal donated three cents from every ton of saleable coal it produces and gave over $25,000 to six schools to help support them through the Covid-19 pandemic. Greg Ellis, "Mining Company Supports School Students and Their Families," *Illawarra Mercury*, October 25, 2021, sec. Business, https://www.illawarramercury.com.au/story/7483842/mining-company-supports-school-students-and-their-families/.
3. Fossil fuels companies have developed a range of learning materials to encourage understanding of their contribution and impacts. Recent

examples in Australia include excursions such as School Mine Tours the NSW Upper Hunter and a controversial primary school incursion provided by Woodside Petroleum where Year 3 students were asked to make an oil reservoir using bread slices, vegemite, and sprinkles. See Emma Wynne and Jo Trilling, "Harmless Fun or Troubling Incursion? Science Lesson Sponsored by Oil and Gas Giant Sparks Debate," *ABC Radio Perth*, August 20, 2021, https://www.abc.net.au/news/2021-08-20/oil-exploration-kids-science-lesson/100388140; "School Mine Tours Program—Upper Hunter Mining Dialogue," *New South Wales Minin* (blog), accessed May 20, 2023, https://miningdialogue.com.au/engagement/school-tours.

4. A tree change is a term used to describe moving from the city to a rural or country setting.
5. In May 2020, Rio Tinto destroyed the Juukan Gorge caves, a 40,000-year-old sacred site to the Puutu Kunti Kurrama and Pinikura peoples in Western Australia, during an iron ore exploration project.
6. These comments are derived from Kari Dahlgren, "The Moral Case for Coal: The Ethics of Complicity with and amongst Australian Pro-Coal Lobbyists," *The Australian Journal of Anthropology* 32, no. 1 (2021): 19–32, https://doi.org/10.1111/taja.12389.
7. Aboriginal Education Officers (AEOs) are Aboriginal people who are employed in NSW public schools with a high proportion of students who identify as Aboriginal. AEOs work with teachers and Aboriginal students and families to support the learning, welfare, and wellbeing of Aboriginal students. AEOs may also represent the school on the local Aboriginal Education Consultative Group which provides guidance for a range of culturally significant educational aims and practices.
8. For more on funding inequities in Australian schools, see Adeshola Ore, "'The Gonski 'Failure': Why Did It Happen and Who Is to Blame for the 'Defrauding' of Public Schools?," *The Guardian*, March 12, 2022, sec. Australia news, https://www.theguardian.com/australia-news/2022/mar/13/the-gonski-failure-why-did-it-happen-and-who-is-to-blame-for-the-defrauding-of-public-schools.
9. Mob is a colloquial term used to refer to a group of Aboriginal people associated with a particular place or nation group. "Country is the term often used by Aboriginal peoples to describe the lands, waterways, sky and seas to which they are connected through songlines. The term Country contains complex ideas about law, place, custom, language, spiritual belief, cultural practice, material sustenance, family and identity." "Welcome to Country," Australian Institute of Aboriginal and Torres Strait Islander Studies (Australian Institute of Aboriginal and Torres Strait Islander Studies, May 25, 2022), https://aiatsis.gov.au/explore/welcome-country.

10. The NSW Department of Education Code of Conduct values statement requires staff to "work openly in partnership with parents, communities and organisations." "Code of Conduct," Implementation document for Code of Conduct Policy (New South Wales Department of Education, October 19, 2022), https://education.nsw.gov.au/content/dam/main-education/policy-library/associated-documents/pd-2004-0020-01.pdf.
11. In NSW schools, the term "faculty" refers to a group of teachers for a particular subject area. For example, all of the science teachers form the Science Faculty and their immediate superior is their head teacher.
12. See "Home | SS4C," School Strike 4 Climate Australia, accessed May 20, 2023, https://www.schoolstrike4climate.com.

5

Photo Bomb: Responding to Online Transgressions

Ana Romero-Iribas and María Almudena Santaella Vallejo

Translated by Sara O'Brien

In Spain, cases of cyberbullying have increased exponentially in recent years. Recent research has revealed that 40 percent of young people experienced online violence for the first time between the ages of eight and nine, with girls affected to a greater extent than boys. Most of these cases were committed by a "friend" or classmate from school. Only 16 percent of cyberbullying cases involved an unknown harasser.[1] In response, the Government of the Community of Madrid in 2016 developed a first-of-its-kind program, "Programa de Lucha contra el Acoso Escolar" ("Plan to Combat Bullying"). This program instituted a battery of permanent and structural measures to prevent and eradicate bullying. Among other things, this program requires specific training for teachers and the creation of a support team for intervention in cases of special gravity or complexity.[2]

--

On Wednesday afternoon at 4:30, the teachers' lounge at Roma School was packed. As a private K-12 school in Madrid, with a committed faculty, highly engaged parent community, and strong academic record, Roma enjoyed a stellar reputation. But today worried voices filled the room as the faculty discussed the rumors that had been circulating about Clara, one of the students in 1ºESO (7th grade). That morning, everyone had received an email from Luis, *Coordinador de la ESO*, asking them to stay after school for an emergency meeting. Now Luis hurried into the room and invited his colleagues to sit as he started the meeting.

"Apologies for the urgency," Luis announced, "but we have a serious problem about Clara S., which you may have heard about already. Inés, as the tutor for the grade, can you explain what happened?"

Inés took a deep breath before she began. She had a soft spot for Clara and hated to relate what had happened to her.

"Last Saturday, Clara's classmates Andrea and Jaime were hanging out at Andrea's house, and they decided to create a WhatsApp profile pretending to be Guillermo, who is apparently a popular older boy who lives in their neighborhood," Inés explained.[3] "For a laugh, they started messaging Clara as Guillermo. The poor kid has always been an easy target—she's so sweet, but definitely immature and a bit awkward compared to her classmates. After a while, they asked Clara to strip in front of her phone's camera, and when Clara took off her bra, they took a screenshot of her, topless, and sent it to friends in the class."

A horrified gasp spread through the room.

"The photo got around, and soon all the other students in the class had seen it," Inés continued. "Some kids even sent it to friends at other schools. When Clara arrived at school on Monday, she had no idea that everyone had seen her topless photo, although she soon found out. She was devastated, and immediately called her mom to pick her up. She hasn't returned to Roma since late Monday morning. To top it all off, one of the other boys forwarded the photo to friends using a school computer. We found out about the situation because one of Clara's classmates was worried about her and came to me to tell me what happened. It's just horrible."

"Thanks, Inés," Luis said. "As you all know, the *Comunidad de Madrid (CAM)* has a protocol we must follow when investigating bullying cases.[4] On Monday, as soon as Inés informed the administration what happened, we met and agreed that we are facing a serious situation indeed: Andrea and Jaime both behaved badly, and Clara herself was reckless. So following the protocol, we set up an investigative committee, which Carlos and I were both a part of.[5] It was important that we investigate quickly, discreetly, and impartially to determine not only whether this was a case of cyberbullying, but also whether any laws against child pornography apply here, since Clara is only twelve years old."

"Oh my God," groaned Juan, the math teacher for 1ºESO. "Those kids had no idea what a mess they were making."

"Yeah—for themselves and if we're not careful, for Roma, too," Carlos affirmed. As a "lifer" who had taught at Roma for twenty years before taking on his current administrative role as *Coordinador de Bachillerato*, or vice principal, Carlos was known for his fierce commitment to the school, and to maintaining its high status in the city.

"Yesterday we interviewed everyone involved in the incident," Luis resumed. "Clara's mother had already asked for a meeting, so we spoke to her first. While she couldn't explain why Clara stripped on camera, she was shocked and upset that her daughter's classmates could treat her so poorly at a sought-after school like this, where we place so much emphasis on moral education. She believes that the school must take action."

"Well, of course!" Laura exclaimed. As 1ºESO social studies teacher, she knew all of the students involved and looked stricken at what she had just heard. "I hope you told her that we would severely punish Andrea and Jaime, and every student involved in sharing those photos, and that we'd have a school assembly to teach all students about respect and digital citizenship."

"Whoa, let's not get ahead of ourselves!" Carlos responded. "Remember that this didn't take place at school, and that Clara's mom has options of her own."

"That's true," Luis nodded. "As a lawyer, Clara's mother is well aware that she could report Andrea and Jaime—and their parents—to the authorities and that she'd have a good case against them. But given that they are so young, and given how much Clara is already suffering, she doesn't want to drag this out. She thinks it's best for Clara to put this mess behind her as soon as possible, and resolving this matter without the courts is the best way to keep Clara from being hurt more than she already has been. So she has asked us to handle the discipline internally, at the school level."

"What did Andrea and Jaime's parents say about all this?" Juan asked, curious.

"Andrea's parents are upset and very angry at their daughter," Luis answered, "although they believe she's too young to understand the significance of her actions. They both work long hours, so Andrea spends a lot of time home alone, and they don't feel they have any good ways to place limits on her screen time. But it's clear they plan to punish her in some way. In fact, I think they'll be reaching out to you for guidance, Raquel."

"I'll be happy to talk with them," Raquel, the school's counselor, responded. "Should I expect to hear from Jaime's parents, too?"

"That's a harder case," Luis sighed. "Jaime's parents assured us that their son couldn't possibly have been involved. He doesn't even have a cell phone, so they insist he wouldn't know how to create a fake profile."

"Wait, so they aren't taking any responsibility?" Laura protested in disbelief. "No wonder Clara's mom expects us to take action, if they won't!"

"It's very important to know how Andrea and Jaime reacted," Raquel pointed out. "Do they understand what they did?"

"Andrea and Jaime are very sorry for what they did," Luis reported. "They knew Clara would be temporarily embarrassed, but it was clear they hadn't thought through the real harm their 'joke' could cause, nor what the long-term consequences might be. I think they're ashamed this all got so out of control so quickly."

"I'm relieved to hear they are ashamed," Raquel commented. "What do their classmates have to say?"

"Most of them felt sorry for Clara when they received the photo; you already know that one of them reported the incident to Inés," Luis responded. "Although of course, a few of them did forward the photo to other students who weren't on the original list."

"How horrible!" Laura exclaimed.

"So what were the committee's conclusions?" Juan asked, hoping to get the full story before Laura launched into more recommendations.

"Well, we determined that the picture of Clara is not legally considered pornography: while it shows her partially naked, it's not suggestive or titillating, and the students didn't take it for those purposes,"[6] Luis explained. "So we're not required to file a criminal complaint, which is good because after all, the children involved are only twelve."[7]

"What about cyberbullying?" Juan inquired.

"While the situation is serious, it represents an isolated incident,"[8] Luis explained. "According to *CAM*, as long as it's not a pattern of behavior, we don't need to report anything to the authorities, though we should revise the student handbook to ensure that the situation doesn't happen again."

"So does the committee have recommendations about what we should do other than revising the handbook?" Juan asked.

"Frankly, this is why we're coming to you," Luis explained. "Clearly we need to do *something* to help our students learn from this as the situation is serious and involves multiple students and their families. But what exactly?"

"Luis, I'm not convinced that the school needs to take any further action—the events didn't happen here," Carlos protested. "We need to deal with the student who forwarded the photo from the school computer, of course, but honestly I'm more concerned about how this incident will impact the culture here, and the school's reputation in the community."

"Wait, what?" Laura burst out in disbelief.

"Have you forgotten about the other school that had a similar incident last year?" Carlos continued. "They were all over the media, and I know their applications this year dropped as a result. It's going to take them a while to recover their reputation. Why should the rest of us pay the price for Clara's foolish actions in a single incident that happened at home over the weekend? The school has already done enough by talking to the students involved—and their families—about the seriousness of the situation."

"Well, given that our mission is to educate, I think we should take some action here," Juan countered, "since it's important that Andrea and Jaime experience consequences for what they have done—and it's not clear that Jaime's parents are going to impose any consequences on their own. But I agree with you, Carlos, that we should resolve this matter privately with the students and their families, without drawing any more attention in the school or the community. Andrea and Jaime clearly didn't understand the full implications of their actions, given their age, and it's in Clara's and the other students' interests also to stop people talking about it so it doesn't get more attention. I've heard chatter in my math class; now that I know what it's about, I can put a stop to it before it gets further out of hand."

"Are we just going to pretend that nothing happened?" Laura exclaimed in disbelief. "Everyone knows about this. Is it fair that one student gets publicly humiliated and we just cover it up? We do the students a disservice if we put their comfort above the reality that actions have consequences. It's a crucial lesson in life, accepting responsibility for what we do."

"Yes, but why make it public?" Juan stressed. "These are twelve-year-olds we're talking about!"

"Let's not forget that this incident *is* public already," Laura responded, "so the consequences should be public as well. We must set an example for all the students: those who took the photo, those who sent the photo, and those who just witnessed the whole thing. Besides, public consequences could help restore Clara's reputation."

"Look," Inés interjected, "I've been talking to Clara—she hasn't stopped crying since Monday. She feels so embarrassed about her actions, and humiliated and betrayed by her friends. I don't know how much time will pass before she feels up to seeing her classmates again. She's shattered, thinking that the entire city is talking about her. I think we need to respect that Clara just wants to forget this ever happened. All the kids are already talking about it; she doesn't want the teachers all discussing it, too."

"We should clearly listen to Clara and her parents—ultimately, she's the victim here," Raquel agreed.

"We can't just let it go!" Laura objected again. "Clara is going through a difficult time, but let's not forget that she brought it on herself, and now she's learning her lesson. The punishment needs to fit the crime, as an example for all students. Andrea and Jaime should clearly be expelled. If we want Roma to remain respected for our moral community, we need to be clear that we will not tolerate this kind of behavior—even if it doesn't meet the legal standards of cyberbullying. The students who stood by and did nothing should be punished, too. And the student who sounded the alarm should be rewarded."

"That student simply did the right thing by stepping forward; knowing they did the right thing is reward enough," Raquel replied. "But I agree that we need a clear plan at least for the other students who forwarded the photo, and for their parents. At the end of the day, they are responsible for the actions of their children until they turn sixteen. And I'm not sure those parents even know what happened here!"

"That's true," Luis responded glumly. "We haven't reached out to them yet, since we wanted to talk things out with you all first. How do we contact them without refocusing the spotlight on Clara? And are we just informing them, or threatening consequences, or what?"

"Don't forget that some of the parents may turn the charges back on us by claiming that 1ºESO students couldn't have used school computers to forward the photos if we had been properly supervising them," Carlos added. "It's a delicate situation."

"Wow, I hadn't thought about our own legal liability," Raquel breathed. "This is hard."

"Exactly why we don't need to pull Roma further into it!" Carlos nodded.

"But as a counselor," Raquel continued, "I do feel we're doing something wrong here at school if twelve-year-old kids think they can treat a classmate this way. Like you, Carlos, I've always taken pride in our work fostering values and character. Shouldn't we be thinking about our own role in this situation–and helping students and parents think about it, too?"

"More than thinking," Laura responded. "Doing. Facing consequences."

"Let's not dwell on this—it happens everywhere," Juan argued. "I still think it's best to just resolve this matter quickly and in private: the students who hurt Clara, and their families, should apologize to her and her mother.

And when Clara comes back to class, her classmates will support her. I know that there are caring kids in her class who will help her put this whole situation behind her. You'll help them with that, Raquel, and I can make sure she feels welcomed in math class, too. And, of course, we're going to need to do some lessons about cyberbullying and the other issues raised here. That's the action you could take, Laura–work digital citizenship into your social studies lessons. But no need to draw this out further."

"So instead we'll sweep it under the rug," Laura countered. "Clara suffers, while everyone else conveniently pretends nothing happened."

"OK, let's not keep circling around the same questions," Luis pleaded. "We need to start making some decisions. How do we balance what is best for Clara, for the other students, and for the school as a whole? Is it up to us to impose consequences on Andrea, Jaime, the other students, or their parents—and if so, what should those be? What do we do about parents like Jaime's, who disavow responsibility, or about parents who might be inclined to hold us responsible instead? And how can we turn this situation into a learning opportunity for the whole class and even the school so we avoid anything like this in the future—but without further traumatizing Clara?"

Conversation

Translation by Maricruz Vargas Ramirez

Ana Romero-Iribas: Welcome to the discussion about "Photo Bomb." If you're ready, I'll ask you the first question: What are the dilemmas in this case? And for whom are they dilemmas?

Carlos-María Alcover: I believe that the principal dilemma in the case is the role played by the young people and the school. In my opinion, the key considerations in this case should be the people involved: the victim, Clara, and all her peers who participated in these events. The students, not the image or the prestige of the school, require care here.

Firstly, those students who participated must recognize their actions and the consequences of those actions. Secondly, what action should the school and families take so that the children's values, attitudes, and, therefore, behavior change to prevent similar incidents in the future?

Thirdly, it's important to promote a change in attitudes and a change in values as much as possible. I understand that any sanctioning or punitive measure is always aimed at immediately changing behavior. But changing behavior does nothing if the values and attitudes that underlie that behavior persist.

In short, clearly the objective is to safeguard—as much as possible—the psychological wellbeing of the students who participated in these events.

I believe that the school's responsibility in this case is secondary, which doesn't mean that the school doesn't need to intervene—of course they need to intervene—but always with the point of view of caring for the students, fundamentally, in both their present and future development.

Helena Regojo Bacardí: The dilemma is also about deciding where the adults should intervene, at school or at home. I agree that we must focus on Clara—how can we support her in the short term and long term?

In our current educational environment, children are faced with enormous problems related to technology. I believe that the more technology we have, the greater the necessity for values education, because children have "atomic bombs" in their hands, to paraphrase the name of the case.

Consuelo Martínez-Priego: It could be said that the dilemma here is between the public and the private. However, every political and social activity has three levels to analyze, each depending on the other. We can distinguish between the legal, the institutional—as in an institution with its own rules—and the moral level, which involves justice and underpins all the others. If we just stay at the institutional and legal levels and never get to the moral or ethical level, we can fall into totalitarianism. We forget about the primacy of the person, and arbitrariness dominates. In other words, the moral level—where we consider things like the good of the person—is the appropriate limit on legal and institutional powers. Attention to people is the realm of the moral sphere. This is the priority, there's nothing more important than the person. You cannot compare the person to anything else. But it's not the only level. In the case we're analyzing, the three spheres are relevant: crimes against the law, to a certain extent, the relevant institutions that must intervene—the school and the families—and the moral development of the people involved: to heal, to learn, to ask forgiveness and make amends.

Carmen Perdices González: For me, the key issue is the final question that appears in the case: "And how can we turn this situation into a learning opportunity for the whole class and even the school, so we avoid anything like this in the future—but without further traumatizing Clara?" I think that action must be taken at the school level and that the school must use this situation to improve. I believe everyone needs to take responsibility, including the school. As the counselor in the case says, what role have we all played: the parents, the students directly involved, and the rest of the students? The dilemma is how the school should respond—with what discretion, with which strategies—so that the response can serve to improve. And on the other hand, to respect Clara's rights and her and her mother's wish not to be the center of attention. Any response should help her overcome this incident and put it behind her. I think this is the challenge: what strategies to use, starting with the idea that each and every person must face their responsibility and the consequences. I believe that everyone needs to ask themselves: what have we done wrong, and how could we do better?

Ana Romero-Iribas: We've given our initial reflections on the case and have expressed different visions. Now I want to take one step back to ask ourselves which values are behind the perspectives you all have shared.

Carlos-María Alcover: The values are clear for Clara's mother. She wants to not only defend her daughter's psychological health but also mitigate the harm that can be done to her reputation in the future. Fundamentally, it seems that Clara's mother is looking to punish those responsible, whether they be those who committed the act or, indirectly, those who may have facilitated it or amplified it in some way.

In my opinion, without judging Clara's mother—because I'm not judging anybody—I believe that she should keep in mind something that many times gets forgotten by educational professionals as well as psychologists and the general population. When it comes to bullying, we always draw a dichotomy between the victim and the bullies, when in reality, one of roles that's frequent but less recognized is the dual role of victim/bully. Clara in this case has been a victim, but her mother and the culture that surrounds her should know that it's quite likely that Clara, in another context, much later, could assume the role of the bully. This possibility of a double role is even more frequent in the case of cyberbullying, and those looking to prevent this type of behavior should consider this.

Thus, Clara's mother should not focus solely on Clara's role as the victim, but rather on the type of behavior that has occurred. Her daughter should know that it's possible that, in another situation, she could behave in the same way and make other classmates victims.

Therefore, the lens applied here shouldn't just be Clara's mother's oversimplified view, in which some students are guilty and others are victims; instead, those behaviors are often confused and combined. As the father of a girl in Clara's situation, I would worry both about my daughter having been victimized and about the possibility of my daughter becoming a bully at some point. For me, dichotomizing these types of problems is the biggest mistake that could be made. At the same time, it's important to make Andrea and Jaime—and all the students who spread the images—aware of precisely that same situation. You all have contributed to a classmate's humiliation, but don't forget that at any time you all can suffer the same humiliation. On the other hand, the school should clarify: what do our own values of diversity, equality, respect mean?

Because when we want to intervene, we always address the children, but we forget to also analyze the teachers' values. We assume that their values are respect for diversity, equality, and freedom, and there are times when this assumption is just that, an assumption. Because there are clearly different opinions within the school on what these mean.

Therefore, we also need to try to identify the values that teachers, school leaders, counselors, and psychologists hold with respect to this type of behavior. We shouldn't assume anything. We might be surprised by how often these types of behaviors occur in schools and go undetected, or if they are detected, go unaddressed. This happens because the values that the adults in the school hold aren't always aligned with prevention and intervention. I'm trying to go beyond this concrete case so that we can have a strategy for intervention in similar cases.

Ana Romero-Iribas: Thanks very much, Carlos. Does anyone have a response or comment about Carlos' thoughts?

Consuelo Martínez-Priego: I want to comment on one argument that seems incomplete if we're talking about a broader context: the intervention with the classmates who solicited the photo, and the classmates who distributed it. To make them conscious of their participation and, as you mentioned, emphasize that they can be victims too, in my opinion, is not sufficient to build moral value in a person. I believe we have to go further. It is not enough to be aware of the moral value of actions; it is also necessary to make students capable of acting well.

Helena Regojo Bacardí: Looking at the values of the participants, I miss one particular value in Clara. I think it is the base of everything: self-worth, self-love. Children need to be educated in self-esteem. Clara clearly has so little self-esteem that she needs to objectify herself to give herself that value. So she agrees to her classmates' request, and it's not just her fault. It's the fault of the educational community, the fault of her parents who work a lot and don't take care of her, and the fault of other parents who say, "My child is wonderful." Or it's the fault of some educators who, maybe, only care about the school's prestige.

Another value is friendship Her classmates are not good friends—as we see from their betrayal, their huge lack of loyalty, and their lack of understanding about friendship—at a moment in adolescence when it's basic to want to belong to a group. It is necessary to teach friendship values in schools, especially at this age. And friendship requires loyalty, not only loyalty toward ourselves and others but loyalty toward the ideas we believe in.

Another value that needs to be at the center is education, not only for the children but also for the parents. Here there are many parents who, perhaps, evade responsibility; and there are many schools that go beyond and try to educate the parents. Because if parents aren't educated on the same content that the child receives at school, the child ends up receiving a different message at home. If we don't have coherence between parents and the school, the kid ends up broken.

Carmen Perdices González: I like the idea of the educational co-responsibility of the school and the parents. In this case, the school takes pride in conveying a moral education. And deep down, when you read the case in depth, you notice they're not doing such a bad job. For example, when I first read about the photo being shared, I thought that everyone had shared it. But when I read it more carefully, I noticed it actually said that most students felt shame and compassion, and only some forwarded the picture. So they're not doing a terrible job. And one girl dared to distance herself from the group's action and come to the tutor because she was worried about Clara. In my opinion, they have reasons to be proud. I think what is misunderstood, in some way, is what the school's prestige means. It doesn't mean to cover things up but rather to say "we can do this better, and we're going to follow these steps to achieve it." From my point of view, that's how you achieve more prestige.

And I think another value that should be taught here is empathy. I think it's precisely a lack of empathy that makes us capable of hurting someone without guilt, or seeing others suffering without helping.

It has always been true that adolescents can lack the courage to confront each other. But I believe that nowadays, there is a new component: lack of empathy. Sometimes, when you ask kids, "Why didn't you do anything?," their answer is: "it's not my problem" or "what do I care?" Don't you feel that pain in your gut when you see a classmate suffer? I believe we need to educate sensitivity, empathy, respect.

Consuelo Martínez-Priego: I think that's right on point. From a very ethical point of view, empathy is essential because it is the affective presupposition of the virtue of justice. All interpersonal relationships are mediated by emotions. Without empathy, without respect, just relationships aren't possible. Justice is an "operative value": the other person occupies a specific place that is like mine, they are a person as dignified as I. And justice is the precedent for a superior bond: friendship, which is really the goal. Mutual respect in school is a place to start, not to end. In terms of values, I believe that everything revolves around justice because it allows the articulation of the individual with the institution. Justice allows us to consider the wellbeing of Clara, and the kids that have been the bullies in this case, and the accomplices, and even the wellbeing of the brave girl who talked to the tutor.

Ana Romero-Iribas: Does the school really have to intervene in situations or actions that happen outside the school, even situations that involve its students and their families, as in this case? I believe this is one of the hot topics this case raises.

Carlos-María Alcover: Given that the event occurred at home, I believe that the school's role shouldn't be sanctioning but rather educating. I think the only person who should really be sanctioned is the student who shared the picture through the school's computer. I believe that the role of the school is to intervene from an educational perspective, not from a sanction or punitive perspective. As a school that cares about their students' moral values, they should facilitate direct contact between the people who participated, precisely to work on empathy.

I don't know if you remember Milgram's experiments about electrical shock, the experiment about obedience and authority. When the participants didn't see the person supposedly receiving the shock and only listened to them, they would administer stronger electric shocks. But when they had the victim in front of them, they were less likely to shock them, which means that empathy increases when you have the other person in front of you. It's harder to hurt someone close to you than someone you don't see.

Therefore, the school's intervention should aim to increase empathy through direct action, in different circles, at different levels. Clara, Andrea, and Jaime should put themselves in the other's role, asking themselves: what would you do if you were in their place? How would you feel in that situation? And the school should build empathy among the students who spread the photo. The intervention should change values and attitudes, and make students aware of the consequences of their actions. I think the families should also be involved because they are co-responsible, in this case because this behavior occurred outside the school. The families should know the role they have—not as guards, because constant surveillance is not only unpleasant but practically impossible with current technology, but to be aware of the possible behaviors of their children. Even though all parents believe that their children never do anything wrong, schools can help them see that this type of behavior is more and more frequent.

Helena Regojo Bacardi: My first reaction was to expel Andrea and Jaime. From the outset, I identified with Laura: expulsion as an exemplary measure, to tackle the problem at its roots. The problem is: how could this affect Clara? And can the school really do it given that the incident took place at home? I don't think so.

So I focus on Clara. How can we help her recover from the damage done to her as a victim of that indignity, in collaboration with her and her mother? They asked for privacy, and I think the right thing is to respect their privacy; maybe it will make it easier for her to turn the page. Or she may want to change schools.

Unfortunately, this is now our day-to-day, and you think, "Oh my God. What have we come to?" Maybe because we didn't stop it from the beginning with extreme measures, right? Now, we clearly need to start preparing the parents because if a kid does this, the parent is responsible. We see it in the [Spanish] Penal Code, as the footnote says: minors under sixteen have no criminal responsibility, but the parents do.

For parents and students, we should introduce cybersecurity issues, the risk online, the risks of pornography, because it's not a joke how far you can go with this.

Consuelo Martínez-Priego: Well, I have loved your interventions. But it is not clear to me why the punitive aspect is so separate from the educational aspect. Teachers do not stop educating when they take measures to make education possible, in the social context of the classroom. That implies punitive elements. There are rules that say: "you shouldn't cross this line." Therefore, I would not so definitively separate education from punitive measures. I don't know what kind of punishment it should be; we would have to think about it a bit, but I wanted to introduce that little reflection.

Lastly, the consequences of their actions. I believe that when a child thinks the consequences aren't going to be public, they have a harder time thinking ethically; the reflection can be superficial. Well, as when people say, "the police are not seeing me," and then they cross the street where they shouldn't. Then, it is worth teaching that, intrinsically, there are things you should never do. And we should know how to teach that—I think that's clearly an ethical education. It transcends the affective field. Some things are a no, even if no one sees them, and some values should always be preserved, even if no one sees them. It happens, for example, with pornography. It seems that nobody sees it, although there is always a second person involved, that you are degrading.

Ana Romero-Iribas: Would anyone like to respond to this point?

Carmen Perdices González: Well, I loved what you just said because I believe that the main goal of education is to help our students to behave in terms of duty. And you asked if the school had to take legal action or not, right? I think that, in this specific case, the school shouldn't take action because, according to the Protocol of the Community of Madrid, there hasn't been a crime. However, I believe that the school must do something because we cannot remove ourselves from the lives of our students. The students are not just people who spend eight hours in school, right? They have another life outside, and as educators, we have to be aware of what is happening there in order to help them grow and, hopefully, to act according to duty.

Carlos-María Alcover: In principle, I wouldn't agree entirely with what you were proposing because I believe, without being an expert in the field, that every sanction or punishment should be proportional to the act committed. In this case, it's Clara who probably feels the worst about herself because she did what she did without being coerced. Of course, the instigators of this situation are Andrea and Jaime, but probably, Clara's psychological damage stems from feeling guilty about what she did, largely of her own free will.

Thus, I can't support expelling the students, nor any other kind of sanction because it wouldn't be proportional to what's been done. And on the other hand, if I can add something else, let's not forget victimization. There are three types of victimization. Primary victimization: The person who is a victim of an action, like this one, suffers psychological and emotional damage. In this case, it would be Clara. The secondary victimization is all the damage done to Clara's reputation by making this case public. But there's another type of victimization, the tertiary, which we often forget, suffered by those who committed the act and all the other people who participated in it.

This means that, deep down, those who commit a crime also suffer precisely because of the damage to their self-image and self-esteem, and because of the effect of the situation on their reputation in the immediate social context. With more publicity and more blaming, victimization affects more people. Of course, the worst victimization is the one that the direct victim—Clara—suffers. But let's not forget that the other participants suffer too. Therefore, I believe that any intervention should be proportional to the act and, above all, the school should avoid the victimization of all the participants, even if they participated to different degrees.

Helena Regojo Bacardi: When I commented on the expulsion, it was as a mother, a visceral response, right? But then you have to rationalize it …

Carlos-María Alcover: Of course, but Clara's mom should also be worried about her daughter's willingness to behave like that.

Helena Regojo Bacardi: I agree with you, Carlos. An emotional response isn't necessarily correct. It has to be analyzed rationally, mainly to ensure it doesn't backfire and hurt Clara even more, as you said.

Ana Romero-Iribas: I believe we're getting closer to a decision. In one way or another, you all have been pointing at possible solutions, but I would like to ask two questions, and you can answer both or just one.

First, what decision would we make? What answer would we have for this case if it was essentially an educational response? Second, should the answer be public or private? Do we have to respect Clara's right to and request for privacy, or is it more important to make an example of Jaime and Andrea for the other students, to educate them and prevent future cases?

Carlos-María Alcover: Well, an answer like this is always formulated in ideal terms, right? Imagining we have the resources to do the best we can do. I believe we should act in circles. Firstly, I believe the school should provide individual psychological support for Clara: to try to understand the consequences of what happened to her, and try to minimize the effects with a psychologist's support. Next, the school should analyze to what extent Clara is, indeed, responsible. Given her lack of self-esteem, which has been pointed out before, she is a vulnerable person in that kind of situation. The school should work on this with her and provide psychological support.

I would also intervene with a psychologist in a second circle directly with Andrea and Jaime, so they can understand and take responsibility for their actions. They must precisely analyze everything behind their behavior and the consequences of that behavior.

And next, I would intervene with all the other classmates that participated directly or indirectly. And how would I do it? Before anything else, I would measure and evaluate their attitudes and values toward this kind of behavior using surveys. From the analysis of those baseline attitudes, I would plan an educational intervention for the whole class to say "this kind of behavior isn't normal; this kind of behavior involves stereotypes, prejudices, lack of values and respect for diversity."

That means focusing on this specific behavior because this is not a case of bullying (a recurrent behavior that could be classified as harassment or as violent behavior). We should try to analyze and intervene educationally with the group of students in order to change attitudes, although changing attitudes doesn't mean automatically changing behaviors. We also know that the ability to self-regulate isn't yet developed at twelve or thirteen years old. That means that you could say to a student, "Would you do this again?" and they would say, "No, I wouldn't do it ever again," but then do it the day after tomorrow.

Hence, we cannot expect great changes with educational interventions in these situations, but we should still intervene. Self-regulation is a slow process, which developmental psychologists know is actually being delayed more and more as a consequence of the modern lifestyle. But we just have to be aware that we are not going to be able to establish very stable behaviors or attitudes through a single intervention at that age.

What teachers and school leaders should do is pay close attention to detect any similar behavior at the school—both cyberbullying and physical bullying—and intervene on each occasion. And of course families also have an essential role in detecting this type of behavior. That is why I mention intervention in circles because it would be a multifocal intervention. I believe it's really important to invite not only adults but also adolescents of similar age, or a little bit older to the school so they can share their experiences in similar situations. Because what adults tell you isn't perceived or accepted in the same way as what your peers tell you.

Ana Romero-Iribas: Consuelo, should the school's response be public or private?

Consuelo Martínez-Priego: I believe it's impossible for it to be private. There isn't any action, besides maybe a good friend's secret, that can be only private.

Ana Romero-Iribas: Then, is it better to solve the matter privately with Clara and her mom or to use a public sanction, visible to all the students?

Consuelo Martínez-Priego: If the intervention is in circles, as has been suggested, the public and community dimensions are covered. But I'd like to add something else: I believe it's essential to intervene when a problem arises, but the school should also rethink what's been done previously. The students' behavior shows that the education they received from first to sixth grade isn't complete. Once the baseline attitudes are identified through the surveys, it can open a space to modify the educational plans regarding values and virtues. During adolescence, emotional regulation is difficult, but before adolescence, it's different. Primary education is when learning is easier, precisely because of the children's emotional stability. So I think there's an opportunity there: what can we do in primary education, in general?

Ana Romero-Iribas: Any idea for a different kind of intervention?

Carmen Perdices González: I think the proposal for an intervention in circles is appropriate. And when we think about sanctions—when they do graffiti, the sanction should be to clean it up. So what has been broken? Clara's image. Then how can we make those involved repair that image? Andrea and Jaime are sorry. I don't know how to do it delicately, but they should offer an apology, maybe a public apology. The other classmates involved could do it, too. Plus, Clara's mom asks for the students to be sanctioned. We can't ignore this. And more importantly, the school should develop a protocol to identify this kind of situation in the future. If they have one already, they should revise it, saying "Hey, look, we missed this."

Helena Regojo Bacardi: Carlos is going to disagree, but I am missing a punitive aspect, at least with respect to cell phone use. These kids have misused their phones, and on top of that, they usurped someone else's identity. We've missed these important things! I loved what you said about concentric circles, and the individual is always the priority. But I believe there should be a negative effect because they created damage. If I just said to the kids, "Well, it's ok, just go with the psychologist, it's ok …." What are the consequences for them? How about, "Hey, you won't have your phone for a month," or enough time that they remember it. If you don't know how to use a phone, I'll take it away for a while. Otherwise, it's just like nothing happened. I'm assuming a parental role here, but other parents might deny their child's guilt. What is the school going to do when you have a parent that denies it, protects the child, and the child gets away with it?

Carmen Perdices González: In this case, I think it could be, for example, a meeting with the parents of Clara, Jaime, and Andrea, where they could express how they feel and what measures they are going to take because it looks like Andrea's parents are going to take action. But evidently, I think we need to intervene with all the families, starting from kindergarten. This is a team; if one leg limps, the team doesn't work.

Ana Romero-Iribas: Thank you all for your participation and for raising such interesting topics.

Consuelo Martínez-Priego *is an associate professor at Universidad Internacional Villanueva, Madrid. She holds a PhD in Psychology from the Universidad Complutense de Madrid, a PhD in Psychology from the Universidad de Navarra, and a Masters in Educational Institutions Management. Her research interests include psychology of emotion; interpersonal relationships (family, friendship, social and political relationships); psychology and philosophy of freedom; and education. She has been an invited researcher at Harvard University, University of Valencia and Instituto Cultura y Sociedad (ICS) of the University of Navarra.*

Carlos-María Alcover *is a professor of Group and Organizational Psychology at the Universidad Rey Juan Carlos, Madrid. He received his PhD in Social Psychology from the Universidad Complutense de Madrid. His research has focused on early retirement and psychological wellbeing, psychological contract and exchange relationships in organizations, conflict resolution in university contexts, and membership and temporal matters in work teams.*

Helena Regojo Bacardí *is Director of Education for Sustainable Development at the Fabre Foundation, an activity that she combines with running a real estate family business. She holds a law degree, a Bachelor of Philosophy from the University of Navarra, and an MBA from IESE Business School. She is also a graduate of the ESADE Business School nonprofit organization management program and has a specialization in psychotherapy and adult accompaniment from the Congruencia-Centro de Desarrollo Humano. Her passions are education, family, and the advancement of women, which she considers essential pillars of fair social human development. She lives in Madrid, is married, and has five children.*

Carmen Perdices González *is a school counselor and teaches students with special educational needs. She holds a Masters in Family Orientation. She is the former President of the Association Mejora Tu Escuela Pública and former Assistant Professor at Universidad Rey Juan Carlos, Madrid.*

Character Guide

Setting
Roma School, primary, secondary, and post-secondary school for students ages 6–18 in Madrid, Spain
Primary Characters

Luis: *Coordinador de la Educación Secundaria Obligatoria (ESO)* (vice principal for secondary school) **Inés:** tutor for 1°ESO (the class for students age 12) **Juan:** math teacher for 1°ESO **Carlos:** *Coordinador de Bachillerato* (vice principal for post-secondary school) **Laura:** social studies teacher for 1°ESO	**Raquel:** school counselor **Clara:** 12-year-old student in 1°ESO **Clara's mother:** lawyer **Andrea:** 12-year-old student in 1°ESO **Jaime:** 12-year-old student in 1°ESO

Discussion Questions

1 In talking about the next step the school should take, Laura advocates for "punishment," Luis mentions "discipline," and Juan references "consequences." What similarities and differences do you see between these three possible approaches?

2 There's disagreement in the case about how much responsibility Clara should bear for this situation, with Raquel characterizing her as "the victim," and Laura arguing that "she brought it on herself." How do you see Clara's role in the photo incident? How does this view influence what should be done in the case?

3 Multiple characters mention the school's reputation as a factor that must be considered as they weigh their options. How do different characters think about the school's reputation? How much should public perception of the school matter as the teachers decide how to respond internally?

4 While this case is set in Spain, this kind of incident plays out all too often in countries across the globe. What details might be different if Clara, Andrea, and Jaime were students in your school? How would these differences impact how you might respond as their teacher?

5 This case raises interesting questions about when children can and/ or should be held responsible for their actions, as in Spain parents are

legally responsible for their children's behavior before the age of sixteen. How much responsibility for this incident do you think Andrea, Jaime, and their classmates should shoulder? How much responsibility do their parents bear? How do your answers impact your thoughts about what action the school should take?
6 How much responsibility should schools take for addressing student behavior that takes place outside the school walls?

Notes

1. "Ciberacoso o ciberbullying," Save the Children, accessed May 20, 2023, https://www.savethechildren.es/donde/espana/violencia-contra-la-infancia/ciberacoso-ciberbullying.
2. This chapter was supported in part by the 21st Century European Teachers Project, a program funded by the European Commission.
3. In Spain, users legally must be at least fourteen years old to create a WhatsApp profile, though the app doesn't verify age.
4. *Comunidad de Madrid* or *Comunidad Autónoma de Madrid* refers to the government of Madrid. *Comunidades* are territorial entities that, within the Spanish constitutional legal system, are endowed with autonomy. They have their own institutions and representatives, and certain legislative, executive, and administrative powers, which in many respects makes them federated entities.
5. Under the law, the investigative committee should consist of the principal, a teacher, and a non-teaching member of school staff.
6. In Spain, pornography is defined in Article 189 of the Penal Code, which lists a series of requirements, including: sexually explicit conduct, sexual suggestiveness, and the representation of sex organs. The definition also includes sexually violent and degrading scenes. The photo described in this case is not considered pornographic, and thus forwarding the photo to others would not be considered "distribution of child pornography."
7. Under Spanish law, children younger than fourteen cannot be convicted of a crime. Instead, their parents would be held responsible for their children's behavior in civil court. Under Article 1903 of the civil law, parents are legally responsible for their children's conduct until those children turn sixteen.
8. By law, cyberbullying requires repeated behaviors, including harassment, persistent and invasive contact with the victim, misuse of the victim's personal information, and threatening the freedom and assets of the victim.

6

Taking the Action Out of Civics?: Polarized Debates over Civic Education

Sara O'Brien and Meira Levinson

Over the past decade, the United States has seen a renewed interest in civic education in K-12 schools, after decades in which spending on civic learning was slashed to create a larger budget for literacy and, more recently, math and science education. This interest in strengthening civic education, however, has also led to disagreement about what kinds of civic learning students should experience in schools. While there is general agreement that students need strong civic knowledge, about the structure of their local, state, and federal government for example, there's strong disagreement about whether students should put that knowledge to use through civic action as part of their education. Some advocate for the development of civic skills and dispositions alongside civic knowledge, calling for student-led civics projects that encourage students to take action in their communities, a form of education sometimes called "action civics." Others have expressed concern that the focus on student civic action diminishes students' ability to develop their civic knowledge. Some states have passed laws restricting student-led civic projects in schools. Texas, for example, prohibits teachers from giving any course credit, even extra credit, for "political activism, lobbying, or efforts to persuade members of the legislative or executive branch at the federal, state, or local level to take specific actions by direct communication."[1]

--

Even after twenty years of teaching, the first day of school was still exciting for Emily Wilson, Social Studies Department Chair at Central High School. The school year wouldn't start for students until next week, but staff were back on campus for meetings. Emily opened her staff email. Scrolling through her messages, she read: Have You Seen This?

The email linked to an opinion piece from the local newspaper, titled "Take 'Action Civics' Out of Our School." It was written by John Warner, parent of a rising Central junior

Kids once went to school to learn reading, writing, and arithmetic. Not anymore. Central High School now requires "action civics," better described as protest civics.[2] In their history classes, students learn to stage walkouts and protests, directed by left-wing educators who use teenagers' temper tantrums for their own political ends.[3] It's indoctrination, and I refuse to stand for it.

Emily felt the attack keenly; she had introduced the action civics model from her old school to the district the year before. Students began by examining their community and identifying issues that needed solving, and then chose a single issue to focus on, working as individuals or in groups. Having chosen their issue, they did research and completed a root cause analysis, looking at the structures and systems that contributed to the presenting problem. They then worked to find community partners and plan some action to create change. Throughout the process, students reflected on what they were learning: about the government, about the community, and about themselves.[4]

The process didn't always run smoothly. Classroom discussions sometimes got heated, as students disagreed about the root causes or about what action to take. And of course, the students did not always create the desired change. But, in Emily's experience, these challenges made action civics uniquely valuable. The heated classroom discussions exposed students to different viewpoints and led to more complex understanding of the topics.[5] In strategizing and taking action, students honed their public speaking skills and learned to navigate spaces of power (like school board meetings or legislative hearings).[6] Emily found that after completing their projects, her students gained a stronger sense of agency, along with increased civic knowledge and skills.[7] Emily proudly recalled one student's words: "This project taught me that I shouldn't be afraid to stand up for what I think is right. It taught me that anyone has the ability to effect change, no matter who they are."[8]

Emily had been excited to bring action civics to her new school. The project became part of the American History curriculum for all juniors;

keeping equity in mind, Emily insisted that students at all academic levels have a chance to participate. Of course, there had been challenges. In fact, Mr. Warner seemed well informed about some parent pushback they had gotten.

Parents must band together to fight this indoctrination, Mr. Warner continued. *The next school board meeting is two weeks from tomorrow. Join me for a conference this Saturday at the New Hope Presbyterian Church, organized by local groups that share my concerns, as we plan to make our message heard.*[9] *I am the tip of the sword.*[10] *There are many others behind me.*

* * *

The subject came up quickly at the department meeting that morning.

"We don't need to devote any time to that drivel," Rose Benson, a veteran ninth grade teacher, stated. "The writer obviously misunderstands action civics and is trying to manufacture a problem where none exists. It's White fragility, plain and simple."

"I sent the article to everyone because I think it's worth discussing," Juan Ramos said. Dedicated to teaching the "general ed" students, who were least likely to go to college and most likely to feel unseen, Juan valued curriculum that elevated student choice and voice. "Across the country, action civics is being lumped in with a host of 'controversial theories' that parents are up in arms about.[11] We can't just ignore this article and hope that protestors won't materialize at the school board meeting. For all we know, there will be news cameras with them. We should talk about how to defend the project."

"I actually think the article makes some decent points," Jim Hennesey, the longest-serving department member, chimed in. "You might remember that I expressed doubts about action civics this time last year. These projects take time away from learning real history."

"I remember your doubts, Jim," Emily responded. "But your students really enjoyed the project, right?"

"Sure, all kids enjoy working with their friends and leaving school to visit City Council," Jim chuckled. "But we're in a crisis of civic ignorance: only half of Americans can name all three branches of government.[12] It's not the right time to be experimenting with civics education."

"Those statistics show that the traditional curriculum doesn't work well, and we know it particularly doesn't work well for kids who look like me," interjected Darren Johnson.[13] "For Black kids, for Latino kids, for other marginalized kids, action civics helps them see themselves in the curriculum.[14] They get to focus on problems that feel relevant to them and their families."

"But not all those families support action civics," Katie Fiske pointed out. "One of the stories in the article came from my class.[15] One group focused on the racial wealth gap, which led to a class discussion about whether meritocracy is a myth. A Black mother called me the next day, furious, because she felt I had told her son that however hard he worked, he'd never succeed the way White people did. She said he felt like he'd always be a victim." Blinking back tears, Katie continued, "I managed to reestablish a good relationship with the student—and the mother—but it was painful, for all of us. I mean, who am I to tell a Black family I know more about racism than they do?"

"I remember that," Darren said. "But, you know, that mom doesn't speak for all Black families. Class discussions like that can do a lot of good."

"That wasn't the only story in the article, though," Jim added. "There was another family angry about affirmative action."

"That was in my class," Juan volunteered. "I had a group examining the barriers to college admissions for minority and low-income students. So the class got into a discussion about whether affirmative action is racist. One parent believed that students were being taught that people of color need a leg up, that they're not as smart as White people. But it led to good conversations."

"I just want to point out," Rose said, "we've got two teachers of color in this department, and they both say that action civics helps kids of color. I trust their expertise."

"With all due respect, Rose," Jim said, "you're not leading these projects. Action civics causes problems between parents and kids, not just parents and teachers. I had one student last year, an incredible athlete, looking at the controversy around transgender kids playing sports. Her parents are religious and don't support transgender rights. The girl was so worried she'd get in trouble at home that she switched groups to work on a pro-life project. But before she switched, she spent days in a panic. Kids shouldn't be tackling these issues, riling everyone up and stressing themselves out."

"The problem isn't the issues," Darren said. "The problem is the pushback."

"Well, more pushback is coming," Jim responded, "assuming we keep the project. I'd certainly support dropping it."

* * *

Thoughts swirled in Emily's head as she walked back to her office. Possibly those teachers who felt comfortable could keep the project—if the district supported that decision. However, this solution contravened the department's commitment to equity. Action civics taught students that their voices had power, and all students deserved that experience. And of course, the decision ultimately wasn't hers; it belonged to the curriculum coordinator for the district, Rhonda Williams. Sitting down at her computer, Emily forwarded Mr. Warner's opinion piece to Rhonda, asking what the discussion was at the district office.

A knock at the door from Principal Dan Ricci interrupted her work.

"I'm guessing that you saw John Warner's opinion piece?" Dan asked.

"I did," Emily said. "I know we got some pushback last year, but I honestly wasn't expecting anything like this."

"I've heard complaints from Mr. Warner before," Dan told her. "A few years ago, he complained about a book with a same-sex kiss. Of course, it was a different world back then; nowadays you see security escorting protestors from school board meetings. Or even arresting people. And Mr. Warner didn't try to pull in other parents that time, not that I remember."

"He seems to have other parents on his side now," Emily admitted. "I was surprised by how many of the parent complaints we got last year were in his piece."

"The whole city is more polarized than ever," Dan said. "My wife's on the City Council, and she says their meetings get pretty heated. I don't even want to imagine our city meetings filled with protestors shouting and news cameras everywhere. It's a real safety threat."

"I don't want to imagine it, either," Emily said.

"I'm no expert in civic education," Dan said. "But maybe there's some way to make these projects less political, maybe some approved topics for students to choose from, topics that aren't so controversial."

"That would undermine a key purpose of action civics," Emily objected. "Students choose issues that matter to them, and many of those issues are political. Besides, having discussions about controversial issues helps students engage with the curriculum and become critical thinkers.[16] That's important."

"Maybe changing what students are allowed to do?" Dan suggested. "They could write letters to the editor, or have a class debate."[17]

"That takes the 'action' out of action civics," Emily explained. "Debates and letters to the editor have a place in the social studies classroom, but action civics empowers students in a way that those traditional methods don't."[18]

"I understand, but a lot of parents don't want their 'empowered' children learning to plan walkouts," Dan countered. "Those parents deserve a say in their children's education.[19] Besides, you know we've been dealing with budget cuts. The last thing the superintendent wants is a costly lawsuit from angry parents. I know that this project worked great at your old school, Emily. But Central is a very different place; I just don't think we're ready for something as divisive as action civics here."

* * *

"Was that Dan I saw in here a while ago?" Darren Johnson asked, appearing in the doorway.

Emily nodded. "I'm sure you can guess why he came. Yesterday, I thought the action civics project was a key part of the American History curriculum. Now I have parents, teachers, and administrators telling me otherwise."

"You've also got parents and teachers telling you differently," Darren countered, handing Emily his phone. "Check out the Central Parents Facebook page."

"Mr. Warner certainly has plenty of supporters," Emily said, scrolling through the comments. Various parents echoed ideas from the opinion piece. One line jumped out at her: "Kids need to learn before they become activists, so they have informed opinions."[20]

"You're focusing on the wrong parts," Darren objected. "There are parents who support action civics, too."

Darren was right. Emily read, "My son hated history for years, but his project changed all that. Now he wants to intern at the State House. I just wish he'd done the project years ago." Other parents shared similar stories of student engagement, not just in their classwork but also in following political news and participating in political discussions at home.[21]

Emily read the next comment aloud: "Maybe the school board isn't the right place to fight. We should talk to our state representatives. Some places have already banned action civics."[22]

"What if we become the school that inspires a new law here banning action civics for the whole state?" Emily asked Darren. "There are well-funded groups behind parents like Mr. Warner.[23] They could make a lot of noise in the capitol."

"It's a risk worth taking," Darren replied, "to do what's right."

"And what's that?" Emily sighed.

"It's clear to me what's right," Darren said. "I've seen this too often here: we do something that challenges the status quo, that lifts up the voices of marginalized students, and people get nervous. And suddenly we don't teach that book or do that project anymore. We decide to wait until people feel ready. We've made a lot of statements about equity and justice recently, but I don't see those statements turning into action. For example, all our new hires last year in the department were White. Now we're looking at eliminating a project that we know helps kids of color because it's making some White people uncomfortable. We have a chance to take a stand for equity here."

A hesitant knock sounded at the door. It was Katie Fiske.

"Come in," Emily told her. "We're just talking about the action civics project."

"That's why I came," Katie said, hovering by the door. "I want to drop the project this year. I'm not eligible for tenure until next year, and I'm worried my contract won't be renewed if anything goes wrong in my classes. But maybe you can still do it in your classes?"

"We'll talk more about it at our one-on-one meeting," Emily reassured her.

"OK," Katie said, heading back to her classroom.

"I imagine Rhonda won't want just some classes doing action civics," Emily said. "Curricular alignment matters to the district."

"Besides, Katie teaches three general ed sections. We don't want action civics to become something only AP and Honors kids do," Darren pointed out.

Emily nodded. "I have to see what they're thinking at the district office. There's a lot to consider."

After Darren left, Emily woke up her computer to find a response from Rhonda.

I did see that article. I've been fielding a lot of questions at the office about action civics! The press attention definitely has some people nervous here, so we'll have to decide how far we push this issue. There may be some rebranding we can do to placate the dissenters. And of course, action civics isn't the only way to shake up the curriculum. The money we have budgeted for the project could fund a guest speaker, maybe, or a new field trip? It's something to think about. Come by the office this afternoon to let me know where you stand.

Emily sat back in her chair. Where did she stand? Should she push to keep action civics unchanged in the curriculum, risking a firestorm of protests and press coverage? Should she accept that the timing wasn't right at Central, putting aside Darren's argument that now was precisely the right time to push for equity? Was there a middle ground, a way to keep some core of action civics while softening the more objectionable pieces? What would Emily tell Rhonda that afternoon?

Conversation

Meira Levinson: What are some of the key dilemmas in this case, and for whom?

Andrew Wilkes: First, Emily, the social studies department chair, appears to be trying to determine whether to retain some version of action civics, whether to discontinue it, or redefine and rebrand it. Second, Darren is wondering about the viewpoint diversity of how parents are represented in how they think about action civics. And thirdly, Rhonda, the social studies coordinator at the district, faces a dilemma about how to engage community members around action civics. So, this is not only a classroom issue, but a community dilemma as well.

Debbie Holecko: Also, Katie, the newer teacher, seems to be interested in the project, but she's worried about her job. That's a real worry, since everything is dependent on how you are evaluated. Dan, the school principal, appears to be interested in the project and sees its value, but is trying to figure out a way to maybe make it less controversial, which probably also lessens the value of the activity.

Robert Pondiscio: I was struck by how much I felt like I did not know about the case. I wanted more context on the school, the kids, their level of preparation, their civic education more broadly. Having taught at a school where civics education was at the core of the K–12 curriculum colors my perception of the particulars of action civics. So, that was the big question in my mind: is this a one off? Where did the action civics fall within the larger context of their K–12 education, and their civic education preparedness in general?

Meira Levinson: Can you say how different answers to those might change your understanding of what the dilemmas are that are at stake?

Robert Pondiscio: For several years I taught the American history seminar to the senior class at Democracy Prep, a network of charter schools based in Harlem, New York. I also mentored students for the Change the World Project. We didn't call it action civics, but it was. It was a year-long capstone project where kids would take on an issue that they chose themselves and were passionate about, and they would spend a year preparing to do some form of activism around that issue.

I felt like the civic education program was very heavy on the activism. Since my background is journalism and policy, I wanted them to see that there are other levers that they can pull to create change in the world. So, the final project in my seminar was to take what they learned in their Change the World Project, and write a policy brief seeking to change some kind of government policy, practice, funding, procedure, etc. Frankly, I was stunned at their lack of preparation to translate that thinking from action to policy. I'm not by any means opposed to action civics, but there was just a tremendous blind spot. I don't want to be unkind, but I felt as if we were preparing them merely to march in other people's armies.

One student organized a die-in in front of the local police precinct to protest police violence, a very moving bit of activism. When I challenged him, "Okay, well, what would you want the NYPD [New York Police Department] to do differently," he really struggled with where to aim his policy brief: to the local level, state level, federal level. But it should be rather obvious that the NYPD is local.

So, if I'm defending action civics, I want to be able to contextualize it within the student's broad suite of civic skills and motivations. If this is the only thing they're doing, then I'm going to be on the side of the people who are criticizing action civics.

Meira Levinson: What you're saying aligns some with Jim, who feels that students lack basic civic knowledge.

Robert Pondiscio: It's a complicated issue. If this is the only thing that kids are doing in civic education in this school, then I'm team Jim. I would have a hard time critiquing his critique that this is indoctrination. If it's within the larger suite of civic skills and knowledge, then it's richer. Then it really is an exercise in cultivating student agency.

Debbie Holecko: I understood the study as the action civics was part of what they would do, and not the whole of what they would do in the civics class. And so I think some of those issues would work themselves out, because you could still be teaching the traditional civics curriculum. My thinking on indoctrination is they have a choice of the topic. These are things that are important to them, and they're applying their knowledge that they're learning in their civics class.

Fernando Reimers: I agree that there are a range of dilemmas in the case, but I do think they're organized in a hierarchy: one of them is the anchor, and depending on how that dilemma is resolved, it conditions what the other dilemmas are. The anchor dilemma is the dilemma that Emily Wilson, the chair of social studies, faces because she has to decide how to respond to this op-ed. The first thing she needs to do is to interpret what this op-ed means. At a minimum, the op-ed expresses the opposition of Mr. Warner, but it could also represent that he and other parents want to limit teaching action civics.

In addition, that op-ed has opened controversy within the department, and in the school more generally, as to whether to continue teaching action civics. What makes this a dilemma is that Emily doesn't know the intent of the parent. Is his op-ed just a way to open up democratic dialogue? Or is he engaged in oppositional tactics such that no matter how Emily responds, he's going to try to steamroll action civics? That's the anchor dilemma. Emily must also decide whether she's going to respond to these autonomously as the department chair. She could lay these on the lap of the principal, or she could say, "No, I am a professional here. And this is my dilemma to resolve," and stand by that, which could cause a lot of hate for her within the school.

Robert Pondiscio: If you're the parent, you say, "Listen, all my kid is ever learning about, or ever doing, is learning about how terrible things are." Where is the room for optimism? Where is the room for gratitude? At a moral level, I would argue you have to love something before you're motivated to fix it. So, we might fall into the perverse trap of actually creating a sense of enervation as opposed to a sense of agency. If kids are always dwelling on the problems that they're facing, then that could be overwhelming after a while.

Andrew Wilkes: I think Darren points to the different curricular experiences of students in the classroom, as well as how the experience of one parent may not be representative of all parents. The op-ed that was written by a particularly spirited and vocal member of our civic committee may not represent all folks' views. And thinking about gratitude with Robert, I'd say that action civics provides the give and take of debate. Students engage democratically about issues that they select. They can weigh evidence, and they can talk about whether they're writing a policy brief or taking some other action. In a lot of Generation Citizen classrooms, students are picking issues like mental health rather than some of the hot button issues that are often discussed.

And so, I think when we consider the question of viewpoint diversity, and how to manage difference conversationally, that's a skill that happens in the classroom. And the case shows us these are skills that are as useful in the workplace as in the public square.

Meira Levinson: As you look at these dilemmas for the various people you've identified, do you see these as stemming from different people holding different values? Or do you see these as stemming from people holding the same values, but interpreting them in different ways? Or maybe they agree on their aims, but they just have different views about how to get there?

Fernando Reimers: I think that there are two types of dilemmas, those that stem from different values and those that stem from different beliefs. Dilemmas that stem from beliefs are easier to solve through democratic dialogue than dilemmas that stem from values, because people's positions can be informed by evidence. Dilemmas that stem from values are harder to resolve because they reflect normative views. These dilemmas are, on the surface, mostly about beliefs, but perhaps one is about values. So, what are the dilemmas? What are the differences in beliefs?

One, there's disagreement about the value of experiential learning versus the intellectualist approach to learning civics. The intellectualist approach assumes that conceptual knowledge eventually leads to procedural knowledge. The experiential approach is John Dewey saying, "No, the only way you actually learn is reflecting from experience." People have different views on that, but there is also an evidence base that we can use to inform those beliefs. The second difference in belief comes from disagreement about the value of engaging students in discussions of controversial topics; there is also evidence that can inform that belief.

The third difference in beliefs is the lack of knowledge about what action civics is, as the op-ed confuses it with indoctrination. Because to the best of my knowledge, Generation Citizen is engaging students in deliberation and decision-making. This is the opposite of indoctrination. And I don't see anyone telling the teacher or the students what movement they should join or how they should think. The organization is actually engaging students in activities that lead them to decide what to do, not deciding for them. If that's true, there is no way you can call that indoctrination, but there may be a different knowledge base about what this program actually is.

And the last difference in beliefs, which may be a borderline between differences in beliefs and values, is connected to Joel Westheimer's thesis on three kinds of citizens: the personally responsible citizen, the participatory citizen, and the social-justice oriented citizen.[24] If you believe that you should educate people who are personally responsible, you may be less inclined to an approach that is about getting people to question norms and rules. The differences in belief in this case may stem from not knowing about these three conceptions. The differences in values stem from preferring some of these over others.

So, because I think this is mostly about beliefs, I am hopeful that democratic dialogue itself can help resolve this issue. It can help bring these differences into the open, and in so doing, opening them up for scrutiny on the basis of evidence, of knowledge based on facts.

Andrew Wilkes: There's also a dynamic of power and influence that's not reducible to questions of belief. For example, Mr. Warner's op-ed reflects over-representation of some citizens getting their views into papers of record relative to others. So, there's a kind of uneven level of voice among citizens that I think initiates the conversation.

I think there's probably two anchor dilemmas, rather than one. One is what Emily decides to do, but then also: to what degree does Emily feel she can influence Dan, the principal? And to what degree does Emily feel that Rhonda can be influenced? Those are questions of deliberation, which in some regards mirror what's happening in the classroom. So, I think there's an ecosystem approach of what happens in the classroom, what happens between teachers and principals, and then what happens between particular schools and districts, which is equally important to highlight in the case, because it has everything to do with the experience that students ultimately have.

Debbie Holecko: There's definitely a misunderstanding by the parent group about what action civics actually involves, because even in the case there was a student who switched from doing something about transgender athletes to a pro-life cause. So, not all the issues are traditionally left-wing issues, because the kids choose them. I think if the parents understand what's happening, they'll be less resistant to their children's projects.

What my eighth graders did was not called "action civics," but, like Robert said, it ended up being action civics. The eighth graders were trying to tie in local history with the American history they were learning. They discovered an old handwritten map and saw that the map showed unmarked graves—it just said, "Colored people buried here." The students were outraged, and they wanted to do something about it. I stepped back, and they got the mayor to come out to our school. The mayor asked them, "Well, what do you want?" And they said, "We'd like a sign up there, at least acknowledging these families because this is wrong." And then they were invited to the landmarks commission meeting. So these students who didn't typically speak out in class were speaking out at meetings. In the end, a company that makes headstones agreed to donate one, which was put in the cemetery.

So, my students felt very empowered. And they did see how local government works. And one girl said that if an eighth grader can make change, maybe anybody can. As a teacher, that really felt good.

Meira Levinson: How political did that activity feel? Were there people, or parents, or community members who you feared might push back? And since you thought that parents in the case wouldn't be upset if they understood action civics better, do you think this is just a communication problem?

Debbie Holecko: I don't know if an organized group like Mr. Warner's would listen. But if they were invited to see what the students were doing, they might calm down. And as far as pushback on the project that we were doing, we did notice some social media posts that criticized the project, and we just ignored that. It never went any further than just social media. But I could see where in some communities it could.

Robert Pondiscio: I wanted to briefly just nod to Fernando's point about values, and our conceptions of what schools are for. I'm professionally closely aligned with E. D. Hirsch Jr.; I'm very much sympathetic to a knowledge-rich education.

So, some of these dichotomies melt away for me. I've spent years standing in that gap saying, "Knowledge versus skills as a false dichotomy. Students need both." And my critique of action civics has tended to focus on programs that lack the knowledge piece and focus just on the skills. Then it just feels like empty calories.

And kudos to you, Debbie, you're absolutely right. Who could possibly object to that project? But I think we're being slightly less than candid with ourselves with this case study. Am I imagining that there was a value judgment implicit in the student who wanted to do a trans rights project and ended up doing a pro-life project? I think, as readers, we were intended to think, "Oh, isn't that too bad?" We are being a little bit less than honest with ourselves if we don't recognize our biases there.

Debbie Holecko: Well, I would argue that maybe it was too bad simply because the student was originally interested in the idea of transgender athletes, but because of the pressure she was feeling from home, she felt like she had to switch.

Robert Pondiscio: I don't want to be cute here, but in writing this case study, those of us who are in this work would never have taken that in the other direction, saying the student really wanted to do something on pro-life but her parents insisted that she do something on trans rights. That would just not happen.

Meira Levinson: We haven't talked about our vision of parents' rights. Are there any dilemmas for parents here? Are there dilemmas for teachers in terms of accommodating parents' wishes about what their students learn or do in the classroom? Obviously there's a huge amount right now of political activism and conversation about this very question all around the United States.

Robert Pondiscio: Who wants to hurl themselves on the grenade?

Fernando Reimers: There is disagreement in the case over whether to prioritize the concerns of some parents, versus the benefits to students, or even the desires of the students. And relatedly, there is disagreement over how to weigh the risk of controversy and the time that it would take to resolve it, relative to the educational benefits of the approach. Even if Emily and Dan think this is a great program, they might conclude that engaging in this dialogue is going to take up a lot of time. Is the opportunity cost worth it? That is one of the issues that Emily and her principal will have to decide. Do we want to invest the time to bring the community along or do we ignore the issue and just think about the students and focus energies on activities of high instructional value for students?

Meira Levinson: Let's imagine that Mr. Warner will not be convinced by Emily offering to show him the students' projects and will in fact continue to organize and potentially bring his organizing beyond just this district to the state house.

We've seen examples of laws, like in Texas, which would, for example, allow Robert's student to write his policy paper but not plan the die-in. And let's assume she's working under the ideal conditions that Robert has posited: the project is part of a robust, knowledge-rich civic education at the school. Should Emily push ahead on this action civics project that she believes in? Or in light of this potential political backlash, should she back off?

Robert Pondiscio: There's a tension here that I think we are not recognizing. I have this sense that the average public school employee in this country simply does not conceive of himself or herself as a government agent, as a public employee. The characters must decide: how are we going to push here? Who are we aligned with? There's almost an assumption of an oppositional relationship with parents, or at least a tension there.

And I'm not pretending to know how to resolve that, but I think it's important to ask ourselves that question. What is our role as educators who are public employees? What is our obligation to be mindful of the conditions in the community, the spirit of the community? I don't want to be crass about it, but what is our obligation to the people who are paying our salary, so to speak? I think a lot of the political discussion about this has been overly broad and facile, like parents saying, "I want control," or teachers saying, "I don't work for the parents." But we are public employees. I think we have to answer that question for ourselves before we can answer these larger dilemmas of who we're accountable to.

Fernando Reimers: Robert, but even if we all agree that teachers in public schools are public employees, and accountable to their employers, isn't part of the challenge that the profession also expects allegiance to the standards of the profession? Let's assume for a moment that we're talking about a medical doctor in a community where everybody loves to smoke, and the doctor begins to recommend that their patients stop smoking. And the community gets very annoyed. We would expect that doctor to essentially stand to the Hippocratic principle, and say, "No, I have a loyalty here to preserve the life of my patients, whether my patient agrees with me or not."

So, why would it be any different for educators? We could imagine extreme scenarios where, for example, a community had an extremist group of some sort. I would hope the teachers would do the same thing that the doctor trying to protect patient health would do, and say, "I'm sorry, we have a commitment to teach democratic values, and your group can't hijack the schools to teach extremely intolerant views. That is not acceptable in a democratic society."

Debbie Holecko: I would argue that we have to think about the role of the public school. So, public schools are not meant to serve every little splinter group that may be very vocal, but are not truly the majority. I think as a public employee, I look at the standards that I'm expected to teach and I stay within those. And parents may come in and say, "Well, I don't want this." And that's where you have the option to put your child in a private school if you disagree with whatever is being taught, because the public schools are following a curriculum that has been decided is best for our community. It's what students should know and know how to do, for the public's best interest. And sometimes parents are not happy with that. They don't want students to be active citizens unless they're active in the issues that they approve of. But it's important for students to understand different points of view. We have such a divided country right now, and it's partially because people don't want to listen to each other and think about things from more than one very narrowly focused viewpoint.

Meira Levinson: So Debbie, can I push you on this? Because I heard Robert saying, "If a law banning action civics passes, that is a representative democracy passing a law that then has implications for the curriculum. And as a teacher, we need to follow the law." And just as you've said, we are teachers following a curriculum built on standards. So, I'm curious, if this law is passed do you then say, "All right. We've had a representative democracy that's changed the curriculum"? Or do you, as a teacher, think, "No, I actually want to be politically engaged in this"?

Debbie Holecko: Not to go off on a completely different tangent, but representative democracy is also questionable when you have gerrymandering of districts so that partisan legislators can pass these laws. But if the law is passed, the law is passed and you can't do much as a teacher.

Andrew Wilkes: Laws like we see in Texas, like what's being considered in South Dakota, Wisconsin, Oklahoma, and a number of other places, essentially seek to strip away access to action civics. But there's a conflict between that legislative arc and social studies standards and state constitutions, both of which are calling for ideals of informed active citizenship. And so, it puts teachers and districts in a bit of a conundrum when you have policy signals from the constitution and standards saying one thing, and laws, which often are unclear as to implementation guidance, saying another.

So, first, it's important to note that laws of the sort that we're talking about are themselves a civics dilemma. Second, if we bracket the question of the legislation, the only way that we can get students feeling empowered to serve on juries, to vote, to join organizations, and to reverse the "bowling alone" trend that Robert Putnam, for instance, talks about, is to have schools support the kind of analysis and the teamwork capacity that help people to associate with one another skillfully, even in the midst of conflict and dissonance, what action civics does at its best. I think that's a part of what Darren is pushing for. Social studies is one of the least racially diverse professions, in terms of teacher makeup. And so, I think it's noteworthy to point out that there's that potential estrangement in the room as well.

Robert Pondiscio: Who is the most effective civic actor in this case study? It's Mr. Warner who wrote the op-ed, because he's the one who provoked a response from a government agency. So, we're viewing him as the sand in the gears here, but there'd be an interesting discussion, to ask, "Is this an example of action civics?" Here's a citizen who was outraged, wrote an op-ed, provoked a response from a government agency, and now we're trying to be like the oyster with the pearl. We're taking the bit of sand and trying to smooth it over, as opposed to saying, "Well, wait a minute. Isn't this what we're trying to teach our kids to do?"

Meira Levinson: The four of you have each thought long and hard about the issues in this case for years now: civic education, student civic action, and the politics of education. How did working through these issues about civic education through this case study compare to other ways that you've thought about these issues?

Fernando Reimers: What the case underscores for me is that there are things that are fair game in democratic politics that are not fair game in education politics when you're trying to teach civic education. In democratic politics, sometimes people resolve conflict through deliberate democratic deliberation, but sometimes they do it through coercion, bribery, or the ruthless exercise of power. And that should be absolutely out of bounds in school politics. In school politics, you have no choice but to engage in democratic deliberation, because that's the essence of educating for democracy.

So, I actually agree with Robert that this individual who wrote the op-ed has to be taken seriously. If Emily decides to engage, I think she has to engage in good faith, giving the fellow the benefit of the doubt, and seeing this as an opportunity to teach the students and the school community what democratic deliberation is. And to me, that means doing the following things. Number one, she has to understand the situation, understand the stakeholders, take the time to listen to the different parties and understand their interests, including his interest. A main stakeholder, of course, should be the students. Others should be the teachers and the parents, and none of those groups are monolithic, which is why this process takes time.

Number two, she has to deescalate the situation through evidence and scholarship. So, for example, if there is disagreement on the value of project-based learning, educate the community, get them to discuss the evidence. Third, she has to identify and make visible for all the criteria which can be used to resolve the situation. What are the benefits of this program to the kids? What is the feasibility of executing it? What are the costs? What are the opportunity costs? What are the political costs? Then she has to brainstorm, with other stakeholders, a range of options and use those criteria to compare them.

And then once the decision is reached, of course, she has to build a political map of key stakeholders and try to create a strategy to manage the politics. This process of deliberation is very different from a political strategy of steamrolling the opponent. I think that would be the worst response because it is a school. In a school, you cannot deny others the right to their point of view. You cannot respond to the ruthless exercise of power with ruthless power, because then you've given up on the democratic missions of the school. You've given up and you've allowed the tyrants to hijack the schools and to teach the lesson that tyranny is all that matters, the worst possible lesson on democracy.

One problem of the moment we're in, a moment of tremendous polarization, where we have lost the most basic habits for democratic deliberation, is that the knee-jerk reaction for many of us might be to shut down the opposing view. Educators have to work extra hard in saying, "No, if I'm going to engage, it's going to be through democratic dialogue." But as I said earlier, because all of this takes time, the first decision has to be: is this worth it in this case?

Meira Levinson: Andrew, I'm curious to hear from you next, given that your job is thinking about policy and advocacy. Has this case been distinctive for you as compared to how you otherwise think and talk about civic education?

Andrew Wilkes: Well, I think this case study is powerful because it's humanizing to hear Jim in conversation with Darren, to hear Emily in conversation with Rhonda and Dan. Hearing these conversations is different from talking through a proposed piece of legislation, or reading a fifty-state summary by a think tank, let's say. But the second thing I think is particularly powerful about the case study method is how it lifts up the values, conflicts, and the differential settings of power. And I say that because I don't fully share Fernando's confidence that schools are deliberative bodies completely unmoored from power and influence. I think school board meetings and department meetings are probably sufficient evidence of that. However, I think it is unequivocally the ideal of schools. And so, I think there's a certain hopefulness about democratic deliberation, and about the exchange of views between citizens that I think this case captures powerfully.

Robert Pondiscio: The case for good or for ill probably reinforced my priors as much as anything else. What I mean by that is, if you want to make the case for action civics, and I'm not suggesting we should or should not, it just cannot be a standalone activity.

Debbie Holecko: As I read it, I put myself in Emily's position and thought, "How would I deal with this?" And I decided that I would just want to meet with parents, and I would want to listen to their concerns. Then I would want to try to calm their concerns with factual evidence, and let them see the choices. I think the way schools are funded is a problem in some places, because that controls what school boards are willing to do. I know in Ohio it's all local. So if the local community is not on board with something, they won't pass the levy, and then you can't operate your school. And I know other states do it statewide. Obviously the concerns of the local community are important. But I think that there's a way that you can just help them air their grievances while explaining why action civics is a worthwhile activity for their child.

Meira Levinson: What do you hope others reading this conversation will continue thinking about?

Fernando Reimers: I hope readers will see the value of engaging in deliberation and considering multiple perspectives. The first thing that anyone needs to resolve a dilemma is a theory of mind, an explanation for why others act the way they do. It would be naive to project onto others the explanations we have for our own behavior.

The beauty of engaging in dilemmas like that is that it helps us practice that perspective taking. So, in this particular case I would hope that Emily would actually write her dilemma down in the way this case is written, and would discuss it with other people before taking any action. Because I think it would lead to more empathic and effective action.

Robert Pondiscio: Preparing young people for active citizenship is both the founding and the forgotten purpose of public education. So, I'm intrigued by this case study and conversation because they bring us back to this purpose. I'm not comfortable now or ever saying, "Do this, don't do that." I don't believe there are right or wrong answers in terms of our approaches, but we have to be sophisticated in our deliberations about them. In other words, you need to situate this kind of learning within a school culture that sees preparation for citizenship as core to its mission, and not merely a fun, or interesting, or engaging activity, or one off.

Debbie Holecko: I would like people to see that the skills in this case are important life skills: bringing up controversial issues, researching them, learning opposing points of view, and figuring out the validity of a source. We can't shield our children from points of view with which we disagree. We need to give them the tools to evaluate, discuss, and even act on these issues that matter to them. And I think that's what action civics does.

Andrew Wilkes: I hope that folks will read it multiple times—that's what I did—to understand the stakes of content pedagogy and applying civics in the classroom. I think specifically the relationships between Emily and Dan and Emily and Rhonda illustrate that there's often multiple and competing actions that happen in schools and in communities. And that folks have to be brought along in order to make that ideal a practical one.

Debbie Holecko *has taught eighth grade social studies in Northeastern Ohio for the past thirty-five years. She is proud when her students show interest in using what they've learned to make the world a better place. One of her best professional moments was when her students were featured in a* New York Times *article about a community project they initiated, ultimately leading to a new memorial marker on the unmarked graves of two local Black families who died in the 1800s.*

Robert Pondiscio *is a senior fellow at the American Enterprise Institute (AEI), where he focuses on K–12 education. A former South Bronx elementary school teacher, he is the author of How the Other Half Learns: Equality, Excellence, and the Battle over School Choice (Avery, 2019).*

Fernando M. Reimers *is the Ford Foundation Professor of the Practice of International Education at the Harvard Graduate School of Education. His work focuses on making education systems more relevant to a sustainable world. He is an elected member of the US National Academy of Education and of the International Academy of Education and has published or edited fifty academic books.*

Andrew Wilkes *is the Chief Policy and Advocacy Officer at Generation Citizen, a nonprofit that works to help young people understand and exercise their civic power through civics education.*

Character Guide

Setting
Central High School, U.S.A. (grades 9–12, ages 14–18)
Primary Characters

Emily Wilson: social studies department chair **John Warner:** parent of an 11th grade student **Juan Ramos:** 11th grade social studies teacher **Rose Benson:** 9th grade social studies teacher **Jim Hennessey:** 11th grade social studies teacher	**Katie Fiske:** 11th grade social studies teacher **Darren Johnson:** 11th grade social studies teacher **Dan Ricci:** principal of Central High School **Rhonda Williams:** social studies curriculum coordinator for the district

Discussion Questions

1 How do different characters in the case think about the purpose of civic education? How do these beliefs influence their views on action civics?
2 Several characters believe that equity is an important reason for all students at Central High to do the action civics project. What connections between civic education and equity work does this case draw? Is this the only or best way for Central High School to promote civic equity?
3 When Katie discusses objections that a Black mother raised to the action civics project, Darren reminds her that one parent cannot "speak for all Black families." Similarly, when Emily focuses on Mr. Warner's op-ed opposing action civics, Darren points her to a local Facebook community page where many parents had expressed support for the initiative. What responsibilities (if any) do schools have to solicit a wide range of parent feedback on their programs? What are some of the challenges to collecting that feedback from the entire parent community?
4 When, why, and how much should parents be able to influence what gets taught at their children's schools? What responsibilities, if any, come with those rights?
5 How should schools work in partnership with the community when the community is polarized on important educational issues, as in this case?
6 While supporters of action civics emphasize that students exercise agency by choosing the topics of their civic projects, opponents like Mr. Warner argue that the issues are truly chosen by teachers "indoctrinating" susceptible young people. How do you think about young people's agency and autonomy—both in the case and in your own context?
7 The case (and the conversation that follows) reflects broader disagreement across the United States about aims of civic education and the relationship between civic knowledge, skills, and dispositions. Is there a "correct" order to how schools should teach these three prongs of civic education? Why/why not? At what age should young people begin taking civic action?
8 Emily worries that controversy over action civics at Central might draw the attention of lawmakers with the power to ban action civics projects across the entire state. How much should these kinds of political considerations impact local decisions?

Notes

1. Texas House Bill 3979.
2. Rebranding action civics as "protest civics" seems to have been coined by Stanley Kurtz of the Ethics and Public Policy Center. Stanley Kurtz, "How Dems Will Push Protest Civics and CRT on Schools," *National Review* (blog), June 1, 2021, https://www.nationalreview.com/corner/how-dems-will-push-protest-civics-and-crt-on-schools/.
3. "Temper tantrums" comes from David Randall of the National Association of Scholars. David Randall, "Oklahoma Education Agency Promotes Progressive Activism Masquerading …," Oklahoma Council of Public Affairs, December 26, 2019, https://www.ocpathink.org/post/perspective-magazine/oklahoma-education-agency-promotes-progressive-activism-masquerading-as-civics.
4. The National Action Civics Collaborative provides an overview of the action civics process, along with links to more detailed materials. See https://actioncivicscollaborative.org/why-action-civics/overview/.
5. Nam-Jin Lee, Dhavan V. Shah, and Jack M. McLeod, "Processes of Political Socialization: A Communication Mediation Approach to Youth Civic Engagement," *Communication Research* 40, no. 5 (October 2013): 669–97, https://doi.org/10.1177/0093650212436712.
6. Ben Kirshner and Kimberly Geil, "'I'm about to Really Bring It!' Access Points between Youth Activists and Adult Community Leaders," *Children, Youth and Environments* 20, no. 2 (2010): 1–24.
7. See data from Generation Citizen about the impact that their action civics curriculum has on students https://generationcitizen.org/our-impact/by-the-numbers/.
8. This student comment is paraphrased from public testimony given by Kaira Watts-Bey, a Generation Citizen student who spoke before the New York City Council's Education Committee in 2017.
9. In Alabama in June 2021, more than forty people took part in a similar conference to "abolish Common Core education standards and ban instruction of Critical Race Theory" in the state's public schools. Brandon Moseley, "Conservatives Hold Conference on Banning Critical Race Theory, Common Core," Alabama Political Reporter, June 28, 2021, https://www.alreporter.com/2021/06/28/conservatives-hold-conference-on-banning-critical-race-theory-common-core/.
10. Maine parent Shawn McBreairty called himself "the tip of the sword" in an interview on Fox News on June 1, 2021, discussing his opposition to an "equity letter" sent by his daughters' school district. Talia Kaplan, "Maine Father Fights Critical Race Theory in Daughters' School: 'We Need

Education, Not Indoctrination,'" Text.Article, Fox News (Fox News, June 1, 2021), https://www.foxnews.com/media/maine-father-critical-race-theory-we-need-education-not-indoctrination.

11. For example, action civics was attacked as a "divisive theory" in New Brunswick, N.C., in June 2021. Kassie Simmons, "Brunswick County Leaders Tackle Critical Race Theory, Other 'Divisive' Theories," WECT News, June 9, 2021, https://www.wect.com/2021/06/08/brunswick-county-leaders-tackle-critical-race-theory-other-divisive-theories/.

12. In 2020, the Annenberg Civics Knowledge Survey found that 51 percent of Americans could identify all three branches of government, the highest percentage since the yearly survey began in 2006. "Annenberg Civics Knowledge Survey Archives," *The Annenberg Public Policy Center of the University of Pennsylvania* (blog), accessed May 20, 2023, https://www.annenbergpublicpolicycenter.org/political-communication/civics-knowledge-survey/.

13. Joshua Littenberg-Tobias and Alison K. Cohen, "Diverging Paths: Understanding Racial Differences in Civic Engagement among White, African American, and Latina/o Adolescents Using Structural Equation Modeling," *American Journal of Community Psychology* 57, no. 1–2 (March 2016): 102–17, https://doi.org/10.1002/ajcp.12027.

14. For example, civic engagement can help urban youth exposed to violence (who are disproportionately low-income youth) build resilience. See Sonia Jain and Alison K. Cohen, "Fostering Resilience among Urban Youth Exposed to Violence: A Promising Area for Interdisciplinary Research and Practice," *Health Education & Behavior: The Official Publication of the Society for Public Health Education* 40, no. 6 (December 2013): 651–62, https://doi.org/10.1177/1090198113492761.

15. This story and the following story about affirmative action are based on parental pushback received by teachers, related by nonprofit organizations that work with educators using action civics in the classroom.

16. Diana Hess at the University of Wisconsin-Madison has spent many years studying the benefits of discussing controversial issues in the classroom. For a good example of her work, see Diana E. Hess, "Discussing Controversial Public Issues in Secondary Social Studies Classrooms: Learning from Skilled Teachers," *Theory & Research in Social Education* 30, no. 1 (January 2002): 10–41, https://doi.org/10.1080/00933104.2002.10473177.

17. For a detailed argument that class debates are preferable to action civics, see Stanley Kurtz, "'Action Civics' Replaces Citizenship with Partisanship," *The American Mind*, January 26, 2021, https://americanmind.org/memo/action-civics-replaces-citizenship-with-partisanship/.

18. Meira Levinson, "Action Civics in the Classroom," *Social Education* 78, no. 2 (March 1, 2014): 68–72.
19. Writing for The Heartland Institute, Robert G. Holland argued, "Let families decide whether they want their children to learn about the principles of self-government that make this country exceptional or if they would prefer that the kids gather petitions to submit to the local waterworks department." Robert G. Holland, "Would Revived Civics End Up Being Progressive Ed Redux?—The Heartland Institute," *The Heartland Institute* (blog), November 19, 2017, https://heartland.org/opinion/would-revived-civics-end-up-being-progressive-ed-redux/.
20. Delaware state representative Richard Collins said this at a Delaware House Education Committee Hearing in May 2021. Matt Vasilogambros, "After Capitol Riot, Some States Turn to Civics Education," *Stateline* (blog), May 19, 2021, https://stateline.org/2021/05/19/after-capitol-riot-some-states-turn-to-civics-education/.
21. Research has shown that action civics can lead to this behavior. Keith Barton and Alan McCully, "Teaching Controversial Issues … Where Controversial Issues Really Matter," *Teaching History* 127 (June 2007): 13–19.
22. In Texas, for example, HB3979 states that "a school district, open-enrollment charter school, or teacher may not require, make part of a course, or award a grade or course credit, including extra credit, for a student's political activism, lobbying, or efforts to persuade members of the legislative or executive branch at the federal, state, or local level to take specific actions by direct communication." See https://legiscan.com/TX/text/HB3979/id/2339637.
23. In June 2021, NBC News found "at least 165 local and national groups that aim to disrupt lessons on race and gender," controversial issues that are often connected with attacks on action civics. Tyler Kingkade, Brandy Zadrozny, and Ben Collins, "'Held Hostage': How Critical Race Theory Moved from Fox News to School Boards," NBC News, June 15, 2021, https://www.nbcnews.com/news/us-news/critical-race-theory-invades-school-boards-help-conservative-groups-n1270794.
24. Joel Westheimer and Joseph Kahne, "Educating the 'Good' Citizen: Political Choices and Pedagogical Goals," *Political Science and Politics* 37, no. 02 (2004): 241–7.

7

Course Correction: Teaching Critical Consciousness in an Anti-CRT State

Yonas Michael, Nicolas Tanchuk, and Sara O'Brien

In the early 2020s, state lawmakers across the United States introduced legislation designed to target certain approaches to teaching about race and racism and other topics related to diversity, equity, and inclusion in K-12 schooling. Between January 2021 and January 2023, following the largest protests for racial justice in US history,[1] forty-four US states introduced or passed such legislation, often banning the teaching of supposedly "divisive concepts" related to race and gender.[2] The language in most of these bills echoed an executive order issued by former President Donald Trump in September 2020.[3] Across the country, the new legislation created uncertainty for many educators, who reported that the laws had a "chilling effect on teaching lessons related to race and racism," contributing to a "[struggle] to provide historical context for current events."[4] This fictional case is rooted in research on the impact of these laws nationally and the experiences of two of the case's authors, who worked as educators and researchers in a state with such a law. The case explores the consequences of this raft of legislation on students, teachers, and school leaders, and the ways in which differences in identity can differentially shape the effects of these laws and the ways they are experienced.

--

"Daniel, do you have a minute?"

Principal Daniel Semere looked up to see Sally Bruce standing in his office doorway at Heath Middle School. Smiling, he motioned for her to sit. The opening bell wouldn't ring for another twenty minutes, so they had time for the conversation Daniel worried was coming.

"I heard back from State," Sally began. "They offered me the position, and I'm going to take it."

Daniel's heart sank. Sally Bruce only worked half time at HMS, but she was an integral part of the team. A White teacher with two decades of experience, Sally taught the sixth-grade Critical Consciousness course, a recent addition to the curriculum designed both to help students think critically about how power and privilege systematically advantage some while disadvantaging others and to help them take action to redress inequities. Sally and Daniel had built the three-week elective course using materials from the Learning for Justice Standards with content anchored to the state-adopted Social Studies and Language Arts standards. In Sally's capable hands, the course was a game-changer for students marginalized by race and gender, as the school's recent climate survey showed.

Now the course's future was in doubt, and not just because of Sally's departure to teach pre-service teachers at the local university. For months Daniel and Sally had been wrestling with the future of the course given increasing pushback within the district. Irate parents had been filing complaints against the licenses of any teachers they believed were filling students' heads with "anti-American beliefs." Sally had already received one complaint, which she jokingly called her "badge of honor."

Daniel fully shared her commitment to the course. As a Black man who had been born in a refugee camp in Sudan and immigrated to the United States as a child, Daniel had a personal and professional stake in creating racially inclusive schools. He'd come to the district specifically to help make equity a reality there, having been handpicked to lead HMS by the previous superintendent, who championed equity work at all levels across the district and put the district's equity plan into action.

But the superintendent had resigned from her position just weeks before, amidst pressure from groups like Heath Parents for Education (HPE), who were up in arms about what they saw as "indoctrination" in the district. The new interim superintendent had already told Daniel that the district was putting equity work on hold in light of the complaints. Now Daniel found himself as the only Black administrator in Heath, trying to decide how much he was willing to risk to continue the work with reduced district support.

To make matters worse, the governor had just signed a law which forbade schools from teaching that "the United States and the state are fundamentally or systemically racist or sexist"—a clause that many teachers and parents alike interpreted as banning any teaching about institutional racism or White supremacy. The law also outlawed teaching students to feel "discomfort […] on account of [their] race or sex"—a difficult feeling to avoid in a course about power, privilege, and systematic advantage and disadvantage.

While it was unclear just how the law would be enforced, many teachers in the district worried that any discussion of race or gender in their courses would leave them vulnerable to complaints—or even legal repercussions. And the Critical Consciousness course had already been flagged as a "matter of concern" on HPE's website. With Sally leaving, the course's future was more uncertain than ever. Whoever took over teaching the course would have a target on their back long before they stepped into the classroom. Could Daniel place one of his teachers in that position? Should he even renew the course for next year?

Pushing these thoughts aside, Daniel turned his attention back to Sally.

"Congratulations!" he enthused. "They couldn't find a better person to work with new teachers."

"Thanks," Sally smiled. "I'm excited, though of course I'm heartbroken, too. I just hate leaving the kids. I brought you some of their work." She held out a paper, covered in purple writing. "It's the identity reflection the students do in the third week of the course. This student wrote about how they never felt school was a welcoming place for queer kids before. They literally wrote: 'This course saved my life.'"

Daniel knew that the course was making a difference—in the recent climate survey, they'd seen a 27 percent increase in students' perceived physical and psychological safety compared to the year before the course ran. But seeing the student's words in their own handwriting struck him deeply. Could he eliminate a course that was having such a positive impact on the students who most needed to feel supported? But given the backlash and the new law, would he actually be able to keep the course in its current form?

"Thanks for bringing this," Daniel said, handing the paper back to Sally. "We're really going to miss you."

***

Later that morning, Daniel popped into the staff room to grab some water. As he filled his bottle, two teachers approached him, their brows furrowed.

"Sally told us about the job at State," Gabrielle Lewis began. She was a literacy teacher in her second decade at HMS. She was also one of the few Black teachers at the school and a surrogate mom to many students, Black and White. "Who are you getting to take over her class?"

"Direct as always, Gabby," Daniel laughed. "I wish I knew the answer to that."

"They'll be in for a rough ride," Gabby sighed. "But we spent years trying to get something like that course off the ground. Just because it's ruffling some feathers doesn't mean we should abandon it now."

"I don't mind ruffling feathers," Daniel said. "But this new law is a serious blow."

"It's downright scary," Brian Hall affirmed. He was a social studies teacher who frequently collaborated with Gabby. A White man who had grown up in Heath, Brian had worked as a community organizer in Chicago before moving back home to start a family. "Honestly, the Critical Consciousness class might be doomed under this law. I've already been wondering whether I'll have to make any changes to my courses. Everything is grounded in the state standards, of course, but will that be enough to keep us from being challenged?"

"I don't think we should make any changes," Gabby protested. "What we're doing is good for kids."

"But teachers are already getting in trouble, and the new law hasn't even taken effect," Brian pointed out. "I know that the complaint against Sally's license didn't influence her decision, but will we find someone else willing to take that risk? I mean, I've got two little ones at home, and my wife's not working. I know I can't afford to lose my license."

"I wouldn't ask you to take on the risk, Brian," Daniel said. "Truthfully, I'm not sure whether I can ask anyone to do it. And I don't want to lose any teachers doing this work."

"But I don't want our kids losing the chance to talk about the systemic challenges that they're facing every day," Gabby insisted. "They're living with all these injustices—racism, sexism, homophobia—on social media, on TV, even in the hallways here! They need help unpacking all that and finding ways to make change."

"Is this one course the only way to do that?" Brian asked. "What if we spread those conversations and projects out into other courses?"

"I know you both would include more social justice curriculum in a heartbeat," Daniel assured him. "But would the curriculum have the same impact if we dilute it that way?"

"And could we be sure everyone would actually teach it?" Gabby added. "If even you, Brian, are wondering if you need to modify what you're teaching, that means a lot of our colleagues won't be willing to touch anything that smacks of social justice." The bell rang, and she gathered up her bag. "I don't envy you, Daniel, making these decisions. Let me know if I can help at all."

"Same here," Brian chimed in. "I know how much this work matters."

***

Daniel returned to his office to find several insistent phone messages from Mrs. Peterson, parent of a sixth grader. He had already spoken to Mrs. Peterson at the beginning of the school year, when she called to ask about opting her daughter Carly out of the Critical Consciousness course. However, Carly had balked at the idea of being separated from her friends and sent to study hall instead, so Mrs. Peterson had relented and allowed Carly to take the course. Based on the messages, she regretted that decision. Sighing, Daniel picked up the phone.

"Mrs. Peterson, it's Daniel Semere from HMS. How are you?"

"I'm angry, Mr. Semere, that's how I am. I'm wondering why my family is being demonized at your school."

"I'm surprised to hear that could be happening," Daniel said. "Can you tell me what you mean?"

"Gladly," Mrs. Peterson snapped. "Carly came home yesterday to tell me that Christians like us have persecuted homosexuals for centuries. She said that her teacher called the legalization of gay marriage a victory."

"In the long struggle for gay rights, it's a huge legal victory," Daniel agreed.

"Well, to a lot of people it's not a victory," Mrs. Peterson argued. "It's a perversion. Scripture tells us that marriage exists between a man and a woman. There's no law that's higher than Scripture."

"Many people disagree with that, Mrs. Peterson," Daniel countered. "And the Critical Consciousness course exists to introduce students to new perspectives."

"And that's the problem!" Mrs. Peterson exclaimed. "You've preached to me before about different perspectives, but you know whose perspective is missing from that class? Mine! If you're going to teach my daughter about the morality of gay marriage, she deserves to hear both sides of the argument. But she's not reading or watching anything that promotes good Christian values. She's reading gay propaganda instead! If you really believe in different perspectives, then put some Christian authors into the syllabus."

"Mrs. Peterson, you have a right to your beliefs. But I won't include readings that devalue LGBTQ students and families," Daniel stated firmly.

"But you have no problem 'devaluing' Carly and her religion?" Mrs. Peterson scoffed. "You're a hypocrite, Mr. Semere, that's all you are. And I'm going to make sure that no child ever has to sit through your course again. You won't be indoctrinating kids for much longer."

With that, she ended the call.

Daniel leaned his head back against the chair. It wasn't the first time he'd been threatened by a parent, and he doubted it would be the last. Would she be filing a complaint against his license? Was the threat more serious? Daniel was weary of weighing threats to his personal and professional safety against the need to support marginalized students and their families. Was renewing the course worth risking his job? His safety? At the same time, how could he claim to be an equity-oriented leader if he wasn't willing to stand up for a course that truly was helping students understand different perspectives, a course that was helping marginalized students feel safer at school?

***

Late afternoon light streamed into Daniel's office. He hoped to send just a few more emails before heading home. But he could hear voices coming down the hallway and sensed that he wouldn't be leaving any time soon.

"Nah, man, we got to tell Mr. Semere about this. It's not right."

Two Black sixth-grade boys appeared in Daniel's doorway, their faces angry. Daniel knew them well. Nicky had been to Daniel's office several times before, sent by teachers who deemed his outspokenness a "bad attitude." His friend Reggie was quieter and had never been referred for discipline, but Daniel always spent time getting to know the incoming students, especially the boys of color. He had been glad to see a close friendship develop between these two.

"What's wrong?" Daniel asked.

"Ms. Hopkins used the n-word in front of the whole class during 7th period!" Nicky burst out.

Daniel sighed. Janie Hopkins was a White teacher who had only been teaching for two years. Though she was well-meaning, she had a lot to learn about the nuances of culturally responsive teaching. He hadn't had reports of her using that kind of language previously, though he'd heard similar complaints about other teachers.

"Go on," he told the boys.

"We were reading the textbook, and she was trying to explain what 'derogatory' means," Reggie began quietly.

"And then she used it as an example! Just said it, out loud, right in front of us!" Nicky interrupted. "And then she just kept talking, like it was no big deal! So I told her, 'You can't say that, Ms. Hopkins.' And she said she didn't do anything wrong—she was just giving an example! And then Reggie … you tell him, Reggie."

"So I raised my hand," Reggie explained, "and I told her that was a microaggression, and Nicky and I and the other Black kids in the class shouldn't have to hear that word."

"We just learned about microaggressions with Ms. Bruce," Nicky put in helpfully.

"So she made me stay after class because she said *I* was being disrespectful." Reggie's voice shook and he looked down at his hands. "But *she* was being disrespectful, Mr. Semere."

"So I stayed with him." Nicky took up the story. "And we stayed there for 20 minutes and she wouldn't admit she did anything wrong."

"I'm sorry, boys," Daniel told them.

"You've got nothing to be sorry about, Mr. Semere," Nicky said. "It's Ms. Hopkins who should be sorry, but she's not. She's the one who should be taking Ms. Bruce's class—why are me and Reggie stuck explaining racism to her?"

Daniel had no good answer. The boys already knew that they lived in an unjust world—they didn't need Daniel to tell them that. For now they needed a sounding board, and not for the first time, Daniel was grateful that he could help Black kids at HMS in this way. Grateful and tired.

"It's getting late. You should be going home," he told them. "I'll take it from here."

As the boys left, Daniel added a conversation with Ms. Hopkins to his mental to-do list for tomorrow. And again he came back to the Critical Consciousness course, which had clearly resonated with both Nicky and Reggie—further proof of its positive impact. Didn't that make the course worth fighting for? But then he thought again about listing Sally's position and placing another teacher in her shoes, facing the possibility of losing their license. And what about the risks he'd be taking on himself? If he lost his license, who would support kids like Reggie and Nicky? But how much could he realistically do with diminished district support? Would he be better off finding another district—or another state—where he could do this work unchallenged? What should his next step be?

Conversation

Sara O'Brien: Take a minute to think: what are the dilemmas in this case? And for whom are they dilemmas? Let's start with the most obvious dilemma, the thing that's probably on everyone's mind.

Chloé Valdary: There's been a course that's been taught, and it's positively affecting people from marginalized communities, and the state is basically trying to shut it down.

Sara O'Brien: What do you see as the dilemmas around the course?

Chloé Valdary: The attempt to retain good staff that's doing the work versus the fact that the staff is actually threatened with unemployment now, or with losing their license or other forms of scarcity. How does Daniel, the person managing all of this, manage all of this, given those barriers?

Rebecca Horwitz-Willis: Another dilemma is whether or not to offer the course at the school next year. And then from the perspective of a prospective teacher, there's the dilemma of whether or not to teach the course if it is offered.

Buddy North: To add to that, the principal Daniel has the dilemma of having the power to suggest whether a teacher should teach it or not. His power influences whether a teacher might accept the position or not.

Rebecca Horwitz-Willis: Buddy, that makes me think about the dilemma of "parents' rights"—or maybe "parents' power" is the better phrase—and how that's in tension with the pedagogy of the school. And the state's power to set parameters for education is mediating the power dynamics between the parents and school in an interesting, problematic way.

Daniel Spikes: I think a broader dilemma is this macro dilemma of the purpose of education: Is it liberatory? Is it functional? Is it just to create robots, people who perpetuate the status quo? Or is it really about liberation, developing critical thinking skills and critical consciousness so that people can become the best versions of themselves?

Sara O'Brien: I find these ideas about power really interesting. Chloé, you were going to jump in before. Did you want to say something?

Chloé Valdary: I really appreciate that point. Whether to change the curriculum or not is a dilemma.

Buddy North: Right, I'm thinking of the wording in the case that the administrators see this as such an issue that they want to change the curriculum to "put equity on hold."

Daniel Spikes: It's also the negotiation about which curriculum is privileged: the null, the implicit, the explicit? Something's always being taught. The question is: what are we intentional about teaching? What are we unintentionally teaching?

Sara O'Brien: Do you see dilemmas for other characters in the case?

Chloé Valdary: Teachers will have dilemmas about whether or not to stay in the program, if it's being defunded, and that affects their livelihood. I remember the interaction between Daniel and the Christian parent, Mrs. Peterson. And I couldn't help but notice that both of these people, in the conflict that they're in, perceive one another in the exact same way. They perceive that their way of seeing is under attack. Jay Z has this quote, where he says that people can experience the same reality but through different dimensions. And I think that if you're not able to see that that's happening, that in and of itself is a dilemma.

Rebecca Horwitz-Willis: Yes, it's a dilemma of perspective-taking or a dilemma of empathy. I think that's a really strong point, Chloé.

Daniel Spikes: I want to piggyback off of what Chloé said, too, about the dilemma for the teachers. I don't know if the word "choice" is the right word to use here, being able to determine whether or not they want to engage in this type of battle or conflict. I think it brings up the question, is Sally leaving because she might have more freedoms in a university setting? The superintendent has already been pushed out. I was working with a district similar to this one that was engaged in similar work. And you see people having to negotiate their livelihoods in terms of trying to figure out: do I want to stay in this space and engage in this work? Or do I want to go elsewhere? It's a constant negotiation that's taking place. Even as an assistant superintendent here in Texas, that's something that we have to negotiate daily: how do we engage in this work, and how much do we push? How little do we push? You're negotiating between "stay in power"—because I had a professor whose voice is always in my head, saying, "You got to be part of the system in order to disrupt the system." So, on any given day, I could just blow up, but I may not be here tomorrow. But then you have the people that are disruptors, or grassroots, who can say a lot more. That's the inherent dilemma that these existing employees are facing.

Buddy North: Similarly, there's a kind of congruent dilemma with the students in the case. Nicky and Reggie are facing a dilemma because of the power that's raining down on them. Their teacher says the N-word in front of them. Then Nicky is faced with the dilemma of how to help his friend Reggie, to stay behind in class and bring that case to the principal.

Rebecca Horwitz-Willis: I'm not sure that this is an ethical dilemma, but I think it's a clear problem that influences many of these dilemmas, and that's how to interpret the new law, which is vague. There are a lot of assumptions that go into how the law either will be or should be interpreted that are framing a lot of these dilemmas, even as the law's impact isn't yet clear.

Sara O'Brien: I appreciate how we are moving from micro dilemmas, like the dilemmas for Nicky and Reggie that Buddy brought up of how to support a friend in this moment where they see injustice and yet are relatively powerless, up to schoolwide dilemmas for Daniel. Does he renew this course? Does he not renew this course? This is the obvious dilemma. But also, how does he negotiate relationships with his staff while being aware of the power imbalance with him as the leader? How should he negotiate relationships with parents who have opposite worldviews and yet are part of his community? Then we have these huge macro dilemmas that Dr. Spikes is talking about: what is education for? Why are we educating the children in this building? And what kind of future are we educating them for?

Daniel Spikes: I love what Rebecca said about how people are interpreting the law. I don't have the right words to really capture what I'm thinking, but it brings me back to Shapiro and Stefkovitch, when they talk about how you should engage in decision-making using multiple ethical paradigms.[5] You use the ethic of care, ethic of critique, ethic of justice, and ethic of community. As I read the case, I assumed that most people were going to use an ethic of justice lens in interpreting the policy, which is lacking the ethic of critique and lacking ethic of care, which is "do what the law says to do" to some extent, as opposed to trying to really understand the intent of the law, critiquing the law even as you interpret that law and thus implement the law. There's a lot of literature that supports the idea that effective leaders can mediate ineffective policies. So even if a law on its surface is ineffective, effective leaders with a critical consciousness—going back to the whole idea behind this course—can still take what they need to do to circumvent the law. They can be politically savvy, in terms of how they go about doing their business.

Buddy North: Daniel, thank you for bringing that up. It made me think of a dilemma that I also want to flag quickly. And maybe it's not a dilemma, but it's an issue: the issue of diluting critical education, rather than just having one class. Should the principal hold the course open or cancel it and try to dilute that content and pedagogy throughout other courses? Would that have the same effect?

Chloé Valdary: I did intuit—I don't know if it would be called a dilemma. but perhaps it would be—a kind of dilemma of perception implicit in the notion that merely changing the curriculum would dilute it. There's an incredible dogmatism that is presupposed in that kind of automatic response. And the absence of awareness around that dogmatism itself presents a myriad of dilemmas for the stakeholders who are trying to navigate this.

Sara O'Brien: What are some of those dilemmas you see?

Chloé Valdary: I do think there is a kind of political savvy, as you said, Daniel, or even philosophical savvy that one could imagine building into a curriculum that could in fact meet the standards of the law and simultaneously get people to think critically. And it's worth questioning the notion that these two things are necessarily at odds with each other and the notion of whether we can be clever enough to figure out a workaround. I'm sorry for another pop culture reference, but I'm reminded of *Hamilton:* you have to be in the room where it happens, right? You could say, if I'm not in the room in this way, then it dilutes the room. That's nonsense on some level. There's this automatic assumption that the course must be this way, because if it's this way, then it's pure, and it's perfect. And if it's not this way, then somehow it's all the opposite things. That frame of perception in and of itself decreases your options, the tools that you can actually pick and choose to serve, ultimately, the purpose of education.

Daniel Spikes: Chloé just lit a fire under me—she made me think about *Weapons of the Weak*, a book by James Scott, where he talks about the everyday forms of peasant resistance. It contradicts the notion that people don't have agency and power, because actually they're acutely aware of what it is that they're doing. They're resisting in ways that we don't normally define as resistance, but it still leads toward liberation, whether that's individual liberation, or whether that's collective liberation. I think about it even in my everyday life. There's an automatic assumption that if we're finding ways to circumnavigate this problematic law, that it is making the curriculum weaker. But, in my everyday walk, there are things that I am negotiating that the outside person may see as a dilution. Going back to what I was saying earlier, we need disruptors sometimes, but we also need people who can stay and disrupt the system from within. It may not seem like they're disrupting, but at the end, their disruption may be even more major than the initial disruption. Sometimes when you'd be taught in history about enslavement, it was almost as though you fell into the notion that some folks were complicit in their own slavery, because they didn't seem to resist. But when I read Scott's work, I saw that slaves would do things like spit in their masters' water as a way to get back at them. That in and of itself gave them a little bit of agency every day. It's very presumptuous of us to assume from our privileged standpoint that a person who's already marginalized, like Daniel is in the case, is "diluting" the course by navigating this process. That navigation in and of itself can be just as powerful, if not more powerful than directly teaching the curriculum. Because that's assuming that directly teaching the curriculum is all powerful, right? So, I agree with Chloé that we're making some assumptions.

Rebecca Horwitz-Willis: Daniel, what you're talking about reminds me of Jarvis Givens's work *Fugitive Pedagogy*, and the work of Black teachers in the American South during Jim Crow schooling, and how so many of them were able to create these incredibly powerful places of learning that were subversive. But with desegregation, the ability to teach that type of authentic, empowering history was diluted by biases—by the standards, though they weren't called that back then. I was also thinking that the text of the policy here feels very different from what we see from students in the case. The text says that you can't teach that the United States is fundamentally or systemically racist, but the examples we have are individual examples. You have the one student who's feeling safer as a queer student at the school. You have the example of the gay rights movement being a march toward progress. And then you have the example of Nicky and Reggie having language for microaggressions. What's actually happening on the ground is not exactly aligned with the law—clearly these lawmakers don't want these things to happen either, for all their political reasons—but it just struck me as interesting. And the language of teaching students to feel discomfort strikes me as an *intent* to feel discomfort, as opposed to an *impact* of feeling discomfort.

Sara O'Brien: I think we're moving now to this question of why these are dilemmas. The fear and uncertainty that the vagueness of the law causes is definitely an important consideration. And a value I had never thought about before, Chloé, is the purity of the curriculum. What values did you all see in the case?

Chloé Valdary: I can't help but notice the irony that there is a deep Christian strand throughout the whole thing, regardless of what side you're on, related to purity. If you trace that strand back to the Puritans, coming over to the new world, that paradigm is underpinning us whether we're conscious of it or not, whether we self-identify as the traditional conservative Christian or the social justice believer, all of this is underpinned by deep recesses of that Puritan purity. And again, for me the strongest dilemma is the failure to perceive that underpinning. This is the paradigm that underpins the conversation. And so often we can see "the other" operating out of it, but we can't see that we're operating according to the same paradigm.

Sara O'Brien: Buddy, you look like you might have some thoughts.

Buddy North: Chloé was making me think that another value that could be named is hypocrisy, but instead *non*-hypocrisy. No one wants to be a hypocrite. And in the case, Mrs. Peterson calls out the school for being hypocrites, because they're not allowing the Christian voice within the classroom. No one sees hypocrisy in themselves, they see it elsewhere. But no one wants to say that they're a hypocrite.

Sara O'Brien: Maybe integrity could be a term for non-hypocrisy? Even Ms. Hopkins, who has used the N-word in front of students and been told that it harmed them, sees herself as acting with integrity. Are there other values at play in the case?

Buddy North: Reading the case, Daniel the principal says to Mrs. Peterson, I'm not going to talk about your views in this classroom. That made me think, why not bring that view into the classroom? Not as a dogmatic tool, obviously, but to critically discuss it.

Sara O'Brien: I wonder, what are the values behind Daniel's refusal to bring that view in?

Daniel Spikes: There are values that are already present, that are not named, which is a problem in and of itself. It goes back to this whole notion of critical consciousness that's permeating everything, or maybe it's a *dis*-consciousness. There are a lot of implicit values, hidden values—and some just plain as day. Sometimes people choose not to talk about them, but there are values that are embedded throughout all of our systems.

Sara O'Brien: What are some of the implicit values that you think maybe not everyone in the case is aware of?

Daniel Spikes: I want to reintroduce this whole notion of what it means to be an American, to hold American ideals. There's a value I think that's controversial, I'm just going to say it: "Make America Great Again." What does that mean? Great for whom? What does greatness look like? And what are American values? What does it mean to be an "all-American"? What are those terms that we just throw out without really interrogating? What values have we attached to those terms? And what identities have we attached to those values?

When people talk about anti-American ideals, the American ideals they're referring to are White, middle class, heteronormative ideas. Anything that is contrary to those traditions, values and ways of thinking is deemed abnormal or anti-American, or not appropriate. So some say to just teach the set curriculum. But the set curriculum is value-laden as well. And not recognizing that it's value-laden is problematic.

Chloé Valdary: I can also try to take a stab at what I think the principal Daniel's value system is. In his response to Mrs. Peterson, I suspect that he is trying to protect the students, and he doesn't want to bring anything in that could threaten their feeling of psychological safety, the feeling of being seen, and the feeling of belonging that these students are experiencing. I could imagine that he's fearful of even bringing in that other perspective, not as a dogma, as you said, Buddy, but as instruction. Because he's fearful that bringing it in will actually cause psychological harm to the students that he's trying to protect.

And I will say, personally, my anthropology teacher in college changed my life because she did the opposite. I grew up in a conservative Christian home, and I was walking around with these dogmas. And my liberal anthropology professor forced us to watch *Jesus Camp*, the documentary about a conservative Christian community that by all measures is dogmatic and bigoted ideologically. And I will never forget the next day I walked into the classroom with all these assumptions about my teacher because she's a liberal professor. And that's not how I was raised. So I put her in a box, already judging her as "other." My teacher got into a shouting match with a liberal atheist student who said that the community in the film should be ashamed of themselves. And my professor said, "If you're not even curious about the ways in which longing for belonging, longing for a sense of community, longing for a sense of security literally distorts our capacity to perceive, and how these psychosomatic anthropological pieces of what it means to be human actually play a role in shaping this community, then you're missing the point of the class entirely." It's like, what!

Now I'm going to get a little more personal. When I hear "critical consciousness," that experience is the standard for me. So the dilemma here is: how can you hold space to ensure that there's psychological safety for the people that you're trying to protect, while also teaching them that it is precisely the absence of psychological safety, the absence of that feeling of home, the absence of that existential feeling of belonging, that's animating all of this stuff over here in the "other" camp, that we're saying no to? That's a tricky finessing that has to take place, and that's a lot for the educator to bear on their shoulders. But when that happens, that's magic.

Daniel Spikes: I also wonder: when we talk about Daniel and his values, I think the people who are saying his values are anti-American ideals want us to say those are the values of Black separatists or Black nationalists. But maybe Daniel has core American values. Or maybe, as Gloria Ladson-Billings might say, maybe that's just good teaching. Maybe Daniel's values are just wanting to be a good educator. Sometimes, we may outsmart ourselves, getting into these conversations about race and class and gender. Those are important because they're embedded within all of these issues, but I think it's just as important to give power back to education.

Rebecca Horwitz-Willis: Chloé, your words resonated with me. I'm looking at this quote, where Mrs. Peterson says, "Carly came home to tell me Christians like us have been persecuting homosexuals for centuries." And thinking about teaching history, there's a way to hold the conservative Christian interpretations up for critique, without demonizing the religion, or the people that adhere to the religion. Or you could hold up the actions that have been executed in the name of that religion as potentially antithetical to Christian beliefs. But here, both sides are walling off their views against any sort of critique, and doing that, you can't get to the deeper issues and the deeper values where there's maybe some commonality.

Daniel Spikes: There's this argument that the course is un-Christian, but there are some very ardent social justice advocates who fashion themselves as Christians and say what others like Mrs. Peterson are engaging in is not Christian. It's worth interrogating the various identities in the cultures that are being talked about here, and our own assumptions about the values that people hold. Because we see the world as we are and not necessarily as it is. That's an Anaïs Nin quote for you. Boom.

Chloé Valdary: That's a great quote. "We see things not as they are but as we are."

Daniel Spikes: (Laughing) I was close!

Rebecca Horwitz-Willis: I think there's potentially some real power in asking why Christianity as an institution has been opposed to homosexuality for so long. Who's benefiting? How is that shifting power to men in a very particular way? I don't know if it's right for this class, but most people in this country identify as Christian and I think it's worth turning that lens inward instead of writing it off. And I'm Jewish, so I might be getting all of this wrong. But I do think that there's analysis that can be empowering and actually turn people toward their faith in critical but loving ways if they have the tools to engage.

Sara O'Brien: I am going to move us into thinking—what should be done in this case?

Chloé Valdary: The last paragraph of this case makes me feel like Daniel feels overwhelmed. When you're feeling overwhelmed, I think that the first thing you should do is pause and breathe.

Sara O'Brien: So you would have him delay making any choice like this? Why?

Chloé Valdary: Because right now, his limbic system is firing on all cylinders. It's trying to decide between fight, flight, and freeze. If he doesn't bring his prefrontal cortex into conversation with the limbic system, to pause, then he's going to make a decision that's highly informed by scarcity.

Sara O'Brien: What would you hope that he would do after taking that time to pause?

Chloé Valdary: I would hope that he would have the courage to ask himself: What am I missing? What am I not perceiving? And what can I learn from every single person I've interacted with here? Whether it's the students Nicky and Reggie, whether it's the conservative parent Mrs. Peterson, whether it's Ms. Hopkins, who he hasn't spoken to, but who caused psychological harm to these young kids. Because, connecting back to the ethic of care, the word "curiosity" comes from the root word *cura*, which means to care. So he could take time to pause, and then use that space to get curious about all of these community members in his orbit and ask himself: How can these individuals educate me? I think as educators, sometimes we—myself included—easily fall into this superiority complex, saying I know what's best. But it's actually relational all the way up and all the way down. So he could get curious, and see what comes to him in the silence.

Rebecca Horwitz-Willis: I want there to be a way to bring the families in community and have a real discussion about the class and the goals, in a way that doesn't first center on the class, but instead first centers on values and community, and then connects up to building transparency around what the class is really trying to do. It just seems like there's such a need for dialogue, for building community, and for building a shared language around the class that isn't just steeped in political rhetoric.

Daniel Spikes: This is a time where you search out allies, and I think you search out White allies. That's especially true for Daniel, who's in a vulnerable position. I think there's an opportunity to bring Sally back into the conversation to help determine how we move forward in a way that will benefit our students. I also think you have to consider this standpoint as well: with any type of initiative, you have to get buy-in from the relevant stakeholders. With any type of vision you're pushing forward, some people will be against it. But there are still ways to get them to buy into that process, as the leadership literature shows. What are the things that everyone can agree on first? How do you build from there? Do all kids need to learn? Yes. All right. Do we have problems in our society? Yes. Right. What are those problems? Why do we have those problems? What are some institutions that can be responsible for addressing those problems? Education is one of the preeminent spaces to address societal issues. We always talk about families as an institution, but we also have to recognize that schools and churches have just as important a role. So what's the best way we can move forward? Because we as educators have responsibility just like you do as a family unit, just like churches, we have a responsibility to meet the needs of our kids. How do you suggest we do it? Hopefully parents will say, "I see what you're saying."

Chloé Valdary: Derrick Bell—the grandfather of critical race theory—complained about *Brown v. Board of Education* because it caused this uprootedness. I went to Langston Hughes Elementary School in New Orleans, which was definitely founded by people during Jim Crow, though I wasn't attending during Jim Crow. But I'm pretty sure the education I received was forged in the fires of Jim Crow. I had to memorize Maya Angelou as a six-year-old girl, "Still I Rise." The education was Black empowerment, but it was simultaneously "America is the land of the free." And the evidence that America is the land of the free is this deeply sorrowful, but also incredibly resilient struggle that has been manifested within my—our—people's struggle and triumph. "Lift Every Voice and Sing"[6] was our anthem, but it wasn't perceived as antithetical to America. It was what made America great. But there's an irony that Derrick Bell pointed out that *Brown v. Board of Education* actually led to *dis*integration because under segregation, what you had was a community in which the family was involved in building the curriculum, the educator separate from the family was involved in building the curriculum, and a lot of community life revolved around the school building. So all of these stakeholders were actually involved, in an embodied fashion. And that's how you got the curriculum, the beautiful curriculum that I was raised with. But now we have societal dislocation and the disruption of something that's supposed to cause integration, irony of ironies. So in this case, everyone's weirdly disembodied. There's no integration of the educators and the parents and the superintendent and the district. So there's an opportunity here for all involved, but especially for Daniel, to think about what integration means as a value and how it might inform the way he thinks about critical consciousness. Derrick Bell talked about this, but that piece is not quite present in the way Daniel's approaching the course so far, in my opinion.

Buddy North: I like this idea of getting curious and caring about everyone: not being furious but being curious, I guess. But it's so hard to not be furious at the fury that's brought to you. Sometimes there's virtue in being furious. I think it goes back to the value of integrity—and hypocrisy. I'm wondering if Mrs. Peterson has lost her integrity. So what does it look like for Daniel to respond with integrity? I would probably be inclined to say that to keep integrity for Daniel would be to stay curious, but it's just so hard to not be mad at things.

Chloé Valdary: Buddy, this question around anger is a really good question. I think I should try to clarify. When Dr. King wrote his "Letter from a Birmingham Jail," other clergymen were asking, Why are you non-violently protesting? You're stirring up trouble. And his response was interesting. He said, the people are angry, and they're going to be angry. The question is, how do we channel the anger? So the question here is not, should Daniel suppress his anger? He totally should not suppress his anger. And so I'm happy that you brought this up, because I will add that he should not only get curious about what the other people have to teach him, he should also get curious about what his own emotions have to teach him. He should direct that curiosity both inward and outward. That can sound like a very unsatisfying answer because it's not in this immediate moment action-oriented, but it is a different kind of action. That rising of anger is intelligent; it's teaching him something very important. But he should be very intentional about how and where to channel it. Because that's exactly what Dr. King was trying to do with the righteous anger that people were feeling during Jim Crow. How do I channel it so that it manifests in such a way to produce the outcomes that we want, which is ultimately a more flourishing society for everyone who lives here?

Buddy North: It's just so very hard to know how to move forward with grace, with an ethic of care, knowing you can't know everything, to make the world better. But I guess one thing that I'll continue to think about is just the value of integrity that's involved in how we compose ourselves. How do we give to others the same grace that we want to give ourselves?

Rebecca Horwitz-Willis is the 2024–2026 Drinan Visiting Assistant Professor at Boston College Law School, USA. She studies the history of race, inequality, and education with a particular focus on how the law and political economy have shaped educational opportunities and experiences by race. Prior to graduate school she worked as a high school educator and a lawyer.

Buddy Boren North is Gwich'in, lives in Seward, Alaska, and is an Assistant Professor of Education at Alaska Pacific University.

Daniel D. Spikes is a P-12 administrator in Lufkin, Texas, and a current adjunct faculty member at Baylor University. He has previously worked as a faculty member at the University of South Carolina and Iowa State University. He focuses on developing critically conscious, equity-focused scholar practitioners.

Chloé Valdary is a former Bartley Fellow at The Wall Street Journal, where she developed the Theory of Enchantment (ToE), an innovative framework for compassionate anti-racism that combines social-emotional learning (SEL), character development, and interpersonal growth as tools for leadership development in the boardroom and beyond.

Character Guide

Setting	
Heath Middle School, U.S.A. (grades 6–8, ages 11–14)	
Primary Characters	
Daniel Semere: principal of Heath Middle School **Sally Bruce:** 6th grade critical consciousness teacher **Gabby Lewis:** literacy teacher **Brian Hall:** social studies teacher **Mrs. Peterson:** parent of 6th grader Carly	**Nicky:** 6th grade student **Reggie:** 6th grade student **Janie Hopkins:** 6th grade social studies teacher

Discussion Questions

1. One of the goals of public education is creating the next generation of citizens. What visions of American identity are present in this case? How do these visions connect to and compete with one another?
2. Daniel has returned to Heath to do "equity work." What does "equity" seem to mean to Daniel in this case? What does it mean to Heath Parents for Education, Gabby, Mrs. Peterson, or the legislators who passed the new state law? How do people's different visions of equity shape the dilemmas in the case?
3. All of the characters in the case are explicitly raced except for Mrs. Peterson. As you read, did you assign her a race (either consciously or unconsciously)? How might the dilemmas change for you if Mrs. Peterson were assigned a race?
4. Mrs. Peterson argues that the critical consciousness course is teaching her daughter values that should be taught at home. How should teachers, school leaders, and districts respond when their own values clash with those of parents in the community?
5. How does the atmosphere of uncertainty created by the new law impact the dilemmas in the case?
6. Daniel characterizes Ms. Hopkins as a beginning teacher who means well, despite her hurtful behavior. As a leader, what are his responsibilities to her professional (and/or personal) development? What are his responsibilities to the boys who have been hurt by her behavior?
7. Public schools in the United States have long struggled to recruit and retain Black teachers and school leaders. How does Daniel's race shape and complicate the dilemmas that he faces?
8. States across the United States are passing similar laws banning lessons that portray the country as fundamentally racist or sexist. Other countries also struggle to teach hard history. Which historical events or concepts cause controversy in your context? How does this case help you think about teaching hard history in schools?

Notes

1. Larry Buchanan, Quoctrung Bui, and Jugal K. Patel, "Black Lives Matter May Be the Largest Movement in U.S. History," *The New York Times*, July 3, 2020, sec. U.S., https://www.nytimes.com/interactive/2020/07/03/us/george-floyd-protests-crowd-size.html.
2. Sarah Schwartz, "Map: Where Critical Race Theory Is under Attack," *Education Week*, June 11, 2021, sec. Policy & Politics, States, https://www.edweek.org/policy-politics/map-where-critical-race-theory-is-under-attack/2021/06.
3. Theodore R. Johnson, Emelia Gold, and Ashley Zhao, "How Anti-Critical Race Theory Bills Are Taking Aim at Teachers," *FiveThirtyEight* (blog), May 9, 2022, https://fivethirtyeight.com/features/how-anti-critical-race-theory-bills-are-taking-aim-at-teachers/.
4. Olivia B. Waxman, "Anti-'Critical Race Theory' Laws Are Working. Teachers Are Thinking Twice about How They Talk about Race," Time, June 30, 2022, https://time.com/6192708/critical-race-theory-teachers-racism/.
5. Joan Poliner Shapiro and Jacqueline A. Stefkovich, *Ethical Leadership and Decision Making in Education: Applying Theoretical Perspectives to Complex Dilemmas*, 5th ed. (New York: Routledge, 2021), https://doi.org/10.4324/9781003022862.
6. "Lift Every Voice and Sing" is often referred to as "the Black national anthem."

8

No Laughing Matter: Can Showing Religiously Sensitive Cartoons in the Classroom Ever Be Justified?

Janet Orchard, Waqar Ahmedi, and Sara O'Brien

England's Counter-Terrorism and Security Act of 2015 (commonly known as the Prevent Act) was a political response to wider concerns about the rising influence of extremist radicalism, religious and political, on the potentially vulnerable. The duty of English schools under this Act is to "have due regard to the need to prevent people from being drawn into terrorism" in all its forms.[1] In summary, the duty to Prevent assumes the following:

- *Protect school families from radicalization and extremism*
- *Identify relevant individual vulnerabilities and changes in behavior*
- *Have a sound understanding of what steps to take if you have concerns about extremism*
- *Teach how to build resistance to extremist ideas and terrorist ideology*

The duty is controversial. Young people's wellbeing is of paramount concern, but critics worry that Prevent reinforces popular stereotypes of Islam and Muslims. This adds to the pedagogic challenges that teachers and schools must navigate when crafting their response to the duty in their particular context. This particular case is set within a Multi-Academy Trust (MAT), a state-funded but independently governed school network led by a CEO. MATs are part of a push away from local education authorities in order to create a more efficient regulatory system, though this claim is contested.

--

"Thank you so much for driving all the way over!"

Imperial Multi-Academy Trust CEO Saima Ahmed welcomed Rebecca Mitchell, Head Teacher of Tate Academy, warmly as she stepped from her car. Although Tate was one of the Trust's longstanding members, it was an outlier, both geographically distant from the other five schools and demographically unusual. Most of its student body identified as "White British," without the racial and ethnic diversity of the wider area.

"The traffic is terrible at this time of day," Saima continued, "but it seems important to meet in person for this discussion, rather than by Zoom."

"I agree," Rebecca nodded, following Saima to the Executive Conference Suite. "Thank you for bringing everyone together at short notice."

"How are things?" Saima queried.

"Not good," Rebecca admitted. "We found more graffiti around the Year 9 boys' lockers this morning. Mrs. Abdi called yesterday to report her daughter being upset by racist, anti-Muslim taunting in the cafeteria. We've increased teacher numbers on lunch duty, but we're still not picking up everything."

Saima winced. "So, you still want to use Jack's expanded *Charlie Hebdo* lesson?"

"'Want' is probably not the right word, but I don't see we have a choice," Rebecca sighed. They joined their colleagues in the conference room. "The graffiti was clearly based on those cartoons. The kids have clearly seen them. We must tackle this directly—we can't carry on skating around it."

"More graffiti?" Maggie Brown groaned, hugging both colleagues. Maggie was Head Teacher at Lyle Academy, one of the most diverse schools in the Trust. Before becoming head, Maggie had taught Religious Education (RE) at Tate for many years, alongside Rebecca, and then worked as an Assistant Head at Lyle under Saima, prior to Saima's becoming CEO. All three remained close, valuing each other's professionalism.

"Unfortunately, yes," Rebecca confirmed. "I don't know what's going on with this Year 9. One class particularly doesn't accept our school's values. I'm worried if it goes on much longer, we'll be challenged for failing to comply with the duty to Prevent—White nationalist radicalism, not the jihadist nonsense our MP is always spouting on about."

Saima grimaced, reflecting on the Trust's latest, unexpected challenge. As part of their response to the "Prevent" duty to protect students from radicalization and violent extremism, all six schools had adopted a specialist curriculum. This supported students at each key developmental stage to understand and discuss sensitive topics, including extremist ideas associated with terrorist ideology, and to learn how to challenge them. Developed by former specialist history teacher and educational consultant Jack Dawson, now with his own consultancy firm, Dawson Corps, the curriculum had successfully helped students think through the complex causes of extremism and terrorism and the different political ideologies that fuel them.

While the precise causes of the unrest at Tate were unclear, something strange had happened there over the past year, suggesting an undercurrent of Islamophobia. Students, parents, and teachers had raised concerns about rising tensions; steps had been taken to "nip the problem in the bud." Unfortunately, further trouble had recently broken out: explicitly anti-Muslim graffiti had appeared in several prominent places, seemingly inspired by cartoons of the Prophet Muhammad published in the French satirical magazine, *Charlie Hebdo*. These became famous after extremists, claiming they were "avenging the Prophet" for the racist and demeaning depictions of Muhammad, killed eleven people in the *Charlie Hebdo* office in 2015. The magazine reprinted the cartoons on the fifth anniversary of the shooting in 2020, just as accused confederates of the gunmen were going on trial. One lesson in Dawson's curriculum referenced these images, asking students to map the complex causation of violent extremism. The lesson didn't include the cartoons directly, but it seemed the graffiti artists, whoever they were, had found them online for themselves.

Rebecca had responded with a request that she knew would be controversial. She wanted to pilot a new resource from Dawson Corps which *did* use the cartoons to help students analyze the imagery to question the anti-Islamic stereotypes presented. As a Muslim, Saima had initially recoiled at the suggestion; she found them personally and professionally offensive and questioned their use, given the Trust's sizable Muslim population. However, the circumstances at Tate were unusual.

Not wishing to further escalate an already volatile situation, Saima called the meeting to discuss Rebecca's proposal. With Saima, Rebecca, and Maggie, the group included Jack Dawson himself and Farid Iqbal, a local imam and governor of Whitworth School, also in the Trust. Having spent too many years being the only Muslim present during such discussions, Saima didn't intend to repeat the experience. She was grateful to Farid for rearranging his schedule to attend at short notice.

"Failing to comply with Prevent and triggering further scrutiny is definitely not what we want," Saima agreed, "but I'm not expecting it to happen here. I'm grateful to Rebecca for initiating this meeting. Our governance agreement requires us to review decisions by individual schools together where there is potential reputational risk to the whole Trust."

"Thank you all for making the time," Rebecca began carefully. "I think it's important to stress the proportionate nature of our proposal. One additional lesson, in our school only, taught to one year group, which we'll plan carefully and simply pilot."

"We're also trying to find out who the perpetrators are, to deal with them directly," Rebecca continued. "In the meantime, we know other students have seen the graffiti and heard the comments. We need to prioritise going through with them why these images are such inaccurate representations and therefore harmful, while recognising people's rights to freedom of expression. By talking about them explicitly in class, we can better establish who may be particularly vulnerable to far-right influence."

"It's certainly worrying, and I do understand your difficulty," Farid responded. "However, one can never justify using these cartoons in the classroom. Many Muslims believe that even respectful depictions of the Prophet are wrong—at best they are inaccurate; at worst they idolise him, 'shirk,' and that is a serious sin. Anyway, these images are hardly respectful."

"I appreciate your concerns," Jack spoke up, "but the lesson Rebecca is proposing to use is specifically designed to address underlying causes of Islamophobia and anti-Islamic radicalization with young people who have encountered the cartoons in some form already. We've trialled it in similar settings. Teachers have reported students better understanding the need to balance being respectful with freely sharing their opinions. That seems important to try in this situation."

"Jack, you know I am hugely impressed by your work," Saima said. "But why would you promote using these cartoons with anybody, anywhere, knowing just how offensive Muslims find them? How could that hurtful portrayal ever be educationally justified?"

"We would definitely not advise using the lesson at schools with significant Muslim representation, like Lyle or Whitworth," Jack reassured her, "given the offence they might cause to staff or others. However, given the severity of the circumstances at Tate, the risk seems justified. It's using the cartoons to promote 'religious literacy', if you like, engaging with what's wrong about the way they depict Islam, what is factually incorrect about the copycat graffiti. Remember, there is political support for using images of the Prophet, where they are carefully structured to teach about blasphemy, free speech, political Islam and so forth."

"But people will be offended," Saima reminded him, "including the Muslim minority students at Tate and their families. What about them?"

"We will be as transparent with those students and families as possible and devote significant time over the next few weeks to speaking with them. We'll certainly hold a community meeting to explain the lesson," Rebecca reassured the group, "and we'll obviously allow Muslim Year 9 students to opt out entirely if they want to."

"Just to clarify—the outright prohibition of cartoons only applies specifically to Muslims who find them disagreeable. It can't be applied to people outside Islam, right?" Jack asked.

"True," Maggie confirmed, "further complicated by the fact that certain images of the Prophet have been used historically by Muslims themselves in Islamic culture, for example in Persia. But there is nothing 'pietistic' or respectful about the images *Charlie Hebdo* chose to publish. On the contrary, they are deliberately provocative, which is why we don't go anywhere near them in my school. Haven't these issues come up before in the council's interfaith network?"

"They have," Farid nodded. "The Sikh representative—do you all know Manpreet?—mentioned a textbook in the States that had printed a hurtful image of Guru Nanak, I believe. Local Sikhs said it was offensive and the state education board took action so children didn't see the image."

"It is helpful to be reminded this isn't just an issue for Muslims," Rebecca observed. "But that may not be how others see it, especially those who aren't religiously literate or sensitive. We can't just let Islamophobia, or the possible risk that our students are being radicalized by members of the far right, pass us by. Our students have clearly seen the cartoons. We can't directly intervene if we're standing on ceremony about how respectful or not it is to show them!"

"I appreciate your concerns, Rebecca, and take your assessment of your pupils' needs seriously," Saima said, gently. "Personally, these cartoons cross a line for me in terms of what it is acceptable to share in a public place. I appreciate that as a Muslim I am in a minority, choosing to live in a Western context, and also that Muslims have very diverse attitudes. However, I am wary of the likely reaction, from Muslim pupils, families, and staff members, if they find out we have condoned using these cartoons in any Trust school.

Remember, Muslim children are brought up to love the Prophet even more than their own family."

"Yes," said Maggie. "I remember a discussion with a Year 9 class at Lyle about their most inspirational person. Quite a few of the Muslim students said the Prophet Muhammad."

"Precisely," responded Farid firmly. "Agreed they are a tiny minority at Tate, but Muslims deeply respect and love all Prophets, including Moses and Jesus. Mockery of them is blasphemous, with insults to the Prophet Muhammad treated most seriously. These cartoons depict him as a bomber, prepared to indiscriminately take life—the very opposite of the message of peace he preached. The Trust condoning showing those scurrilous images in one school would be insensitive, Rebecca, and all the community meetings in the world won't change that reality."

"Plus the press will get wind of it," Maggie interrupted.

"Exactly!" Farid declared. "Imagine the media frenzy!"

"I'm afraid we may be facing a media frenzy already," Rebecca interjected. "That graffiti around the lockers, who knows how many students took pictures with their phones? At a minimum, all our Year 9 students need the chance to talk them through, informed by well trained, experienced specialist teachers. Just now, they're coming across them unsupervised with their friends. Can't we do this carefully, proportionately, while supporting the relatively few people who might be offended?"

"Look," said Farid, "Not everyone feels as strongly about this as I do, but quite a few members of my community would be extremely upset if they got wind of the cartoons being used in lessons locally. I would say there is a real risk of protestors turning up outside the school …"

"I understand your concern, Farid," Saima acknowledged. "But let me play devil's advocate. Experts in the school and in critical thinking believe that with the cartoons already accessible and known to kids, the way forward in extreme situations like this is to discuss them in a safe and supported space, sensitively, to build resilience."

Maggie shook her head. "Critical thinking can be developed without showing or repeating the very things that cause offence. Would we, seriously, use the n-word, or show porn, to make a point and to 'build resilience'? My Head of Media Studies was teaching race representation to her GCSE group. She thought about using the *Charlie Hebdo* cover which satirised the George Floyd murder. The class was really divided about whether Katie should show the cartoon at all. A couple of the Black students said they were keen to see it—but she decided against it."

"So, who gets to decide what's offensive—the Black students or the White teacher?" Saima asked.

"And we've already tried talking about the cartoons without showing them," Rebecca reminded everyone.

There was a pause.

"There is no explicit advice from anyone in this area," Jack conceded. "The DfE, the LA, any of the professional associations, have the same guidance everyone can access, like the 'Educate Against Hate' stuff. My materials grew from something that happened a few years ago when I was teaching History. Members of my department wanted to show Nazi cartoons in their lessons on the Holocaust which ridicule Jews, also very offensive. They consulted Jewish parents, and a local rabbi. Turned out most did think using the cartoons was of educational value, even the rabbi, because they communicated how the motivation behind them was to demonise and discriminate. Isn't that where the *Charlie Hebdo* cartoons are coming from?"

"But Farid doesn't feel like that. And I'm not sure showing cartoons of the Prophet can be justified in a similar way," Maggie objected.

Jack reflected. "I am concerned that both antisemitism and Islamophobia are at an all-time high; yet neither kind of prejudice gets the attention they deserve. We don't want to play into the hands of people who will exploit local Muslim families' reactions if these images upset them. But we should be calling out the Islamophobia connected to these cartoons. It's part of our duty of care in schools."

"I will agree there, Jack," Farid conceded. "These things we keep saying about British values—respect and tolerance. They need to be modelled in the classroom."

"As well as promoting political freedom and our responsibility to uphold democratic principles," Rebecca chimed in. "How can we say that we're committed to those values when we don't apply principles of freedom of speech ourselves? The images are not illegal; they are out there. The most responsible course of action is to directly address them in the classroom."

"We train all teachers before this lesson," Jack added. "Anyone using the cartoons needs to appreciate the sensitivity of the topic and know about Islam. They mustn't promote stereotypes themselves. We don't expect non-specialist or cover teachers to pick up and run with this lesson."

"Whatever is decided, we must maintain our reputation for covering contentious issues well, and keep the community's trust and support," Maggie declared.

This was one thing, at least, that everyone could wholeheartedly endorse.

Glancing at the clock, Saima saw they had only a few minutes left. She had hoped they might reach a clear decision on using the cartoons by now. Should the Trust allow Tate school to use them, or not?

Conversation

Sara O'Brien: What are the dilemmas in this case? For whom are they dilemmas? What did you think was the biggest dilemma in the case?

Shammi Rahman: From a teaching point of view: if you are planning lessons in citizenship, and you want to encourage these conversations, how far do you take your lesson on freedom of speech, especially if your teaching team is not as confident and as comfortable as you are? I think the dilemma would be for the person who's planning the lesson, who's instructing other colleagues to lead on these lessons.

David Kerr: For me, the biggest dilemma here is: what do you do about the anti-Muslim feeling in Tate Academy as predicated by the year nine boys' graffiti around the lockers and the taunting in the cafeteria? This clearly needs to be dealt with, but it becomes a dilemma as to how you do that and who's involved in it. It ripples out all the way from Tate. This is a Multi-Academy Trust (MAT), but Tate doesn't fit in with the other four schools in the area, in terms of its population, which is described as White British. That anti-Muslim feeling doesn't just come from the pupils. It must also come from their peers, their parents or guardians, the community. The case refers to the local MP talking about jihadist nonsense and not White nationalism, and lack of guidance from DfE [Department for Education] and the professional association. So the MAT, and Tate in particular, is left struggling about what to do.

Sally Elton-Chalcraft: In addition, there's a dilemma of how to treat and respect your colleagues. Maggie, Rebecca, and Saima have worked together, and they understand each other's problems and where each other are coming from. Then there's the extent to which you trust Jack Dawson with his consulting company, and also Farid, the local Imam and Governor. I was reminded of Judy Pace, who's done some work on what it means to be a teacher who is either a container, containing discussions, or a risk-taker. You can put Jack into that latter category. So it's a dilemma about how the people on the ground listen to and work with each other so as to not step on somebody else's toes.

Shammi Rahman: I'm also now thinking, bad behavior is bad behavior. If you are running a school, and you are tiptoeing around this provocative behavior, is this a dilemma? Or is this a management issue? Going back to what David was saying—I agree with you, it's an issue of language. Having worked in education, I've heard comments from educated colleagues about being "White British." And I've had to remind colleagues that not all British people are White. What do we even mean by that concept? Are we not looking at these Muslim children as British? Are we looking at them as outsiders? Even the way we talk and the language we use around the issue may be a problem.

David Kerr: I think that the dilemma occurs because of the wider connotations and challenges. The challenge of being a MAT, no longer on local authority controls. You haven't got specialist advisors, plus these schools look like they might have been kind of chucked together—Tate is a kind of outlier that joins that MAT. Then in the real world, we've recently had the Shawcross review of Prevent, which basically said Prevent is spending too much time on far-right White extremism and should really be tackling jihadist Muslim extremism.[2] That sets the wider context in the press and elsewhere. So this behavior issue is influenced by that context. Then within the case you've got Jack Dawson, who's a bit of a chancer. Whether this goes badly or goes well, he's going to get loads of extra publicity for his program, so he may have ulterior motives there. It worried me that he said that this new resource had been trialed in similar settings— that's like pouring fuel on the flames. Remember the poor teacher in France who got beheaded outside the gates of his school for showing the *Charlie Hebdo* cartoons?[3] That wider context explains why they're tiptoeing around the issue.

Janet Orchard: For some people, this isn't a dilemma. There are right answers. I think there are a lot of people who would say you should never show those *Charlie Hebdo* cartoons or anything like it—that they are offensive and should have no place in a classroom. Perhaps on a more charitable reading, Jack Dawson is representative of people who are pro-freedom of speech and very uncomfortable with the idea that anybody should be censored. So you've got strongly held views in direct opposition to each other. Then, as others have so eloquently said, there's a real lack of support, a sort of power vacuum and insufficient guidelines for people to operate within.

David Kerr: You also have the Muslim minority pupils at Tate who need to be considered, because schools are supposed to be safe places for all pupils.

Sally Elton-Chalcraft: The safeguarding point is interesting. It's thought of as a hallowed thing, safeguarding, but actually, in terms of Prevent, it puts some of the Muslim community at risk. The Prevent policy in the UK was designed to prevent terrorism, but what has actually happened is that there has been a "chilling" of conversations about controversial topics. Also, Muslims are seen as "at risk" of being radicalized or "risky" to society—many folk have written about this. And in that respect Prevent has been counterproductive.

David Kerr: Prevent guidance has a major safeguarding dimension, which is the one that everyone jumps on. But if you read the actual literature, the Department for Education (DfE) in England additionally introduces a duty to prepare pupils for life in modern Britain by developing their understanding of "fundamental British values," including democracy, the rule of law, individual liberty, and respect for and tolerance of different faiths and beliefs. So Prevent has a teaching and learning focus—the idea being that young people should be exposed to controversial issues and build up the resilience to deal with them. Yet schools often drop out from that responsibility because it's just too challenging. Thus Tate brings in this expert Jack Dawson to write their materials and perhaps train all teachers. A lot of teachers would shy away from it, or leave it where they could to the Religious Education (RE) or citizenship experts. There hasn't been substantial training in this area. For example, at the University of Reading I get about an hour a year with all our new teacher trainees to explain it to them.

Janet Orchard: Maybe people not wanting to do this are being very responsible because they've had an hour on their PGCE [Post Graduate Certificate in Education] from somebody like you, David, and they know they're not experts in this. It might take more than a consultant and some bespoke materials to actually do the kind of teaching and learning job you're talking about.

David Kerr: There's also the possible press reaction. So many schools in the UK and elsewhere, when they put their head above the parapet, suddenly the whole of the national press comes down on the school. So there's a real fear about schools being put on the firing line, instead of getting support, and there's a real lack of safety in the community.

Shammi Rahman: I would say responsibility for the dilemma must lie with the school leaders to educate themselves. Because they have to educate themselves about every aspect of leading school. Are we as a society, first of all, doing enough to prepare our leaders? And are our leaders putting themselves in a position where they're open to being educated, particularly if they're leading a school where a large percentage of families are from diverse communities? And particularly if it's an all-White senior leadership team, which is pretty much most of our schools, what responsibility are they taking upon themselves? It's not about blaming, it's about recognizing what our responsibilities are. If you are going to put yourself forward to lead in a very diverse community where these issues can come up, educating yourself is part of safeguarding, not just the children, but also staff and teachers. I understand that sometimes we don't have the specialists or the experts. But often I am described as a "hard to reach person" in the community. I am not hard to reach. I'm out there, I'm speaking places, I'm going to events. But I am described as a hard-to-reach member of the minoritized community. But if you're not reaching out to us and saying that you need support, I feel that sometimes we're making—not excuses, that doesn't sound very fair, because I understand leaders are so overwhelmed. But fundamentally, if we're going to lead a school, we need to start increasing our knowledge and reaching out to people who can support us rather than constantly relying on others.

David Kerr: I actually think they've been very responsible in the case about getting the right people there: the CEO, the head teacher, someone who's taught at Tate, Jack Dawson, plus the local Imam and governor. They're ticking all the right boxes.

Sara O'Brien: I will just highlight, as you've been saying, that one of the reasons this is so tricky is that we've got dilemmas reverberating at all different levels. You've got the classroom level, which Shammi started us off thinking about pedagogically: how do you address controversial issues in the classroom? And then we're bringing in questions of who gets to decide what those lessons look like, and who has the expertise to do that? These are issues at the school level. Then there are the questions of leadership. What are the responsibilities of leaders, and who is responsible for making sure that those leaders are prepared to tackle so many different issues? And then moving up to these really societal wide issues: where's this Islamophobia coming from? So the next question that we think about is: what are the values and principles at stake here? Do the characters in the case hold different values and principles?

Shammi Rahman: There's no question it's about freedom of speech. People move to this part of the world because they can be free to practice and believe what they believe, so I think that is a really important value. If you are going to use cartoons like that in an academic environment amongst mature adults who can actually have sensible conversations around it, maybe that's a bit more doable, because you can have that even with Muslim colleagues who are open to the idea of discussing and talking about controversial issues. But if you're going to present that to a young group of children, then we're talking about something very different. I've worked in education, and been a big supporter of discussing controversial issues in the classroom. I used to show images—artwork and such—of the Prophet Muhammad, peace be upon him, to make the point that there are multiple views and there's artwork depicting the Prophet Muhammad, peace be upon him, in a positive light.

If you're going to show those sorts of images for the purpose of discussing things that shouldn't be closed down, which I think is absolutely correct, then you can't just isolate one community, because it feeds into Islamophobia. If you're going to talk about something controversial, maybe take things that we hold sacred in secular societies and discuss those as well. And maybe choose offensive pictures from different communities. Why isolate one community over another? I think that's where the problem comes from.

Sally Elton-Chalcraft: I just want to add on the idea of blasphemy, which, in this particular scenario, the young people don't really understand. Maggie talks about how critical thinking can be developed without showing or repeating the very things that cause offence, like using the N word or showing porn. It's more about getting to the heart of what these things are, and understanding, like Shammi said, that different groups have different traditions, different values. Trying to explain that to groups of young people who don't share those values or traditions is quite difficult. I think that's why RE teachers are always given the job, aren't they? Because traditionally, we are the people that help young people take their own shoes off and try to put on the shoes of somebody else. And that's very, very challenging to do.

Janet Orchard: I think that citizenship education does that as well. I'd be interested to hear David's response to this. Could you share with us what you think the values and principles are at stake here that citizenship education would address?

David Kerr: I'll try. It's pretty complex, isn't it? For those outside the UK, Fundamental British Values [as defined in the original Prevent legislation] includes democracy, the rule of law, individual liberty, and respect for different faiths, beliefs and cultures. They're all in play at lots of different levels within this case study. There's liberty, rights, freedom, particularly for young people. It's a question of whether the adults involved have had any other training that might have made them more sensitive to different views. And it ultimately comes down to respect, doesn't it? There's a lack of respect here for different faiths, beliefs, and cultures. But citizenship education is in place to address these kinds of issues, because it's one of the few subjects that actually helps kids understand the society in which they're living—the rest of the curriculum is backward looking. The issue you've got is a lack of training. There aren't enough citizenship specialists across the country. I don't know if there are any in this MAT. It's interesting that the RE person is there, the history person is there, but there's no citizenship or PSHE [Personal, Social, Health, and Economic] coordinator there. There's a vacuum which they're not necessarily addressing. Whereas I would have thought with trained citizenships specialists, they would have started in primary school to help kids understand what discussion and debate are really about, how you need clear rules and to take people's considerations into account. That builds a kind of tolerance and respect as they move through school and allows them to gain more maturity to tackle these issues. It looks like the year nine boys are partly letting off steam, chucking their weight around. This is coming out in anti-Muslim sentiment. It's a question of how you make them aware that their behavior is not acceptable. That's the difficult bit not helped by bringing the *Charlie Hebdo* cartoons into it.

Also, do they not have a set of printed values for the academy trust? A lot of these schools now send home contract agreements to parents and pupils. And it's absolutely clear, from their motto and all their publicity and everything, what the academy chain stands for. For whatever reason, Tate doesn't seem to fit in with those values, so I wonder whether Tate's been given a bit too much slack alongside the other five schools where Islamophobia doesn't seem to be an issue. Maybe this situation is a culmination of Tate not feeling part of the Trust's common practices and common principles, despite staff moving around between the academies. It looks like, reading between the lines, everyone's tiptoed round Tate for lots of different reasons.

Janet Orchard: It's one thing to impose a contract on people. But if people don't identify with those common values then you're on a defensive back foot from the start, trying to persuade people, or, in this case, potentially coerce people into toeing the party line.

David Kerr: And it goes back to choice—or lack of choice—in the education system. In terms of Tate, parents likely don't have a choice, that's their local school. It's quite interesting to consider why minority Muslim parents would send their kids to Tate given the culture there. How are they dealing with that culture on a day-to-day basis, let alone with this particular incident for year nines? I'd like to know a bit more about the context and the socio-political makeup of this Academy, because you would have thought the Academy would be dealing with this kind of issue much more proactively given how Tate is an outlier. One of the big things that happened a few years ago was a recognition, particularly in northern schools, that there were divided communities, and so they started creating school partnerships. Bringing communities together in safe spaces or students or visiting each other's schools, breaking down those barriers, and making people realize there are differences, but there's also quite a lot of similarities. I'm not sure if this has been considered in Tate's Academy chain.

Shammi Rahman: I completely agree with you, David. What's really at stake is what children in the school are learning and what they're not learning. The best place for them to learn how to have these conversations, to agree to disagree, to have really meaningful conversations is at that age, and in a school environment. It's a really precious time. But the school doesn't have that citizenship expert, or someone who knows how to train teachers, to make something positive out of this volatile situation. Because the pupils are showing that they are interested in what's going on in the world, they have got something to say whether we like it or not. These young children are probably your best group of kids that you can teach, because they are engaged, though it's all very negative. The graffiti says that these children are crying out for education or support. You've got such a great opportunity to take that fire, however negative it might be, and develop these young people. They're children at the end of the day. So going back to that question, what are the values and principles at stake? It's care, it's resilience.

David Kerr: But they need to understand the law as well.

Shammi Rahman: Yes, they do.

David Kerr: If they're spraying graffiti and making anti-Muslim comments outside their school, they're in danger of getting arrested. Because they are breaking UK laws, and schools are fundamentally places that are based on democracy. They only work because of rules and regulations. Otherwise, it'd be absolute chaos. So it makes you wonder what has allowed Tate to get to a situation whereby pupils are doing graffiti and feeling confident enough to make those taunts in a cafeteria, probably with staff around. It makes you question the kind of behavior policies that are in place in this school, and the kind of slippages you might be getting there, because these are raising red flags about other things that could be going on. And that raises issues about the management, not just of that school, but of the academy.

Janet Orchard: Those comments really show how vulnerable Tate is. I mean, this school's in trouble. An Ofsted [Office for Standards in Education, Children's Services and Skills] inspection could judge them "inadequate" [the lowest grade]. I wonder though, whether instead of the problem being the school's policies, the issue is the (lack of) capacity to enact them. If this is an outlier school, maybe at the bottom of the pile, the one that children end up going to through lack of choice, presumably, it's harder to attract staff to that school. You've got to be pretty dedicated to go and work in a school that's ended up at the bottom of the pile. I do feel really sorry for the people at Tate and for Rebecca. I feel like they're doing their best, and they're just in this relentlessly difficult situation.

David Kerr: Then why would you suggest showing provocative cartoons? That's just crazy, if the stakes are so high. I think Jack Dawson says it's a risk. It's much more than that! It's a bomb that's going to go off, if it goes horrendously wrong, which it invariably will do. Those kids will take it home to their parents, it will be on the front pages of the Sun newspaper tomorrow, and demonstrators will be piling into Tate within the week.

Sally Elton-Chalcraft: I think it's also the ethos of the school and how teachers work with these young people. Jack Dawson has created this consultancy group, which trains people. Isn't that really a curriculum deliverer type ethos? I think some of the other teachers are trying to emulate an ethos of skills and concept building and working *with* the young people rather than *on* them.

Shammi Rahman: These comments, anti-Muslim comments, will have happened over a period of time of colleagues turning a blind eye, because children do not just all of a sudden get the confidence to write this stuff in the canteen overnight. This will be a culture issue. Talking about Prevent, how much preventative work has been done to educate these young people so they don't get to this point in the first place? How much of the curriculum has been education about religion and worldviews, citizenship? It's really got to boiling point. And now we've got to try and do something about it.

David Kerr: The other group we're not really talking about here is the Muslim minority at Tate. There must be a massive safeguarding issue going on here. This is probably the tip of the iceberg. How are they feeling about getting taunted in the cafeteria, graffiti coming out? Are their parents not up at the school, perhaps complaining? They must feel under threat, plus there's the male-female dynamic—these are Year 9 boys. I mean, if Ofsted comes they're in serious trouble. But they probably know that already, which then calls into question the leadership of the multi-Academy trust.

Sara O'Brien: What are some of the things that might be done in the case?

Sally Elton-Chalcraft: In the case study Saima's looking at the clock thinking "I've not got much time, we've got to make a decision," and also she is said to "wince" and feel hurt. I think it's a bit like rearranging the deck chairs on the Titanic. It's a much bigger picture, the way Tate was described as an outlier school. Maggie "hugs" Rebecca, but all that shows is that they're feeling sorry for each other, but they're not really working together to solve this particular issue. I'm not quite sure that any of them are realizing that, because education seems to be straying toward teachers being cast into the role of curriculum deliverers, policy followers, and ticking the box for Ofsted, rather than really thinking about preparing young people for a future life where they are aware of complex issues, and aware of the fact that people will think and do and behave differently from them.

Shammi Rahman: It's a long-term problem that has accumulated over time, and it's going to need a long-term solution. And I don't think it's just about the teachers, it's systemic. They should be looking at the systems within the school, helping the leaders, and dealing with the types of views that exist in their local area. Where is the Muslim community in all of this? Are the pupils' views very different to their parents' views? How far do the governing bodies of the trust and those individual schools reflect the community? If parents are sending their children to Tate, they might have a genuine interest in helping with these issues. Who's reaching out to them? So for me, I think it's a much broader solution. It involves the community, and not just the school community. Leaders within the local area cannot opt in, they *have* to do the work. Because if they're going to lead in those communities, they need to understand the complexity of the issues. We've got some amazing lecturers and scholars that are experts in this.

I think if schools collaborate better with leadership, communities, and experts, they're going to gain more.

David Kerr: For me, the Academy Trust needs to work as an Academy Trust. You can't have outlier schools. If you're really an Academy Trust, then you need to treat all your schools equally. And you need to recognize the strengths and weaknesses of those schools. They must have a real policy to address the prejudices, which perhaps needs to come through more cross-school working partnerships, so there are new ideas flowing in and out, through teacher exchanges and pupil exchanges, where they move across to see what goes on in different cultures, different religions, different beliefs. There might be some resistance to that, but you need to break that down. And I agree with you, Shammi, that they need to know where they can get expert help and have conversations about core training for all teachers in the school around how to handle issues. This has got to be a long-term project. Because these are deeper seated issues within the community, within our education system, unfortunately, in England, that need to be constantly addressed. And finally, they must get citizenship in their curriculum and get some experts in there and start working with their primary schools, because these issues don't suddenly appear at age eleven, or fourteen. They start in the feeder primaries.

Janet Orchard: Building on what David said, if Saima is as wise as I hope she is, she listens to the cry for help from Rebecca. And she says, we can't let you use the *Charlie Hebdo* cartoons, we don't feel that it's going to make the situation any better, and potentially could make it a lot worse, but clearly, there are big issues here. And those of us who don't want you to use the cartoons need to put our money where our mouths are, get together, and support you. Because you shouldn't be having to deal with this by yourselves. We need to work with you to come up with a better solution than the one that you've suggested.

Shammi Rahman: Absolutely. Collaboration is key. You need different members of the community, with different academic backgrounds, different levels of knowledge and experience. I think when leaders are left on their own, it's not fair on them—they're already rushed off their feet. The collaborative approach is strongest because you've got backup, and you know that you can go to different people who genuinely care about making improvements. You know your community best, and you will know what might work and what might not, but you might have to take a few risks.

Sally Elton-Chalcraft: I also wonder where Jack Dawson and his company fit with all this. Because he obviously is very passionate. A lot of the people in this particular meeting are very supportive of what he's trying to achieve. They might not necessarily agree with the way he's trying to do it. I think it makes it difficult for Saima because she has to say to Rebecca, we don't want to use Jack Dawson's resources. How will that play out? Does he change his resources?

Because the DfE has put forward this idea of Prevent, these little companies are springing up here, there, and everywhere. Some of them are very good, and incredibly well intentioned, but at the end of the day, they're out to make money. That can actually muddy the waters.

Shammi Rahman: It goes back to, again, leadership and decision-making. If you're going to go to somebody for advice, you look at their credibility. How have they worked in schools, what's their background? If we look at our universities, there are specialists who have dedicated whole careers to this topic.

Janet Orchard: I think as a result of this conversation, my view would be you can actually "park" the freedom of speech discussion from this case, because that doesn't feel to me to be the driving dilemma. I'm coming round to agreeing that the key issue here is racist behavior, which is illegal in schools in England, and which, were it called out properly, should result in serious punishment. Those issues in this case seem to be more fundamental than whether you have the right to say what you think, even if other people find it a bit offensive. There's bigger fish that need to be fried in this situation, and the freedom of speech thing is a red herring.

David Kerr: It's a problem that Prevent is just seen as being about safeguarding, rather than its teaching and learning aspect. If we had a culture in our schools that, from a young age, encouraged children to have discussions around controversial and sensitive issues, then you'd build up a culture where you think before you speak, and you think before you act. I'm sure some of these Year 9 boys are not aware of the wider implications—they're mimicking—but they need to understand how dangerous that is in terms of breaking the law, and also its implications on others. And if that means they need to be shown how their feelings could easily be hurt by certain depictions of things that they hold important, then so be it. But you can't do that unless that culture is in place. And that that culture is not in place in our education system. So Prevent is a kind of sticking plaster, which explains why no one quite knows what to do with it, because it flip flops around. Should it be about far-right extremism? Should it be about jihadist systems? It should be about extremism generally, trying to safeguard and protect our young people, because schools are meant to be safe spaces. And the trouble is we go from issue to issue without looking at what the underlying culture is. We've gone away from having any values in the national curriculum and elsewhere—school doesn't stand for anything.

Sally Elton-Chalcraft: I hope this conversation gets people to think about what the purpose of education is, not just this particular scenario. I think we've all come to the agreement that it's not just a matter of, shall we use the *Charlie Hebdo* pictures or not? It's more about: what is our ethos about teaching and learning and education?

Sally Elton-Chalcraft is Director of the Learning Education and Development Research Centre at the University of Cumbria, where she has taught undergraduate, post-graduate, master's, and doctoral students. She is editor of Teaching RE Creatively (2nd ed., Routledge, 2023) and joint editor of Professional Studies in Primary Education (4th ed., Sage, 2022). She is convenor of the Religions, Values and Education special interest group for the British Education Research Association.

David Kerr is Co-Head of ITE at the University of Reading overseeing initial teacher education courses at undergrad and postgrad level. He is an expert in Citizenship education having been integral in putting Citizenship into the National Curriculum (England). He has also produced three training manuals on Handling Controversial Issues in partnership with the Council of Europe.

Shammi Rahman is a Race Equality Adviser for HFL Education in the UK. She previously taught Religious Studies for eighteen years in secondary schools in Beds and Milton Keynes. She serves as a member of the Advisory Board for Children's Commissioner for England, is a member of the OCR RS Subject Consultative Board, and serves as an executive leader on the NATRE secondary team.

Character Guide

Setting	
Imperial Multi-Academy Trust (MAT), a network of six schools in London, England	
Primary Characters	
Saima Ahmed: CEO of Imperial MAT **Rebecca Mitchell:** head teacher at Tate Academy **Maggie Brown:** head teacher at Lyle Academy	**Farid Iqbal:** imam and governor at Whitworth Academy **Jack Dawson:** educational consultant

Discussion Questions

1. Several characters mention free speech as a reason to bring the cartoons into the classroom. How should rights to freedom of speech impact the Trust's decision whether or not to show the cartoons?
2. The characters in this case bring many kinds of expertise into the room: several are former religious education (RE) teachers, two are current

school leaders, one is the leader of the Multi-Academy Trust (MAT), two are practicing Muslims, one is an expert in curriculum design. Which forms of expertise strike you as most important as they grapple with their choice? Why?

3 The Prevent duty comes into the conversation several times. How do different characters in the case view their legal duty? How does this legal duty connect to their ethical responsibilities as they consider whether to show the cartoons?

4 Muslims are a minority population in England—Saima identifies herself as "a Muslim […] choosing to live in a Western context." And there are few Muslim students at Tate school. Yet a significant number of students in the wider Trust are Muslim. How should these demographic details influence the way the group thinks about showing the cartoons?

5 Farid brings up key "British values—respect and tolerance." How do the different characters in the case seem to interpret those values?

6 Rebecca suggests that her local MP (Member of Parliament) is more concerned about "jihadist nonsense" than about "White nationalist radicalism," even though she feels her students are more prone to the latter than to the former. To what extent should the Imperial MAT take the broader political context into account when deciding what Tate Academy should do in this case? How should school leaders in general navigate mismatches between their own judgment and what politicians are raising concerns about?

Notes

1. "Revised Prevent Duty Guidance: For England and Wales," GOV.UK, April 1, 2021, https://www.gov.uk/government/publications/prevent-duty-guidance/revised-prevent-duty-guidance-for-england-and-wales.
2. In February 2023, the British government published an independent review of the Prevent program, spearheaded by William Shawcross. Shawcross' executive summary declared:

> My purpose has been to ensure that the government's approach to preventing radicalisation and terrorism is as successful as possible. I found a programme that is broadly right in its objectives, admirable in its intentions and that fulfils many of its functions to good effect. However, there is room for improvement.

> Prevent must return to its core mission—countering all those ideologies that can lead people to committing or supporting acts of terrorism. This can only be done if Prevent properly understands the nature of these ideologies and how they attract and suborn individuals.
>
> It is correct for Prevent to be increasingly concerned about the growing threat from the Extreme Right. But the facts clearly demonstrate that the most lethal threat in the last 20 years has come from Islamism, and this threat continues.

William Shawcross CVO, "Independent Review of Prevent" (House of Commons, February 8, 2023), https://www.gov.uk/government/publications/independent-review-of-prevents-report-and-government-response.

3. In October 2020, French teacher Samuel Paty was beheaded by extremists after showing cartoons of the Prophet Muhammad to his middle-school class. The assailant had responded to a video message on YouTube with accusations against the history teacher.

9

Faith in Mr. D.: Accommodating Religion in Schools

Lauren Bialystok

Toronto, Ontario, is an enormous magnet for immigration and one of the most multicultural cities in the world. Canada adopted an official policy of multiculturalism in 1988, eschewing any state religion or assimilationist policy. Its liberal values about diversity are ensconced in the Canadian Charter of Rights and Freedoms, which also protects equality on the basis of sex and gender identity. Although education is a provincial responsibility, the public school system in Ontario still displays vestiges of the terms of Canadian Federation in 1867, in which British Protestants and French Catholics came to a compromise about colonial rule. Each branch of Christianity was allowed to provide its own schools, but the Protestant schools became increasingly secular over time, to the point that overt endorsement of any religious denomination now contravenes the law. Catholic schools, meanwhile, remain fully publicly funded and committed to denominational teaching, even where their tenets collide with broader liberal values. No other religious schools in the province have public funding. Middle or junior high schools, like the one in which this case takes place, are common schools, so the proportion of racial or religious minority students is usually an accident of their geographical location. The case reflects the sometimes uncomfortable coexistence of religious neutrality and religious preferentialism in Ontario policy.

--

"Happy Tuesday, Mr. D.," a student said cheerfully. The principal smiled and replied, "Hi, Karim. Shouldn't you be getting to class now?" But it was still ten minutes before the bell.

Peter Dikastis was distracted; it had been the most stressful month of his career. A scandal had broken out when he had allowed Friday *jummah* prayers to take place in the cafeteria of his public middle school. It seemed like a perfect fix for a problem with both religious and educational dimensions: the adolescent students, especially the boys, had been leaving school each Friday at lunch time to attend prayers at the mosque and not returning for the rest of the school day. Teachers and other students were complaining about the disrupted class time. The school had a majority Muslim population and was located in an urban middle-class community full of immigrants from Pakistan, Iran, India, and other South Asian origins. The Friday *jummah* prayer, Peter had learned, is the most important one of the week for Muslims and was considered obligatory for males. When Mr. and Mrs. Farouk, the parents of a Grade 8 student, proposed that an imam visit the school and conduct the half-hour prayer on site, the principal jumped at the chance to accommodate his Muslim students and improve attendance at the same time. Mrs. Farouk and several of her friends took care of all the set-up and supervision. But the media descended on the school with a torrent of questions and sparked an angry public debate. Conservatives in particular were decrying the "mosqueteria" and the fact that the sermon, the *khutbah*, was delivered in Arabic. Some warned that the sermon could contain intolerant messages, or even recruit students to violent causes. Commenters on news websites told Muslim immigrants to "go back to their home country." Police apprehended a person who had posted flyers outside the school offering a reward of $1000 for a video of students praying in the cafeteria. Meanwhile, liberal columnists worried about the blurring of religious freedom and the separation of church and state. Peter had grown up in Canada and thought its multiculturalism policy was straightforward. He was quickly learning otherwise.

The previous week, the board's superintendent had issued a press release saying that the in-school prayers would be suspended while the school explored its options. Last Friday at the designated prayer time, some 100 students gathered in the schoolyard and prayed in peaceful protest of the policy's suspension, while outside groups, including the Jewish Defense League and a Hindu nationalist group, sparred with Muslim parents on the sidewalk. One thing Peter knew for certain: he didn't want that chaos and tension again this week. The superintendent told Peter privately that she would support whatever he decided—and that she would check in at the end of the day.

At 9:00 sharp, the bell rang and Mr. and Mrs. Farouk knocked on the principal's door. He swallowed and tried to remind himself what he had prepared. "Mr. and Mrs. Farouk," he began, "I am so grateful for your advice, but as you know—"

"We have another solution," Mr. Farouk interrupted. "We see that bringing the imam into the school over the last few weeks caused too much controversy. We have a son in high school—you remember Khalid—who is a *hafez*. He can lead the service."

Peter paused as he digested this idea. "Would the sermon still be in Arabic?" he inquired.

Mrs. Farouk recoiled slightly, but it was Mr. Farouk who answered firmly, "Yes, it must be in Arabic."

The principal thought this over. The proposal was certainly less likely to provoke outrage than the first iteration of prayers in the cafeteria, with the imam at the head. And it would satisfy the goal of letting observant students pray without leaving school. But he wasn't sure it was just the imam's presence that made this issue inflammatory. He was responsible for everything that happened on school property. How could he be sure that the high school prayer leaders were following board policies?

Mrs. Farouk, who had been silent until now, seemed to read Peter's thoughts. "Mr. Dikastis, we see that this is not easy. But surely you are familiar with the school board's accommodation policies."

He had re-read the policy so many times in the last several weeks that he could recite it from memory. *Accommodation is considered appropriate if it promotes equal educational opportunity and meets the individual's creed-related needs.* The policy was sensible enough, and it followed from the Canadian Charter of Rights and Freedoms. He just wasn't so certain what "equal" meant here.

"Of course, of course," Peter replied. "As you know, we have the largest middle school Muslim Students' Association in the city." Peter was especially proud of the school's positive reputation in the community. Just a few years earlier, he had navigated some delicate conversations about a new sex education curriculum by working closely with parents who had religious objections to the material. The media had praised him then. "But I've heard from some other parents …." He trailed off. Perhaps this wasn't the right time to mention other parents.

"Yes?" Mr. Farouk asked, seemingly ready to solve any challenge.

"Well," the principal continued, "it's just that I'm not sure we accommodate the non-Muslim students so well. At least one Hindu student missed a field trip last year that coincided with Diwali, and we didn't accommodate him."

"Mr. Dikastis," Mr. Farouk said, "everyone is equal. But 400 of the 550 students at this school are Muslim. And *jummah* prayers can only be performed in a congregation. The Prophet Mohammad, peace be upon him, said that offering Friday prayers is equivalent to one entire year of praying and fasting alone. This Diwali story is not the same thing."

Peter wasn't sure what to say. He stood up and extended his hand. Mr. Farouk shook it firmly. As the parents walked to the principal's door, Mrs. Farouk turned around and said, "We all want our children to stay in school."

***

As the lunch bell rang, Jennifer Armstrong and Celeste Duval settled into the staff room with their sandwiches.

"Can you believe this thing about the Friday prayers?" Jennifer said, pushing aside a newspaper. She was a perky early-career math teacher known for her wit.

Celeste, a mid-career French teacher, rolled her eyes. "I know! They're making such a big deal out of it! But now I can finally teach my fifth period class on Friday. Before they fixed this, I'd be teaching to a half-empty classroom and have to repeat everything on Monday."

Jennifer put down her sandwich. "Celeste, it *is* a big deal! Those prayers are *sexist*. Do you know they make the girls stand behind the boys?"

Just then Peter walked in the staffroom and dropped a stack of envelopes on the table. "What are you two talking about?"

Jennifer turned to the principal and explained, "I was just saying to Celeste that you were right to call off the prayers in the cafeteria."

"Well, they haven't been called off exactly …" he answered.

"Good!" Celeste said. "I don't mind students leaving class for half an hour. I don't want them to disappear for the whole afternoon!"

"If the prayers only take half an hour," Jennifer shot back, "then why can't they go to the mosque and come right back? Why are we making a whole big fuss to accommodate students who are cutting class? We should be giving them detentions!"

"We thought of that," Peter replied. "The mosque is too far away to walk. And the bus only comes every 40 minutes. The timing has to be exactly right for them to get back for sixth period, and even then, they would still miss all of fifth period."

"Speaking of periods," Jennifer continued, her voice rising, "did you know that menstruating girls are not allowed to participate in the service? It's so obviously sexist."

Peter took a breath. Jennifer was echoing some of the toughest points he had encountered in the recent public backlash. Gender equality was as important in the board's equity policy as religious equality. In fact, in the last two years alone, Peter had attended three PD days on accommodating trans and non-binary students. Now he had the kids divided into two sexes, with the boys in front, in his own cafeteria. It didn't sit right.

"Jennifer," Celeste prodded, "you were raised evangelical. Are you going to tell me that we shouldn't accommodate our religious students because they treat men and women differently? All religions do."

"But school is supposed to be a secular space," Jennifer insisted, "where kids can figure out who they are."

"I agree with you on that," Celeste said. "But it's not our place to tell people how to figure out their religion. In fact, when prayers were only at the mosque, more boys went than girls. Now there's more equal opportunity."

"More opportunity? Or more pressure?" Jennifer asked rhetorically, tossing her sandwich wrapper in the garbage.

***

The bell rang. Peter was grateful for an hour alone in his office, without any meetings.

But a few minutes later there was a knock on the door and Zahra Suleimani approached his desk. Zahra was a straight-A student and the Secretary-Treasurer of the MSA.

She began, "Sir, I heard that some people have been talking about girls sitting behind the boys at *jummah*. I just wanted to tell you—"

"Yes?" Peter asked.

"I just want to pray and honestly I don't even want to pray in front of the boys and have them see me from behind."

"Thank you, Zahra, that's good to know. Is there anything else you'd like to tell me?"

Zahra hesitated a moment, then said, "Well, Mr. D., it's just, as you know I'm Secretary-Treasurer of the MSA and I do a lot of the organizing and stuff, but ... well, Hassan said I shouldn't talk to journalists about the cafeteria prayers."

Peter was perplexed; Zahra had spoken so articulately to the local news at last week's protest. Why would Hassan, the President of the MSA, be anything but proud? He motioned for her to elaborate.

"It's just, he said I wasn't dressed very ... religiously, and that it made us look bad."

As Peter absorbed this information, Zahra quickly continued, "Never mind, I shouldn't have said anything. You know, a lot of people don't understand what Muslims are like. I love my faith and I just want everyone to be respected."

***

Peter was glad to be spending his evening in good company. Mitch Gallagher and Steven Fromm were two of Peter's closest friends. Mitch was a lawyer at the Ministry of Education, and Steven was Vice Principal at a private Jewish school. Peter was also glad that his wife, Arlene, had met them at the restaurant after work.

"So how's life in the eye of the storm?" Mitch teased, taking a sip of his drink.

Peter sighed. "I'm trying to accommodate everyone," he explained, "but I seem to keep running into limits."

"It's one of the reasons I moved to a parochial school," Steven said. "At my old school in the public board, they tried to accommodate me and the few dozen Jewish students, but they kept scheduling assessments on Jewish holidays, there was no kosher food in the cafeteria, and all the extra-curricular tournaments ran on Saturday—*shabbat*. It's a Christian system, whether they call it that or not. You have your hands tied."

"Being Christian doesn't mean being exclusionary," Mitch retorted. "All the schools in the province are required to provide a multi-faith room—even Catholic schools!"

In the Canadian province where Peter lived, Catholic schools were fully funded from kindergarten through to Grade 12. No other religious denomination had any public education funding.

"A multi-faith room doesn't solve this, though," Peter replied. "The only way for our Muslim students to fulfill their religious obligations is to go to mosque during school hours—or to bring the mosque to the school."

"Or change school hours!" Mitch joked.

"Exactly my point!" said Steven. "Public schools can't run on twelve different clocks. Maybe these students should move to an Islamic school?"

"That puts a completely unfair burden on religious minorities," Mitch replied. "Not everyone can afford to go to a school like yours. The public system may still run on a Christian schedule, but it's our job to make schools inclusive for everyone."

"That puts an unfair burden on school administrators!" Peter cried, surprised at his own fervor. "Why should only Catholic schools be funded? Maybe the solution is to fund all religious schools, and then families can choose." Arlene squeezed his shoulder.

"You know that's not going to happen, Peter," Mitch said. "It's in the Constitution and no politician wants to touch it. We have to give Muslim students equal opportunity—even if the Catholic students can go to mass without leaving the school."

"And get credit for it!" Arlene piped in.

"Well, yeah," Mitch said. "It's an exception to the separation of church and state. Catholic schools get to endorse Catholicism. But Peter can accommodate these students without endorsing Islam."

"I don't know if I can," Peter confessed. "I don't understand Arabic; does that mean I'm endorsing what they're saying in prayers?"

"Have you thought about asking them to provide a translation of the service?" Steven asked.

"Then he'd really have to answer for whatever they're saying in there!" Arlene said.

"People say all sorts of things on school property," Mitch pointed out. "Peter doesn't endorse all of it. He doesn't even speak French! Does that mean they have to cancel French classes?"

"That's different," Arlene said. "They're not praying in French class."

"But students pray in the multi-faith room," Mitch reminded her. "Why is this different?"

Peter's phone rang. The call display showed the name of the superintendent. What should he decide about Friday prayers?

Conversation

Lauren Bialystok: Welcome, everyone. I'm delighted to have you all with us. I'm going to start by inviting you to talk about what you think the dilemmas are in this case and for whom they are dilemmas. I'm going to ask Kevin if he wants to start this conversation, but everyone will have a chance to weigh in.

Kevin McDonough: One dilemma that jumps out at me is what I would call the main dilemma for Peter Dikastis, the principal—whether to allow or accommodate the school prayer request by Muslim parents. There are practical aspects to the dilemma. One is that the choice impacts school attendance for half a day per week for a majority of the school population. Whether or not he decides to accommodate will have significant academic implications for students and teachers. Ethically, my sense is that there are a couple of different value dimensions to the dilemma. One is a conflict between the value of the school's obligation to provide equal educational opportunity for all students and on the other side the commitment to liberal principles of non-discrimination and gender equality. There's also a concern for respect for the religious liberty of students and parents, and the school's obligation to provide a secular education. I understand secularism as the idea that schools should be autonomous from religious influence, that their educational mission shouldn't be reflecting particular religious views.

Rebecca L. Starkman: I was really stuck on what felt like a dilemma to me—how is a religious need being defined in the case? Are we defining this by the majority? Is this need for accommodation coming from the parents? Is it coming from the logistical reality of the number of students that are leaving? Is it coming from a particular definition of Islam? Are there a diversity of religious needs in the school community that aren't coming to the fore based on different theological positions? Is this a need simply because of the logistical necessity of the disruption to the classroom? So is this coming from the teachers?

Philippa Carter: The school is majority Muslim, but they're still in a system where Christian rules and regulations predominate. Carols and Christmas, candy canes, Christmas trees. It troubles me that the principal seemed to quickly decide that setting up a prayer space in the cafeteria was the right approach. Why was that the solution in his mind? If the mosque really wants and the parents really want their students to attend Friday prayers, can the mosque not provide a school bus?

I feel like this is the public school system engaging in enforced religious behavior. Those students are under pressure—I'm particularly worried about the girls—to attend a religious service that's being held on school grounds. This is not a problem the school should be solving in the way they think it's been solved. I think that this religious creep in our public school system is something that needs to be looked at quite differently than the way that we're looking at it. This may mean in urban centers like Toronto adjusting Friday teaching schedules across the board. I think we can find a creative way to have these students go off the school grounds to participate in prayers, and it should not be mandatory for Muslim students to actually do this on a Friday. I'm really worried that that's what's happening.

Lauren Bialystok: Thank you. It's a valuable perspective because I think what you're saying is that the way we even say what a dilemma is or isn't takes for granted certain features of the situation. If we weren't so wedded to things like the school system, which as you aptly pointed out is not secular at all in practice, then we would see that this doesn't have to be viewed as a dilemma of inserting the needs of a religious minority into some otherwise inflexible and secular system. Let's go to Rizwan.

Rizwan Mohammad: I think that we should also consider a dilemma regarding student self-determination. How do we support student self-actualization in this kind of context? Another dilemma is the difficulty of communicating about public expressions of religion. I think it carries over into our broader society. My experience in Ontario's public schools, and working with students in the years since I left, has suggested to me that this is an ongoing dilemma for students, for teachers, for administrators, and for parents. I have seen the way that some people disagree about religion disagreeably, or don't talk about it at all, or talk about it in very simplistic and reductive ways.

Lauren Bialystok: Can I also ask you to come back to the point that Rebecca made earlier about what counts as a religious need?

Rizwan Mohammad: I think Rebecca's point is really, really helpful. As a student who started out being a member of the only Muslim family in my primary school in the Durham District School Board in the 1980s, I was alone in requesting accommodation for prayer. My sisters didn't request prayer accommodation. They made their own choices based on their own comfort level. So I found myself in my Vice Principal's office at lunch hour to pray, by myself. He would make rounds at that time, and it was a non-issue. There was no problem. Our arrangement was completely informal, no internal consultation, no external discussion. He heard my request, and his solution was simple: "Just use my office."

When I got to high school, I found myself waiting in the principal's office with a whole bunch of other Muslim students, who happened to all be male, making a request for prayer space that day. We had to go through more bureaucratic processes to do that. One of the things we found once the prayer room was announced was that we had to negotiate as students how we were going to pray because we pray differently. For example, Shia students will often have need of certain materials to ensure that the prayer space is sacred and pure that Sunni students don't need. There's a whole discussion that has to be had. And then how do they as a group communicate with one voice to the administration in a way that's not confusing?

Allysa Khan: I've been itching to speak. Overwhelmingly, all of my participants in my research did participate in Friday Prayer Groups, and all of my participants were female. When you are in a secular school space or in a public school and your administrators and your teachers don't know the nuances of the religion, there is a misconception about what this prayer really represents, why there's a need for it to be congregational.

There's a further nuance that this prayer is generally understood among Muslims to be obligatory for the male students, and not for females. I believe the case study underscores the fact that it was majority males that were leaving the school to go to the mosque to pray, whereas the females weren't. But when the prayers started happening at the school, more females were indeed participating. And this is a sentiment that is echoed by my participants as well. The females were attending the prayers when they were in schools because religious accommodation was provided, and it was something that they wanted to do.

There are also other prayers that happen throughout the school day that aren't accommodated by the school. Students were asking for accommodation for these prayers, but because they weren't understood in the same manner as the *jummah* prayer, students were having a lot of difficulty having this religious accommodation enforced. What they ended up doing in many cases was to ask their teacher to leave class to go pray. Their teacher didn't really understand that there was supposed to be an accommodation for prayers that happened daily, so the teacher would say, "No." The students would then informally meet in corridors, or under the stairwell, or outside of the building. However, there would be other students in the hallways, or if they were under the stairwell, people would be walking up and down, changing to the next period or class. A lot of the students would get their clothes stepped on, or onlookers would see them in this precarious position and make comments. The students wanted to have this accommodation, and they wanted to be able to fulfill the religious obligation inside of the space of the school in a way where they felt safe.

I think it's very common to think about this idea of being pressured into prayer, but on the flip side there are some who genuinely have this desire to fulfill a religious obligation. But they have to be a student at the same time. How do you reconcile being a student but also being a Muslim and wanting to bring those two parts of your identity together in a way that is physically safe for you, in a way that you don't have to leave your school, where you can feel comfortable and safe and not under the gaze of non-Muslim students who don't fully understand what you're doing?

Lauren Bialystok: Thanks, Allysa. I think you're really putting your finger on an aspect of the dilemma that is not so much about space but is about multiplicity in the school system. I want to pull out two things. As soon as we're talking about accommodation and conflicts of values or balancing religious equality with other forms of equality, we are taking for granted a liberal framework, which, among other things, asserts a distinction between public and private, a distinction between different aspects of ourselves, between religious and non-religious ways of thinking or doing things, which doesn't resonate with many religious people's actual experience—that their selves are not divisible in that way, that they are a religious person everywhere they go and in everything they do, and that is part of the fulfillment of their obligation. So it's nonsensical to talk about entering into a secular space and checking their religion at the door and only picking it up again when it's time to go out. I think that's really important in terms of the limitations of using a liberal framework for labeling the dilemmas and trying to resolve the dilemmas.

And I like your examples, which bring up at least two dimensions of this challenge for me. One is that because we're in a liberal framework and accommodation only follows on recognition—the liberal dynamic of making a need or an identity visible in a pluralistic society in a way that requires other people to change what they're doing—it may be the case that recognition is more easily earned for some religious needs. For example, congregational prayers or prayers that an imam can say are mandatory or mandatory for males may be more likely to be recognized than other religious needs, which may be no less significant to the person who wants to practice them, but are perhaps less coordinated or have fewer identifiable rules or are harder to get an imam to say to a principal that this is the exact place of this prayer in our religious observance. Ironically, then, it sounds like you have some students, especially the female students, needing recognition for other religious needs, which are less intelligible within this liberal accommodation framework. Therefore, they're actually having to sacrifice some of their other liberal goods like educational equality and personal dignity goods of being in a safe space and not being subjected to unwanted gaze or unwanted comments. So it backfires. The principle of accommodation and equality for everyone is backfiring if the need itself cannot be made intelligible within a framework that the school system and the liberal society understands.

Another thing that you touched on is that from an ostensibly secular, ostensibly multicultural liberal perspective, we think we know what is good for girls or what gender equality means, but the things that we might do to promote gender equality within a religious context may also backfire because they do not play out in that non-liberal or non-secular context in the ways that we expect. So the assumption that, for instance, it's worse for girls to pray behind the boys or that there would be pressure on the girls to pray if the *jummah* prayers were held in the school are actually presuppositions following from a non-religious liberal framework of accommodation, and it's important to attend to what the people involved are saying about their own needs.

Rizwan Mohammad: Just to respond quickly to Allysa. Much of what you described and your reflections about what you observed struck a chord with me. That's what I've also seen from a community member's perspective and also somebody who has been mentoring students. I wanted to add another dilemma. Who should be weighing in on decisions like this? The case highlights a problem of consultation and who has the knowledge, the experience, the credibility, and the authority to come up with a meaningful solution for students.

Kevin McDonough: I hope this isn't going back too far in the discussion, but I wanted to probe the idea you put out there, Lauren, that it's limitations to the liberal framework of accommodation that are the problem here. It's hard for me to imagine how in a diverse society and in a diverse school where there's a large majority of Muslim students, how something like a liberal framework can be avoided as a basis for thinking about these things. If that's true, it's important to think about how we think about the liberal framework of accommodation.

One distinction that seems important to me is between liberal frameworks that insist on a hard public-private distinction, where religion is relegated to the private realm and the public is free of religious expression. I think multiculturalism is one way of doing that, and laïcité is another model of liberalism that does it. In multiculturalism, religious and other forms of diversity belong in the private realm, so a system of separate schools for religious groups makes sense on that model, where religious differences are respected but confined to a private realm. Maybe there's a multicultural massaging that can be done to work out different prayer rooms for different groups or something to recognize diversity, but that seems likely to run into practicality or feasibility issues. The laïcité model says the public space of citizenship and dialogue is really all about non-religious principles, and religion should be banished. From that perspective, accommodation appears like, the phrase was used earlier, religious creep. If we let religion in, it's creeping into a realm where it doesn't belong.

I think both of those models do have some significant limitations, but there are other liberal frameworks that bring into view advantages from a secular point of view of having a robust religious dialogue about a lot of these issues. Let's start with what's in the case, and then move to Allysa's examples. One of the things that strikes me about the case is that you've got parents and students and teachers and a principal who are all extraordinarily engaged. They're not alienated from one another, they're not hostile, not adversarial, and work out in a dialogical way a solution that meets everyone's needs. I think that's really important from this kind of citizenship model of liberalism where reasonable accommodations initiate a dialogue that's aimed at helping students to develop skills they need to co-construct the society. The idea is that in a religiously diverse society, many citizens have religion at the center of their identity. So if we're going to show values like mutual respect, we need to be able to talk to people who have different religious faiths. Or, if you're non-religious, you need to be able to appreciate what it means to have a religious faith.

There are tons of opportunities in this whole dialogue about accommodation, regardless of the outcome, to foster those values. So it really matters a lot, for example, whether the principal is dismissive of these questions or whether there's an honest, good faith attempt to listen, to find a solution that does meaningfully seem like an honest attempt to those who are asking for the accommodation. And students can learn a lot from that, too. And learn things that are important for being liberal citizens in a religiously diverse society, to figure out ways to combine, as Allysa puts it, their Muslim identity and their identity as students.

The problem isn't that liberalism can't accommodate those needs for accommodation but that efforts need to be made to recognize them as being in need of accommodation and to find good principles for why to justify the accommodation. Things like respect for human dignity and not putting people in humiliating positions seem like they can easily be framed in secular terms. I just wanted to defend liberalism and say that maybe what we need is a more sophisticated, flexible liberal framework for accommodations.

Lauren Bialystok: Thank you, Kevin. Philippa, thanks for your patience. It's your turn.

Philippa Carter: I want to touch on a couple of things. The first is an observation that I have had with conversations with students at the post-secondary level. It's not just about young women who are feeling coerced to behave in certain ways, but it's also young men. I do not object to spaces dedicated for various religious activities that students feel mandated to participate in during the school day, I think it's important to acknowledge that, and it would never ever occur to me to prohibit a student from stepping out of a class, or students, to go pray. I mean, if the class is so rigid that if they leave for ten minutes on an ordinary weekday then somehow the whole system is going to fall apart—that's nuts to me. That's not right, and it's not fair.

Overall, my feeling is that if students need to pray at a particular time, they should be accommodated. Absolutely. But I don't think it should be happening on school grounds. Part of the problem we're dealing with is that we have a very Victorian school system, for all of its innovations. Here's an example. We know that teenagers do better if they don't have to be at school by 830 a.m. in the morning. As far as I know, the research has demonstrated that, but we keep sending our teenagers to school on the public transit during rush hour. We've had no consideration, as far as I can tell, of the Christian holidays that make up—heck!—the agricultural roots of our culture that make up when school holidays and so on take place. I think this all boils down to a much broader discussion of what we want our education system to do. I have no objection in principle to religious accommodations, but I think we need to move toward a place where if you have a majority of your students who are saying that they want to go to the mosque .... Am I going to say that? Yeah, I'm going to say this. If Muhammad cannot go to the mountain, then the mountain must come to

Muhammad. But it doesn't have to be in the actual building where the teaching is taking place.

Rebecca L. Starkman: I'm wondering if there needs to be a distinction made between the *jummah* prayers and daily prayer. I am wondering if there are limits to the accommodation capacity specifically for the *jummah* prayers because, and please correct me if I'm wrong, by virtue of needing to be enacted communally—therefore cueing particular gender practices of hierarchicalized seating and exclusion based on sex, periods, bodily function that could be interpreted as discriminatory—it really is pushing the limits of what the public school principle of gender equity is advocating for. I hit this all the time in my own work. I hit this impasse in my own life as a religious, Orthodox, feminist, Jewish person. It's so hard to find a way to reconcile liberal gender equity approaches and faith-based gender practices derived from a different perspective, a different point of truth, a different way of operating, a different authority.

Allysa Khan: I think there's something to be said for taking into consideration the diversity not just of religious sects but the diversity in beliefs and how they evolve over time, specifically with females. I want to point out a few things about how these Muslim Student Associations and Friday Prayer Groups are changing. The first is that there are many schools where I interviewed participants where they ran female-only Friday prayers, and there were also female-only Muslim Student Associations. There were also instances where female students were able to take on leadership roles in a religious manner in the school system that they were not able to in a community or mosque system. For example, in quite a few of the Friday prayer groups—I'll take for granted that all of us have the understanding that these Friday prayers are led in Arabic by males—females started taking on religious leadership roles where they were leading a preamble to the Friday prayer called the bayan. This is something that the students who I interviewed said that they were proud to be able to take on because it helped them work through a lot of what they themselves were grappling with. They're advising some of their peers, they're internally working through their own struggles, but then they're also addressing the congregation in a leadership role. They felt that this is really innovative because in the conventional setting they don't have those opportunities. Because it is a religious obligation that is being fulfilled in a non-religious space, females were reinventing ways to see themselves as leaders.

Another thing I wanted to address is the diversity within the beliefs of female Muslims who attend these prayers. There is resistance. There is agency. These females are not seen as being agentic or having resistance because we are viewing Islam and Muslim females through a liberal lens, where sometimes that liberal lens can be clouded by misconceptions of what the religion is—Who are these female adherents? What do they look like? Are they being forced into doing things? My research and my own experiences as a teacher and as a practicing Muslim female have shown me that there's a changing face to this. For example, going to the prayer. If they're not hijabi, and they don't wear full-length clothing, they still want to be in this space, they still want to pray, and they push back. They say, "This is the school space, I have the opportunity to do it here, and I don't want to have to go to the mosque to do it because there's rigidity in the mosque that I don't have to encounter in the school space." I think it's important to really understand that there's such a diversity in the beliefs of each new generation of Muslim females that is really changing how Islam is being practiced.

In so many school boards, so many schools that have a large Muslim student body, it's the females who are doing the organizing and advocating to even have these groups, to have the accommodations. And then when they do get pushed back, they find ways to circumvent the lack of accommodation. I think it's important to think about just how much diversity there is because these young women are trying to blend their identities as Muslims, as Canadians, and as students. There is a re-imagining of how their identities are played out in the school system. Some of them identify first and foremost as Muslim, some of them don't, but they come to these spaces to explore or to navigate how to blend their identity or come up with an identity that is Muslim-Canadian, Muslim-Canadian-female. Having the ability to do this in the school space where they're afforded these opportunities that they would not be in the larger community or in a religious setting such as a mosque is very important for them.

Lauren Bialystok: I'm going to go to the question of what you think should be done about these dilemmas, which I believe you've already started to answer.

Philippa Carter: I'm worried about individual dignity. There should be way more flexibility. If a school starts half an hour early to accommodate the fact that a lot of the students are going to go off to the mosque on Friday afternoons and not come back, don't schedule important stuff for academic purposes on Friday afternoon. Change the scheduling so that students who need to attend communal prayer in the community can go and do that, but I don't think the answer is to try to accommodate it in the school.

Lauren Bialystok: If I could just clarify your push one last time; is it your feeling that this form of accommodation is tantamount to endorsing?

Philippa Carter: Yes!

Lauren Bialystok: Thank you for clarifying. I think the question about endorsing is critical from a values perspective. Rizwan, I'm going to you next.

Rizwan Mohammad: One of the things that for me is worth a longer discussion is about endorsement. What amounts to endorsement? What amounts to accommodation? What's the line? I'm not convinced that in a pluralistic society that the dilemma Mr. D. is faced with is tantamount to endorsement. I could be wrong, and I'm open to debating it further. If I go to a Jewish service, I'm not endorsing the beliefs. If I go to Catholic mass, I'm not endorsing the liturgy. I think Mr. D. could say to the superintendent: "I want to convene an interfaith, reasonable accommodations committee. It's going to have people of different faith backgrounds, and it's going to have different student representatives. It's going to have some teachers, it's going to have some parents, and what we're going to do together is, communally, try to figure out what's reasonable and what alternatives there are and try to think creatively." I think one of the misconceptions, and this is a pillar of Islamophobia, is that Islam is not at its foundation a rational teaching that is open to engagement in dialogue. There has to be meaningful consultation. I don't think it's productive to pursue a non-liberal framework in this situation. I really don't know what that would look like.

Rebecca L. Starkman: What's come out of my research is a need for much more understanding about what it means to be a person of faith—what does it mean for someone to feel obligated to pursue a religious practice that's going to lead them to ask for accommodations or to make decisions on their own that might lead to situations of vulnerability, situations of risk, exposure? We need to find some way for greater understanding and dialogue among those who have different worldviews and who are moving through life from a different starting point or choosing to make different value or principled decisions. How do we have that conversation in a school so that it doesn't come down to the nitty gritty of who is entitled to what type of accommodation?

Lauren Bialystok: Thanks, Rebecca. Kevin, what would you do?

Kevin McDonough: From near the beginning of this case, I wanted to be on the side of a reasonable accommodation approach because my view of liberalism, the one that I find most compelling, is one where citizens can negotiate difficult issues and differences. I think this case is a great case of how civic learning could happen informally as part of the ethos of the school. So I want to be on the side of reasonable accommodation. I think that would involve a lot of really difficult and skillful leadership, whether it's the principal or the superintendent or some sort of collective body.

The issues that Allysa raised about the agency of Muslim women strike me as ultra-important. I think it's right to point out that there's a danger of complacency on the liberal side to see women as passive victims and to neglect the ways in which, even in the context of gender inequality, agency is still there and needs to be supported. I think that the response is that liberals need to really be attentive to that. If you're committed to individual autonomy and equality, the moral imperative is to pay attention to the ways in which you're denying opportunities for agency and growth on the part of those that are assumed not to have it. If there's going to be a liberal justification for accommodation then the emphasis has to be on exactly the kinds of things that Allysa is talking about, like including and amplifying the voices of those who are ignored or silenced and to encourage their agency. We need to point out how encouraging the agency of Muslim girls and students is also empowering for everyone else because they learn more about the reasons behind how other people see the issues. It's a collective thing.

Allysa also mentioned something that I think is a real problem for liberalism. The more you get into the position of supporting that kind of agency educationally, the more the danger that you're going to be seen as interfering or meddling in intra-religious matters. That's not something a liberal state should be doing. They shouldn't be telling Muslims how to be Muslim. Ultimately, my response is that the emphasis has to be on the educational benefits of this kind of dialogue—encouraging the students to see themselves as agents who are becoming part of the story of the construction of society as it changes and evolves, rather than as bits and pieces in an unchanging mosaic. We're not taking sides on the question of what it is to be Muslim or the meaning of Islam. These are skills of autonomy, critical deliberation. We remain neutral with respect to religion, but we're committed to a liberal education—that is, neutral in its justifications, not its effects.

Lauren Bialystok: Thank you. One of the things I like about the way you've reframed this in terms of the educational goods at stake, Kevin, is that you've also—maybe inadvertently or indirectly—answered the question of what a discussion like this might yield and what the exercise of writing and talking through case studies can afford us. This educational exercise seems to be a good model of the kind of dialogue that you're urging schools to prioritize. Presumably, even when the case isn't about religious accommodation but about other ethical dilemmas in school, there is something to be gained from prioritizing the view that whatever solution is taken should be enhancing the education of the students and all the people involved. It should be furthering dialogue, not trying to come to a solution that squares away all of the messy bits and shuts down dialogue. Of course, that in itself is arguably a very liberal conceit, but I think one that most of us can get behind.

Philippa Carter received her PhD in Religious Studies from McMaster University, Hamilton, Canada in 1992. She is now teaching professor in the Society, Culture & Religion undergraduate degree program at McMaster.

Allysa Khan is a secondary school English teacher with the Peel District School Board in Ontario, Canada. She completed her PhD in education at the University of Toronto with her dissertation, The Politics of Identity and Space: Muslim Female Students' Discourses on Their Experiences in Secondary Schools. *Her work* examines how Muslim females in religious student groups develop and negotiate their identities both in secular schools and in religious student organizations.

Kevin McDonough is Associate Professor of Philosophy of Education at McGill University, Canada. His research focuses on questions of how citizenship education relates to issues of justice and inclusion in diverse democratic societies.

Rebecca L. Starkman received her PhD in Curriculum and Pedagogy from the Ontario Institute for Studies in Education at the University of Toronto. Her research explores intersections of youth religiosity, gender, and public education.

Rizwan Mohammad is a graduate of the University of Toronto specializing in Islamic Studies. He has over a decade of experience conducting research on Islamic thought and Muslim life, training leaders of Muslim Students' Associations, and serving Muslim organizations across Canada. His recent advocacy work on behalf of Canadian Muslims focuses on promoting changes in policy and legislation related to public safety, hate crime, online harms, ethical use of technology, and religious freedom.

Character Guide

Setting	
An urban middle school in Ontario, Canada (grades 7–8, ages 12–14)	
Primary Characters	
Peter Dikastis: school principal **Mr. Farouk:** parent of a Grade 8 student **Mrs. Farouk:** parent of a Grade 8 student **Jennifer Armstrong:** math teacher **Celeste Duval:** French teacher	**Zahra Suleimani:** student, secretary-treasurer of the school's Muslim Students Association **Mitch Gallagher:** lawyer at the Ministry of Education **Steven Fromm:** vice principal at a private Jewish school **Arlene Dikastis:** Peter's wife

Discussion Questions

1 How does Peter's legal responsibility to provide religious accommodation to his students compare to his ethical responsibility to do so?

2 Jennifer raises concerns about the different ways boys and girls are treated during the *jummah* prayers. How should Peter balance the school's commitment to both gender equality and religious equality?
3 How should Peter's conversation with Zahra influence his decision about the *jummah* prayer?
4 How should Peter weigh the school's demographics in his decision-making, given that nearly three-quarters of the students at the school are Muslim?
5 Why is the language the service is conducted in such an important consideration to the different characters in the case?
6 How should Peter balance the school's commitment to secular education with the responsibility to provide accommodation to students of all religions?
7 Peter worries that allowing *jummah* prayers to take place in the cafeteria signals that he "endorses" what's said in the prayers. Why is he concerned? What's the difference between accommodation and endorsement?
8 How should the public dialogue around prayers in the cafeteria influence Peter's dilemma (if at all)?

10

Conclusion: Expanding the Conversation

Sara O'Brien, Meira Levinson, Ellis Reid, and Tatiana Geron

As democracy faces threats around the globe, schools play a crucial role as both democratic spaces and sites of civic education. However, as the case studies and conversations in this volume show, what civic education should look like and what role schools should play in civic life are contested. Even where there is broad agreement that civic education matters, teachers, school and district leaders, students, parents, and policymakers face dilemmas as they try to turn educational ideals into reality. Yet this mission is critical: in increasingly polarized times, schools are one of the few places where we engage with diverse others and step outside our "bubble," as Nikki Spencer describes it in the conversation about "A Parallel Universe" (Chapter 2). Reflecting on a student's conspiratorial views, Spencer notes, "There is no other platform I can think of other than schools where you might create a forum where these views might be challenged." Her comment highlights the important role that schools play as democratic spaces in fragile democracies.

The cases in this volume are designed to be read and analyzed but, more importantly, they're designed to be discussed, ideally by groups that hold viewpoints as diverse as those presented in the cases themselves. Engaging in democratic discourse is hard. It asks us not only to bring our deeply held views and beliefs to the table but also to engage thoughtfully and earnestly with people who might hold views and beliefs antithetical to our own. We hope that normative case studies make this task of engaging in democratic discourse easier—even just a bit. Thus we devote this conclusion to discussing how these cases, and their accompanying conversations, function as teaching tools for the classroom and discussion tools for democracy.

Using the Cases for Democratic Dialogue

Over the years, the editors of this volume have facilitated countless case discussions: in small and large groups, in person and online, with unlimited time and within strict time limits. In this section, we explain how to organize and run discussions using the cases in this volume, whether those discussions take place in a classroom, a teacher's lounge, a conference room, or a community meeting space.

As noted in the introduction, our approach to facilitating case discussions emphasizes thoughtful deliberation over active problem-solving. Our protocol deliberately leaves the question of what should be done (along with questions of why and by whom) until quite late in the conversation. Schools are highly action-oriented places. Educators have too many tasks to do and too little time in which to do them. Our approach to case discussion asks participants to put off the moment of decision until they have had a chance to think through the ethical nature of the dilemmas presented and the complex context around these dilemmas, taking the luxury of time that educators rarely get but desperately need to develop ethical sensitivity and practical wisdom. We encourage anyone using these cases to take the same approach. Our discussion protocol can be found in the facilitation guide in the Appendix.

Preparing for Case Discussions

We generally recommend allotting at least an hour to a case discussion, to allow enough time to dive into the dilemmas presented by the case and reflect on what connections participants make to their own professional and personal lives. Ninety minutes is even better. Under serious time constraints, discussions can even run under sixty minutes if facilitators eliminate the reflection. The facilitation guide lays out the protocol for a full case discussion, from introductions through reflection. While this guide is designed for a ninety-minute discussion, it includes a number of modifications that enable a shorter conversation.

When we run case discussions, we prefer to have groups of six to twelve people, which allows for diversity of perspective as well as plenty of opportunity for participation. If faced with the choice, we recommend making the groups slightly too large rather than too small. Facilitators can always break larger groups into pairs or trios to increase opportunities for participation, but it's hard to cultivate diversity of thought in groups that are quite small. And while having a dedicated facilitator for each small group can enrich the experience, we have also run cases with very large groups using just one facilitator for whole-group discussion and leaving small groups to largely self-facilitate.

The cases and conversations in this volume work together to highlight key challenges in civic education across many contexts, but each case can also be read alone, without any additional background knowledge. The cases are designed to be read fairly quickly, in about ten minutes by a fluent English speaker. While all of the cases are presented here in English, on our website (justiceinschools.org) you can find some of the cases in the languages of their contexts ("Photo Bomb" in Spanish and "Feeling Exposed in Online Class" in Dutch, for example).

There are many ways to help users prepare for case study discussions. In academic settings, instructors often send the case out to students before they will discuss it. In some instances, it's helpful to send extra preparation materials with the case. Questions about the context can sometimes distract students from the important ethical questions that the case raises, so while this volume does contain a context paragraph and footnotes for each case, consider whether students will need any additional background materials. Some instructors also send philosophical writings, empirical studies, or other academic texts to help focus their students' thinking as they read the case. In professional development settings, we sometimes send cases and accompanying supplementary materials out to educators before the discussion, but we also sometimes build time into our session for participants to read the case (or a reader's theater adaptation) at the event, depending on the needs and norms of the group we're working with. For events like a community meeting, when we're unsure exactly who will be coming, we have participants engage with the case at the session itself. If you do send out the case before your event, make sure that users have enough time to engage with the case thoughtfully before they will come together to discuss.

Setting the Conditions for Discussion

Because these case studies are designed to help make challenging conversations a bit easier, we believe it's important to set the conditions for discussion before asking the first question. Our protocol asks users to dig into challenging questions that draw on core values, principles, and beliefs. While discussing these values through the lens of a case study does provide some distance that makes conversation easier, these discussions still raise strong reactions. To help create an environment where people feel comfortable sharing their thoughts, we take time for introductions if we don't know the group members or they don't know each other. We also frequently build in an icebreaker question (about a favorite food or activity, for example) for some community building. We then set norms for the conversation, which we can return to should the conversation become heated. Norms help to create shared expectations for civil discourse. Read on for a list of norms that we often use in our discussions—keep in mind that we always ask discussion participants whether they wish to discuss any of the norms listed or add new ones.

Discussion Norms

• Respect Yourself and Others
  ○ (E.g., Actively listen; maintain confidentiality; and challenge ideas, not people)
• Acknowledge the Different Backgrounds and Experiences of Others
  ○ (E.g., Consider the role of your identities and power dynamics)
• Accept Challenge and Anticipate Discomfort
  ○ (E.g., Push your thinking; hold yourself and others accountable; and contribute to the conversation)
• Keep an Open Mind
  ○ (E.g., Allow for growth; listen before responding; and stay engaged)
• Embrace Uncertainty and Non-Closure

Norms adapted from "Leveraging Norms for Challenging Conversations," Developed by Whitney Polk in collaboration with Dr. Aaliyah El-Amin. Harvard Graduate School of Education, 2016.

Our protocol often leads to discussions that lean into analytical thinking and focus on the world of the case. As we've noted, this analytical lens, focused on characters and stakeholders outside ourselves, can make it easier to discuss the hard dilemmas that the case raises. We deliberately encourage users to think about viewpoints very different from their own and try to empathize with the people who hold them. However, there are many ways to enter a case discussion, as the conversations in this volume show, and case readers often find themselves identifying with different characters and dilemmas in very personal ways. The discussants featured in this volume frequently draw on their own personal experiences as they consider the dilemmas raised by the cases. In the discussion of "High School at the Coal-Face" (Chapter 4), for example, Kristy Pascoe starts the conversation with a vivid memory from her own time teaching at a school much like the school in the case. The dilemmas that the educators in the case face are Kristy's dilemmas, too. Likewise, in the discussion of "Photo Bomb" (Chapter 5), Helena Regojo Bacardi shares the "visceral response" that she had to the case "as a mother"—a gut reaction that two twelve-year-olds deserve to be expelled for creating and disseminating their classmate's topless photo, a course of action that Bacardi ultimately decides can't be justified "when you have to rationalize it." These cases stir up a variety of feelings in addition to more analytical thoughts and questions. Facilitators may choose to capitalize on these strong feelings of identification to bring readers into the world of the case, perhaps by asking them to choose a moment or line that struck them on a personal level.

In addition to sharing discussion norms, we take a moment to define the concept of a dilemma before we begin the discussion protocol. As seen in our facilitation guide, we define a dilemma as "a situation where there is no one right answer and it is hard (even impossible) to realize all important values and principles at once." In addition to the perennial usefulness of defining terms that the group will be discussing, sharing our definition of a dilemma helps to ground the conversation in values and emphasizes that there are no "right" courses of action that the case points readers to. Explicitly naming this focus on values and principles and de-emphasizing answers is yet another way that our protocol aims to give users the time and space to dive deeply into ethical challenges that are so often lacking in schools themselves.

Running a Standard Case Discussion

While there are many ways to discuss the cases in this volume, we do generally use our standard protocol when leading case discussions. As the facilitation guide illustrates, if time allows, we recommend beginning the conversation with a quick recap of the case. As an example, Daniella Forster begins the discussion about her case "High School at the Coal-Face" (Chapter 4) with a brief summary. The character charts printed at the start of each chapter in this volume can be helpful for reviewing the details of the case as well.

We also frequently pause after the first question in order to summarize the dilemmas raised by discussion participants. Because normative case studies include so many dilemmas, it can be nearly impossible to remember all those raised in the first ten to fifteen minutes of conversation. Lauren Bialystok gives an excellent summary of the dilemmas raised in the conversation about her case "Faith in Mr. D." (Chapter 9), which could be used as a model. While this task of summarizing might feel overwhelming to first-time facilitators, it becomes easier with subsequent facilitations as discussion leaders grow familiar with the dilemmas that are frequently raised. As they listen, facilitators might look for thematic connections between the dilemmas raised or consider at what level the dilemmas are located (classroom, school, district, or national level, for example). The conversation about "Course Correction" (Chapter 7) offers an example of this kind of summary.

Running Virtual Case Discussions
Over the past few years, we have facilitated many more virtual case discussions than we had in previous years. (Indeed, seven of the eight conversations printed in this book were conducted virtually!) We have found that our standard protocol works well for these discussions, though we have learned a few tips for translating the discussions into this virtual medium. As Bjorn Wansink notes in the conversation about "Feeling Exposed in Online Class" (Chapter 3), online facilitators miss "that '*fingerspitzen*'-feeling [context sensitivity]" that in-person facilitators rely on as they use nonverbal cues from participants to shape the conversation. Because establishing community can be tricky in the virtual space, we make sure to devote plenty of time at the beginning of our online discussions to introductions and icebreakers. Asking participants to keep their cameras on also helps to build community. We use the chat feature regularly during our virtual discussions. We might ask participants to write a response in the chat, for example, and then use a "waterfall" technique by asking everyone to post their response at the same time. Participants can then read each other's words and reflect on them; we often restart the conversation by asking someone to expand on what they wrote in the chat or asking participants to share patterns that they see. We particularly rely on these techniques for quieter groups and for larger groups, when we want to ensure that everyone gets a chance to share their thoughts.

Case adaptations

One common way that we adapt our cases is by creating reader's theater versions, read aloud immediately before the discussion. We often use reader's theater scripts in workshops when we haven't asked participants to read the case before arriving. These adaptations take the form of scripts that shorten the case slightly and divide the text into dialogue for the different characters and a narrator. Before students or educators discuss the case, we select volunteers to act out the roles in the script in front of the rest of the group. Reading the reader's theater case generally takes about ten to twelve minutes. Hearing the words spoken aloud can make the experience more engaging and make the characters and dilemmas seem more real, including for adult groups comprising graduate students, education professionals, or academics. We particularly appreciate this modification when running case discussions with very large groups. On our website (justiceinschools.org), you can find reader's theater scripts for many of the cases in this volume. You could also create script adaptations yourself using existing scripts as a model.

The cases in this volume can also be adapted based on the context in which they'll be taught. While we have run insightful, productive discussions of these cases with students and educators from many countries, there can be value in altering a case so that it better fits the needs of the context. As an example, in the German case "A Parallel Universe" (Chapter 2), sixteen-year-old Peter dominates classroom discourse with conspiracy theories that have distinctly anti-Semitic undertones. In arguing that the teachers must do more to protect Jewish students from these views, Peter's teacher Mr. Berger insists, "These 'theories' do not belong in the classroom, not in this school and not in this country with our history. It's simply not acceptable." While this argument resonates across contexts, instructors might consider adapting the case to include conspiracy theories rooted in their own country's challenging history. Here in the United States, for example, with our history steeped in racism and xenophobia, we might adapt the case so that Peter spouts White supremacist views, like the increasingly prominent conspiracy theory that immigrants of color are being brought to the United States to replace the White population and render Whites politically powerless or even extinct.[1] Adaptations such as these can make the dilemmas raised in the case feel more pertinent and urgent for readers.

But of course, even with a structured protocol, discussions sometimes go off the rails. We do not mean to suggest that the cases in this book are a magic key that can unlock productive dialogue. The sad reality is that we live in fractured times. Even those deeply committed to engaging in democratic discourse can stumble. Sustaining democratic discourse, while challenging, is the work of every citizen. We hope that the cases in this volume and the tips that we have shared here prove helpful for facilitators wishing to open such dialogue in their contexts.

Using the Conversations as Tools for Learning

Conversations as Models of Facilitation

One important function of the conversations in this book is to serve as models of facilitation. While our protocol provides the basic structure for a case discussion, facilitation has the power to deepen discussions and push conversations in different directions. Like classroom educators, facilitators often exist in silos. They rarely have the chance to be observed by or receive feedback from fellow facilitators in order to improve their craft; likewise, they rarely get the opportunity to observe and learn from their peers. Therefore, we hope that the conversations in this volume can serve as a model for strong facilitation moves. As an example, we appreciate how Ana Romero-Iribas regularly invites discussants to respond to one another's ideas in the conversation about her case "Photo Bomb" (Chapter 5). Daniella Forster and Meira Levinson, facilitating conversations about "High School at the Coal-Face" (Chapter 4) and "Taking the Action Out of Civics?" (Chapter 6), respectively, both ground the discussion in the world of the case by connecting the discussants' comments to views held by specific characters, whom they reference by name.

At the same time, we hope that the conversations can serve as texts that invite reflection and critique. For example, in her facilitation Daniella Forster comments on the "alignment" in her discussants' viewpoints several times. What are the benefits and potential drawbacks to focusing on alignment in diverse groups? What would be the benefits and drawbacks of exploring divergence instead? As another example, in the discussion of "No Laughing Matter" (Chapter 8), the discussants quite quickly dismiss the idea of using offensive *Charlie Hebdo* cartoons in the classroom, even to dissect the Islamophobic stereotypes they promote. How might the conversation look different if facilitator Sara O'Brien had pushed the group to delve into the reasoning *for* using the cartoons, given their strong feeling that using the cartoons would be "crazy," in the words of David Kerr? When is it appropriate for facilitators to step into the role of devil's advocate? How strong a role should they play in shaping the conversation when participants are leading it elsewhere? We hope that readers of these conversations—particularly those who facilitate case discussions themselves—will take time to reflect on these types of questions to analyze and critique the conversations presented here.

Here are some possible activities that instructors and professional development leaders might employ to help users analyze the conversations as models of facilitation:

- *Analyze facilitation moves.* This activity might be especially helpful in professional development for educators or in university settings with students training to be teachers. Where do users see facilitation moves they'd like to emulate in their own practice? Where do they find moments that they might have facilitated differently? How might different facilitation moves have altered the conversation? These are useful questions for individual reflection and small-group or whole-group discussion.
- *Find starting points for new conversations.* Conversations by nature include forks in the road, moments in which one possible pathway is abandoned as a discussant and/or the facilitator leads the group down a different path. Users might analyze the cases for such moments and then use these moments in different ways. Students in undergraduate or graduate settings might take them as a starting point for a written commentary or a new conversation. Educators could create questions that they want to explore with their own students. In a professional development setting, the facilitator might in fact use these moments as the starting point for conversation that happens on the spot with participants.

Conversations as Insights into the Cases

Beyond their use in exploring the power of facilitation, the conversations offer substantive insights into the dilemmas raised by the cases, providing rich moments to explore through reflection and discussion. Clearly, there are too many such moments throughout this volume to name, but as an example, the conversation about "Taking the Action Out of Civics?" (Chapter 6) brings to light important insights into the ways that schools function as spaces of both civic preparation and civic engagement. Fernando Reimers probes the different values and beliefs that stakeholders bring to their conceptions of civic education. What kind of citizen should schools aim to create: the personally responsible citizen, the participatory citizen, or the social-justice oriented citizen? This framework offers a lens for reading the characters' disagreements about the action civics program and the school's broader civic education curriculum. However, in response, Andrew Wilkes leans into schools as sites of civic interest and action themselves and the ways that the "dynamic of power and influence" makes them inequitable sites of civic engagement: "[Concerned parent] Mr. Warner's op-ed reflects over-representation of some citizens getting their views into papers of record relative to others. So, there's a kind of uneven level of voice among citizens that I think initiates the conversation." Yet Robert Pondiscio points out that, ironically, the concerned parent in question is practicing exactly the kind of civic skills that the action civics project hopes to nurture: "Who is the most effective civic actor in this case study? It's Mr. Warner who wrote the op-ed." These comments provide insight into the ways that opportunities for meaningful civic engagement are inequitably distributed across American society, highlighting the importance of preparing future citizens—from all backgrounds—to bridge the gap.

The conversations also open new lines of inquiry into the cases and the dilemmas they raise. In the conversation about "Feeling Exposed in Online Class" (Chapter 3), for example, discussants explore the dilemmas that protagonist, a civics instructor, faces after her online controversial issues discussion is interrupted by an incensed parent who has been listening off-screen. In the conversation, Belinda Kleijweg raises interesting questions about the civic nature of the online classroom by lamenting the instructor's lack of "control" in online classes, where "everyone has an equal slice of the screen." Does this unusual equality make the online classroom too unpredictable to be used as a space for civil discourse or instead the perfect space for civic discourse, being perhaps more democratic than the typically hierarchical in-person classroom? An instructor or facilitator might use the conversations in this volume to generate similar questions to spark discussion among their learners.

Conversations as Tools for Surfacing Intuitions and Assumptions

The model conversations presented here also raise interesting questions about the intuitions and assumptions that operate within the cases themselves. As Lauren Bialystok reminds us in the conversation about her case "Faith in Mr. D." (Chapter 9), "The way we even say what a dilemma is or isn't takes for granted certain features of the situation." As an example, in the conversation about "Course Correction" (Chapter 7), Chloé Valdary starts a discussion examining the assumptions that the protagonist, a middle school principal, holds about the critical consciousness course that's under threat. Should we immediately assume, as the principal does, that spreading the curriculum from that one course into multiple classes would "dilute" the material? Building on Chloé's comments, the discussants unpack the principal's assumption by asking questions about the nature of resistance and the dogmas held by people on both sides of the ideological divides in the United States. Similarly, in the conversation about "No Laughing Matter" (Chapter 8), Shammi Rahman questions school leaders' use of the term "White British" in the case, leading to a discussion of the ways that Muslim students are viewed in the school in question. Are there underlying biases in the school culture causing Muslim students to be viewed as outsiders, which might contribute to the rising Islamophobia that the educators in the case are now trying to quell? By interrogating the assumptions that lead the characters in the cases—and sometimes the discussants themselves—to take certain aspects of the dilemmas for granted, these conversations help educators, students, and community members look at ethical questions in new ways.

At the same time, the conversations raise interesting questions about the intuitions and assumptions that readers themselves bring to the cases. The cases and conversations in this volume take place across a variety of national contexts and thus provide insights into how ethical dilemmas are framed in those contexts. Yet they also invite us to reflect on the ways that we ourselves frame the dilemmas, as well as the intuitions and assumptions that underlie that framing. As an example, we have run case discussions of "Photo Bomb" (Chapter 5) with many international groups and have been continually fascinated by the myriad views on how much responsibility the twelve-year-old girl whose topless photo has been captured and shared by her classmates should bear for her situation. Many American readers have cast the young girl solely as a victim of her classmates' cruelty, critiquing as unfairly sexist the notion (raised in the case) that the girl is at fault. Yet the Spanish discussants featured in this volume speak about the girl both as a victim and as someone who must be "feeling guilty about what she did, largely of her own free will," according to Carlos-María Alcover, an interesting tension to explore. What do we mean when we talk about the girl's "responsibility" in the case? What assumptions shape our thinking—and how are these assumptions shaped by the cultural norms and mores of our contexts? How does our assignment of "responsibility" for the incident at the heart of the case impact our decisions about how the school should respond—and about how all schools should view their responsibilities to educate students in digital citizenship? While this example is one that has long intrigued us, all of the conversations in this volume offer such moments that provide users the opportunity to reflect on the unconscious values and beliefs that shape their own ethical decision-making.

Here are some activities that instructors and facilitators might employ when using the conversations as tools for surfacing institutions and assumptions.

- *Analyze the assumptions at play—in the conversations and our responses.* It's very hard—for all of us!—to spot the assumptions that we bring to case discussions, given the unconscious nature of assumptions. However, when users read conversations about cases that take place in contexts very different from their own, it can provide an opportunity for them to compare their own reactions to those of the discussants, surfacing assumptions at play in the conversation. Instructors and facilitators might encourage learners to "get curious" about their reactions to the conversations, as Chloé Valdary suggests the principal in "Course Correction" should do (Chapter 7). What can the conversations teach us about the ways that ethical dilemmas are viewed in other contexts? What do our reactions to the viewpoints in the conversations reveal about our own intuitions and assumptions, whether they are similar to or quite different from those held by the discussants?
- *Consider which viewpoints are missing.* While we have made every effort to create diverse groups of discussants for this volume, there's only so much diversity that can be packed into a four-person group. Users might analyze the conversations presented here to consider not merely which views are present but also which views are missing. University instructors might assign students to conduct interviews to solicit a wider variety of viewpoints on the dilemmas in the case or even organize their own discussions and generate their own transcripts. Facilitators leading professional development might draw on the expertise and diversity in the room to surface viewpoints that are currently missing from the conversations recorded for this volume.

Conclusion

While the cases and conversations in this book have many uses, we hope that, at their heart, they serve as models of what it looks like for diverse groups to engage in dialogue about challenging issues with no easy solutions. The cases themselves are carefully constructed to show multiple contrasting, reasonable views on complex ethical challenges. The conversations serve as even stronger models. Like students and educators who will discuss the cases presented here, the discussants in this volume puzzled out their views on complex ethical challenges in real time—no easy task! Yet the resulting conversations illustrate what it looks like to consider new viewpoints, revise one's thinking, and disagree respectfully, key skills for democratic discourse.

However these cases and conversations are used, whether in classroom, professional, or community settings, we hope they provide one tool in the important work of shoring up democracy. Schools are vital democratic spaces, where not only young people but also adults encounter new viewpoints. The civic lessons imparted in schools extend well beyond the civics classroom, as the cases and conversations in this volume show. We hope that this work shines a light on those civic lessons, both implicit and explicit, and provides an opening for conversations about what democratic citizens around the world hope those civic lessons will ideally impart.

Note

1. Called "the great replacement," this conspiracy theory has inspired mass shootings in the United States and is unfortunately becoming increasingly mainstream. According to a 2022 poll, one in three American adults believes in some version of this conspiracy theory. Odette Yousef, "The 'Great Replacement' Conspiracy Theory Isn't Fringe Anymore, It's Mainstream," *NPR*, May 17, 2022, sec. Race, https://www.npr.org/2022/05/17/1099233034/the-great-replacement-conspiracy-theory-isnt-fringe-anymore-its-mainstream.

Appendix

Case Discussion Facilitation Guide (for 90 minutes, with notes for modification)	
Before the Discussion	
Consider the goals for your discussion. • Who is your audience? How well do they know each other? • Why is this group coming together? Determine which materials you will need. • Will you distribute the case before the discussion? (Is it reasonable to expect participants to read it before the event?) • Will you devote time during the event for participants to read the case or perform the reader's theater script (see Case adaptations)? • Are there any other materials that you wish to distribute alongside the case? Determine group size(s). We recommend ideally 6–12 people per discussion group. • Will you run one whole-group discussion yourself? • Will you break a large group into smaller groups? Will those groups be self-facilitated or will you require a team of facilitators?	**Notes**: When we run case discussions in undergraduate or graduate courses, we generally ask students to read the cases—and any accompanying academic sources—before the discussion. When running professional development with in-service educators, we sometimes ask our participants to read the case in advance, but we also often rely on reader's theater scripts, knowing how many demands teachers have on their time. Consider how you can maximize participation and learning for the group that you are working with.
Introductions (5–10 minutes)	
Ask each member of the group to share their names and pronouns (if desired), along with any additional information that may be useful (professional role for educators, academic major for students, etc.). You may also include an icebreaker question for community building.	**Notes**: For virtual discussions, we often have discussion participants call on the next person to help the introductions run more smoothly. **Modifications**: If all members of the group already know each other well, you can omit introductions.

Discussion Norms (5 minutes)	
Share a list of discussion norms for the conversation with participants. Once participants have had a chance to review the list, ask whether they wish to discuss or amend any norms or to add any new ones.	*Notes*: You can find a list of norms that we often use on page 178. *Modifications*: If the group meets regularly, you can likely do a quick review of existing norms here.
Case Recap (5 minutes)	
Ask a volunteer to share key case details, using the character and setting chart at the beginning of the case. Other participants can chime in with ideas they feel have been missed. The goal of the recap is to remind participants about the "facts of the case" before they begin discussing the dilemmas.	*Notes*: While it's nice to have members of the group provide the recap, to save time you could present a short written recap or have the facilitator give a recap. *Modifications*: If you are using a reader's theater script, you should omit the case recap. Be sure to budget 10–12 minutes for the group to perform the script.
Discussion: What are the dilemmas? (15–20 minutes)	
Before diving into the discussion, establish a common understanding of the term "dilemma." We share the following definition: • Dilemma: A situation where there is no one right answer and it is hard (even impossible) to realize all important values and principles at once. Begin the actual case discussion by asking participants to surface the dilemmas in the case, using the following questions: • What are the dilemmas in this case? For whom are they dilemmas?	*Notes*: We often ask discussion participants to start by naming the most obvious dilemma, the one that's likely on most people's minds. Then we move to exploring dilemmas within that main dilemma and to looking at other dilemmas that might not be so obvious. *Modifications*: If you are short on time, you can shorten this section to 10 minutes. But we recommend giving the group as close to 15–20 minutes as possible.

Discussion: Why are these dilemmas? (15–20 minutes)	

Before asking the next question in the protocol, give a short summary (2–3 minutes) of the dilemmas raised. Then, use the following questions:
• Why are these dilemmas?
  ○ What values or principles are at stake? Do people disagree about which values matter, which should take precedence, or how they apply in this case?
  ○ What practical and/or policy considerations are at stake? Do people disagree about which considerations are relevant, which should take precedence, or how they should be addressed in this case?
	Notes: You may wish to provide discussion participants with a list of possible values that might be at stake in the case.
	
	Modifications: If you are short on time, you can shorten this section to 10 minutes. But we recommend giving the group as close to 15–20 minutes as possible.

Discussion: What *might* be done in this case? (5–10 minutes)	

Have discussion participants brainstorm possible courses of action that might be taken in the case. These can address any of the dilemmas raised and may be explored within the case or be totally novel. Use the following questions:
• What choices are available, and to whom?
  ○ How does each of these choices frame and address the issues at stake?
  ○ For each choice, what is gained? What is lost?
	Notes: You may wish to give participants time to brainstorm or discuss in pairs before opening this question to the group, if time allows.
	
	Modifications: If you are pressed for time, omit this section and instead move to the next question of what should be done.

Discussion: What *should* be done in this case? (5–10 minutes)	
Ask participants to consider what should be done in the case, using the following question: • What do you think should be done in this case, and by whom? Why?	**Notes**: Remember that there is no one best course of action in these cases (though some courses of action are definitely better than others, and some actions would be wrong to take). Participants should not be looking for the "right answer." Be sure to ask people to explain why they believe that the course of action they chose should be taken.

Reflection (10–20 minutes)	

Before ending the discussion, ask participants to reflect on the case and their experience discussing it. Use (some of) the following questions:
• What have you learned from talking about this case that might apply to other ethical dilemmas in education?
  ○ What principles or values are you thinking about for the first time, or thinking about in a new way?
  ○ What policies or practices are you thinking about for the first time or in a new way?
• What value is there, if any, to talking through a case like this with others?
  ○ What did you learn about yourself?
  ○ What did you learn about others?
  ○ What did you learn about your institution, organization, or broader context?
  ○ What did you learn about the process itself?
• What have you learned from this case and/or discussion that you'd like to take back to your own classroom/school/context?
• Is there anything else you want to bring up or discuss?
	Notes: *It's nearly impossible that you'd have time to ask all of the reflection questions listed here! Think about which questions will be most helpful for the group that you're facilitating and choose one or two accordingly.*
	Modifications: *If this group is coming together for a specific purpose, you may want to tailor the reflection to that purpose. In the past, we have used this reflection time for discipline or grade-level teams to chat about implications for their classrooms, for example. We have also used this time for teachers across a district to reflect on the ways the case discussion helps them think about new policies being implemented. In our experience, discussion participants find this chance for reflection very meaningful—be sure to leave enough time for it in your discussion.*

Bibliography

Australian Institute of Aboriginal and Torres Strait Islander Studies. "Welcome to Country." Australian Institute of Aboriginal and Torres Strait Islander Studies, May 25, 2022. https://aiatsis.gov.au/explore/welcome-country.

Barton, Keith, and Alan McCully. "Teaching Controversial Issues ... Where Controversial Issues Really Matter." *Teaching History* 127 (2007): 13–19.

Buchanan, Larry, Quoctrung Bui, and Jugal K. Patel. "Black Lives Matter May Be the Largest Movement in U.S. History." *The New York Times*, July 3, 2020, sec. U.S. https://www.nytimes.com/interactive/2020/07/03/us/george-floyd-protests-crowd-size.html.

"Code of Conduct." Implementation document for Code of Conduct Policy. New South Wales Department of Education, October 19, 2022. https://education.nsw.gov.au/content/dam/main-education/policy-library/associated-documents/pd-2004-0020-01.pdf.

"Commercial Arrangements, Sponsorship and Donations." Implementation document for the Commercial Arrangements, Sponsorship and Donations Policy. New South Wales Department of Education, November 16, 2022. https://education.nsw.gov.au/content/dam/main-education/policy-library/associated-documents/pd-2009-0399-01.pdf.

Dahlgren, Kari. "The Moral Case for Coal: The Ethics of Complicity with and amongst Australian Pro-coal Lobbyists." *The Australian Journal of Anthropology* 32, no. 1 (2021): 19–32. https://doi.org/10.1111/taja.12389.

Ellis, Greg. "Mining Company Supports School Students and Their Families." *Illawarra Mercury*, October 25, 2021, sec. Business. https://www.illawarramercury.com.au/story/7483842/mining-company-supports-school-students-and-their-families/.

GOV.UK. "Revised Prevent Duty Guidance: For England and Wales," April 1, 2021. https://www.gov.uk/government/publications/prevent-duty-guidance/revised-prevent-duty-guidance-for-england-and-wales.

Hess, Diana E. "Discussing Controversial Public Issues in Secondary Social Studies Classrooms: Learning from Skilled Teachers." *Theory & Research in Social Education* 30, no. 1 (2002): 10–41. https://doi.org/10.1080/00933104.2002.10473177.

Holland, Robert G. "Would Revived Civics End Up Being Progressive Ed Redux?—The Heartland Institute." *The Heartland Institute* (blog), November 19, 2017. https://heartland.org/opinion/would-revived-civics-end-up-being-progressive-ed-redux/.

Jain, Sonia, and Alison K. Cohen. "Fostering Resilience among Urban Youth Exposed to Violence: A Promising Area for Interdisciplinary Research and Practice." *Health Education & Behavior: The Official Publication of the Society for Public Health Education* 40, no. 6 (2013): 651–62. https://doi.org/10.1177/1090198113492761.

Johnson, Theodore R., Emelia Gold, and Ashley Zhao. "How Anti-Critical Race Theory Bills Are Taking Aim at Teachers." *FiveThirtyEight* (blog), May 9, 2022. https://fivethirtyeight.com/features/how-anti-critical-race-theory-bills-are-taking-aim-at-teachers/.

Kaplan, Talia. "Maine Father Fights Critical Race Theory in Daughters' School: 'We Need Education, Not Indoctrination.'" Text Article. *Fox News*, June 1, 2021. https://www.foxnews.com/media/maine-father-critical-race-theory-we-need-education-not-indoctrination.

Kingkade, Tyler, Brandy Zadrozny, and Ben Collins. "'Held Hostage': How Critical Race Theory Moved from Fox News to School Boards." *NBC News*, June 15, 2021. https://www.nbcnews.com/news/us-news/critical-race-theory-invades-school-boards-help-conservative-groups-n1270794.

Kirshner, Ben, and Kimberly Geil. "'I'm about to Really Bring It!' Access Points between Youth Activists and Adult Community Leaders." *Children, Youth and Environments* 20, no. 2 (2010): 1–24.

Kurtz, Stanley. "'Action Civics' Replaces Citizenship with Partisanship." *The American Mind*, January 26, 2021. https://americanmind.org/memo/action-civics-replaces-citizenship-with-partisanship/.

Kurtz, Stanley. "How Dems Will Push Protest Civics and CRT on Schools." *National Review* (blog), June 1, 2021. https://www.nationalreview.com/corner/how-dems-will-push-protest-civics-and-crt-on-schools/.

Lee, Nam-Jin, Dhavan V. Shah, and Jack M. McLeod. "Processes of Political Socialization: A Communication Mediation Approach to Youth Civic Engagement." *Communication Research* 40, no. 5 (2013): 669–97. https://doi.org/10.1177/0093650212436712.

Levinson, Meira. "Action Civics in the Classroom." *Social Education* 78, no. 2 (2014): 68–72.

Levinson, Meira, and Jacob Fay, eds. *Dilemmas of Educational Ethics: Cases and Commentaries*. Cambridge, MA: Harvard Education Press, 2016.

Littenberg-Tobias, Joshua, and Alison K. Cohen. "Diverging Paths: Understanding Racial Differences in Civic Engagement among White, African American, and Latina/o Adolescents Using Structural Equation Modeling." *American Journal of Community Psychology* 57, no. 1–2 (2016): 102–17. https://doi.org/10.1002/ajcp.12027.

McCoy, Jennifer, Tahmina Rahman, and Murat Somer. "Polarization and the Global Crisis of Democracy: Common Patterns, Dynamics, and Pernicious

Consequences for Democratic Polities." *American Behavioral Scientist* 62, no. 1 (2018): 16–42. https://doi.org/10.1177/0002764218759576.

Moseley, Brandon. "Conservatives Hold Conference on Banning Critical Race Theory, Common Core." *Alabama Political Reporter*, June 28, 2021. https://www.alreporter.com/2021/06/28/conservatives-hold-conference-on-banning-critical-race-theory-common-core/.

New South Wales Mining. "School Mine Tours Program—Upper Hunter Mining Dialogue." Accessed May 20, 2023. https://miningdialogue.com.au/engagement/school-tours.

Ore, Adeshola. "The Gonski 'Failure': Why Did It Happen and Who Is to Blame for the 'Defrauding' of Public Schools?" *The Guardian*, March 12, 2022, sec. Australia news. https://www.theguardian.com/australia-news/2022/mar/13/the-gonski-failure-why-did-it-happen-and-who-is-to-blame-for-the-defrauding-of-public-schools.

Randall, David. "Oklahoma Education Agency Promotes Progressive Activism Masquerading …." Oklahoma Council of Public Affairs, December 26, 2019. https://www.ocpathink.org/post/perspective-magazine/oklahoma-education-agency-promotes-progressive-activism-masquerading-as-civics.

Reid, Ellis, and Meira Levinson. "Normative Case Studies as Democratic Education." In *The Cambridge Handbook of Democratic Education*, edited by Julian Culp, Johannes Drerup, and Douglas Yacek, 129–45. Cambridge: Cambridge University Press, 2023.

Save The Children. "Ciberacoso o ciberbullying." Accessed May 20, 2023. https://www.savethechildren.es/donde/espana/violencia-contra-la-infancia/ciberacoso-ciberbullying.

Schain, Martin A. "Shifting Tides: Radical-Right Populism and Immigration Policy in Europe and the United States." Migration Policy Institute, August 2018.

School Strike 4 Climate Australia. "Home | SS4C." Accessed May 20, 2023. https://www.schoolstrike4climate.com.

Schwartz, Sarah. "Map: Where Critical Race Theory Is under Attack." *Education Week*, June 11, 2021, sec. Policy & Politics, States. https://www.edweek.org/policy-politics/map-where-critical-race-theory-is-under-attack/2021/06.

Shapiro, Joan Poliner, and Jacqueline A. Stefkovich. *Ethical Leadership and Decision Making in Education: Applying Theoretical Perspectives to Complex Dilemmas*. 5th ed. New York: Routledge, 2021. https://doi.org/10.4324/9781003022862.

Shawcross CVO, William. "Independent Review of Prevent." House of Commons, February 8, 2023. https://www.gov.uk/government/publications/independent-review-of-prevents-report-and-government-response.

Simmons, Kassie. "Brunswick County Leaders Tackle Critical Race Theory, Other 'Divisive' Theories." *WECT News*, June 9, 2021. https://www.wect.com/2021/06/08/brunswick-county-leaders-tackle-critical-race-theory-other-divisive-theories/.

StatLine—Statistics Netherlands. "Bevolking; geslacht, lft, generatie en migr. achtergrond, 1 jan; 1996–2022," May 31, 2022. https://opendata.cbs.nl/statline/#/CBS/nl/dataset/37325/table.

The Annenberg Public Policy Center of the University of Pennsylvania. "Annenberg Civics Knowledge Survey Archives." Accessed May 20, 2023. https://www.annenbergpublicpolicycenter.org/political-communication/civics-knowledge-survey/.

Vasilogambros, Matt. "After Capitol Riot, Some States Turn to Civics Education." *Stateline* (blog), May 19, 2021. https://stateline.org/2021/05/19/after-capitol-riot-some-states-turn-to-civics-education/.

Waxman, Olivia B. "Anti-'Critical Race Theory' Laws Are Working. Teachers Are Thinking Twice about How They Talk about Race." *Time*, June 30, 2022. https://time.com/6192708/critical-race-theory-teachers-racism/.

Wynne, Emma, and Jo Trilling. "Harmless Fun or Troubling Incursion? Science Lesson Sponsored by Oil and Gas Giant Sparks Debate." *ABC Radio Perth*, August 20, 2021. https://www.abc.net.au/news/2021-08-20/oil-exploration-kids-science-lesson/100388140.

Yousef, Odette. "The 'Great Replacement' Conspiracy Theory Isn't Fringe Anymore, It's Mainstream." *NPR*, May 17, 2022, sec. Race. https://www.npr.org/2022/05/17/1099233034/the-great-replacement-conspiracy-theory-isnt-fringe-anymore-its-mainstream.

Zuboff, Shoshana. *The Age of Surveillance Capitalism: The Fight for a Human Future at the New Frontier of Power*. First Trade Paperback Edition. New York: Public Affairs, 2020.

INDEX

Aboriginal
   community 57, 67 n.5
   culture 59
   education 52, 59
   knowledge 61, 64
   people 56, 63, 68 n.7, 68 n.9
   values 59–61
Aboriginal Education Officers (AEOs) 52, 68 n.7
accommodation 7–9, 103, 156–71
action civics 7, 91–108, 110 n.6, 184
adolescence 80, 86
affirmative action 94, 112 n.15
agency 92, 99–100, 106, 125, 168, 170–1
Annenberg Civics Knowledge Survey 112 n.12
antisemitism 17, 27, 141

Bell, Derrick 130–1
Beutelsbacher Konsens 24, 26
Brown v. Board of Education 130–1
bullying 6, 71–2, 79, 85

Canada 8, 155–6, 171–2
care 17–18, 32, 35, 77, 80–1, 124, 129–30, 132, 141, 148, 150, 156
Charlie Hebdo cartoons 7, 136–7, 139–41, 143, 146, 150–1, 182
chilling effect 7, 115, 143
Christianity 18, 119, 123, 126, 128–9, 155, 160–2, 167
citizenship 6, 37–9, 41, 45, 108, 146–7, 149, 166
civic
   education 2, 4–8, 10–12, 32, 35, 45, 91, 98–9, 106–7, 175, 177, 184

engagement 112 n.14, 183–4
knowledge 7, 91–2, 99
learning 2, 5, 91, 170
mission 7
classroom 5, 7–8, 13, 17, 19–21, 23–4, 26, 28–9, 31, 35–40, 44–5, 51, 56, 62, 64, 83, 92, 95, 97–8, 100, 102–3, 108, 117, 126–8, 138, 141, 143, 145, 158, 162, 176, 181–2, 184, 187
climate change 1, 9, 49, 54, 60–2
collaboration 4–4, 45, 82, 150
collaborative ethical inquiry 3–4
communication 5, 43, 91, 102
community
   Aboriginal 57, 67 n.5
   Christian 128
   engagement 59
   Muslim 143, 148–9
   school 6, 49–50, 52, 106, 149, 162
   values 59–60, 104–6, 128, 144, 150–1
Comunidad de Madrid 72, 89 n.4
congregational prayers 164–5
conspiracy theories 1, 5, 13, 15–16, 18–21, 23–7, 181
controversial issues 5, 16, 23–4, 31–3, 36, 38, 40–2, 44–6, 95, 108, 144–5, 184
Counter-Terrorism and Security Act (Prevent Act) (UK) 135
Covid-19 13–14, 16, 19, 31, 33, 37–40, 50
crime 36, 42, 74, 76, 78, 83–4, 89 n.7
critical consciousness 7, 116–19, 121–2, 124, 127–8, 131, 185
critical race theory 7, 130
critical thinking 7, 11, 15–16, 18, 23, 26, 28, 46, 122, 140, 146

curiosity 129–31
curriculum 23, 33, 58, 61–4, 92–9, 105, 118, 122–7, 131, 137, 146, 148–52, 157, 184–5
cyberbullying 71–2, 76–7, 79, 85, 89 n.8

democracy 1–2, 8, 43, 98, 105–7, 144, 146, 148, 175–6, 187
Department for Education (DfE) 141–2, 144, 151
dialogue 8, 11, 18, 23, 53, 59, 100–1, 103, 130, 166, 170–1, 181–2, 187
discussion 3–5, 8–11, 15, 19–26, 28, 31–45, 92, 94–6, 101, 104, 106, 117, 130, 136–7, 140, 142, 146, 151, 163, 166–7, 169, 171, 176–86, 189–92
diversity 3–4, 7–8, 11, 46, 79–80, 85, 98, 100, 115, 136, 155, 162, 166, 168–9, 177, 186

education
　Aboriginal 52, 59
　achievements 16, 65
　aims of 2–4, 11
　citizenship 45, 146, 152, 172
　civic 2, 4–8, 10–12, 32, 35, 45, 91, 98–9, 106–7, 175, 177, 184
　justice 3–4
　online 34, 39–40
　primary 35, 86, 152
　private 6, 55, 71
　public 8–9, 53, 57–61, 104–5, 108, 160–4
　secondary 35
emotion 21–2, 39, 41, 44, 81, 84, 86–7, 131
empathy 81–2, 108, 123, 178
endorsement 9, 155, 169–70
engaged ethical inquiry 3
environment 9, 16, 25, 29, 38–9, 53–4, 56–61, 145, 147
equity/equality 4, 8–9, 80, 93, 95, 97–8, 116, 120, 159, 162, 164–5, 168, 184
ethical sensitivity 10, 176
extremism/extremist 137, 143, 151

facilitation guide 10, 176, 179–80, 182–3, 189–92
families 6, 16, 20, 25, 55, 58–9, 74–8, 81–2, 85, 87, 94, 102, 109, 120, 130, 139, 141, 144, 161
family engagement 20, 22–3, 25, 27, 59, 82, 130–1
fossil fuels 49, 55, 63–4
free speech 1, 139
Friday prayer 8–9, 156, 158, 161–3, 168–9
friendship 23, 80–1, 87, 120
Fugitive Pedagogy (Givens) 126
fund/funding 6, 49–56, 61, 63–5, 107, 155, 160–1

gay marriage 119
gender 8–9, 115–17, 128
　equality 8, 159, 162, 165
　equity 9, 168
　inequality 9, 170
Generation Citizen 100–1, 111 n.8
Gesamtschule (comprehensive school) 13, 24
girls 9, 15, 22, 42, 71, 79, 81, 94, 102, 130, 158–9, 162, 165, 171, 185
Givens, Jarvis 126
great replacement 187 n.1

HB3979 113 n.22
Heath Parents for Education (HPE) 116–17
Higher School Certificate (Australia) 53, 57
Hirsch, Jr. E. D. 102
Holocaust 38, 141
homework 16, 22, 28
homosexuality 119, 128–9
hypocrisy 120, 126–7, 131

indoctrination 58, 64, 92–3, 99, 101, 116
inequity/inequality 9, 36, 47, 132, 170
integrity 127, 131–2
intellectualist approach 101
interdisciplinary ethical inquiry 3

INDEX

Islam 135, 139, 141, 161–2, 168–71
Islamophobia 137–9, 141, 145, 147, 170, 185

judgment 10–12, 103
jummah prayers 156–9, 164–5, 168
justice 81
   educational 3–4
   ethic of 124
   social 65, 101, 118–19, 126, 129, 184

King Jr. Martin Luther 131
knowledge 4, 7, 23, 26, 37, 40, 58, 61, 64, 91–2, 99, 101–4, 145, 150, 166, 177

laïcité 166
Land Rights Act (Australia) 57
leadership 9, 130, 132, 144–5, 149–51, 168, 170
legislation 7, 36, 105, 107, 115, 172
liberalism 166–7, 170–1
loyalty 80, 104

MBO-Holland 31–4, 45
media 5–6, 15, 20–1, 26, 32, 34–5, 49, 75, 102, 118, 140, 156–7
microaggressions 121, 126
mining industry 6, 49–50, 52–65
Mob 53, 68 n.9
model conversations 2–3, 8–11, 184
Muhammad, Prophet 137, 139–40, 145, 154, 154 n.3, 167–8
Multi-Academy Trust (MAT) 7, 135–6, 142–3, 146, 149
multiculturalism 8, 155–6, 165–6
Muslim 7–9, 135–49, 153, 156–8, 160–4, 166–72, 185
Muslim Student Associations 168

National Action Civics Collaborative 111 n.4
Native Title Act (Australia) 57
normative case studies 2–12, 175–6, 180
norms 1, 11, 101, 177–9, 185, 190

Ohio 108–9
Oklahoma 105
online classroom 31, 34, 36, 38–40, 184
Ontario school 8, 155, 163, 171–2

pandemic 5–6, 13–14, 16–17, 31, 36, 38, 40
parents
   community 71
   and kids 94
   rights 10, 103, 122
   and the school 80–3, 122
   values 100–1
   voice 15, 23, 59–61, 123, 184
pedagogy 5, 40, 45, 62, 108, 122, 124, 145
polarization 1, 11, 107
police 40, 83, 99, 156
political activism 91, 103, 113 n.22
population 13–14, 31, 79, 137, 142, 156, 162, 181
pornography 72, 74, 83, 89 n.6
power industry 59
practical wisdom 10, 176
Prevent Act 135
privacy 1, 32, 82, 84
propaganda 15, 58, 119
public deliberation 23
punishment 76, 83, 151
Putnam, Robert 105

Querdenker movement 5, 13, 16, 18–19, 21, 23

race 7–8, 56, 115–17, 128, 140
radicalization 7, 42, 135, 137–8
relationship 5, 16, 39, 52, 55, 63, 81, 87, 94, 104, 108, 124
religion/religious 7–9, 94, 128, 135–6, 138–9, 144, 149–50, 155–7, 159–72
Religious Education (RE) 136, 144, 146, 152
representation 101, 138, 140, 184
respect 5, 7, 11, 16, 23–4, 33, 36, 43, 55–6, 73, 75–6, 78–82, 84–6, 94, 138–44, 146, 162, 166–7, 171

responsibility 6, 8, 19–20, 25, 39, 42, 49, 74–5, 77–81, 83, 85, 130, 141, 144–5, 155, 185–6

safety 5, 19, 34–7, 42, 46, 95, 117, 120, 127–8, 144
school
   control 33, 108, 184
   culture 6, 46, 108, 185
   duty of care 141
   funding 49–50, 53, 160
   K-12 6, 71, 91, 98, 109, 115
   primary 29, 51, 146, 150, 163
   private 55, 105
   public 8–9, 25, 49, 53, 57–9, 68 n.7, 104–5, 155, 160, 162–4, 168
   secondary 13, 152, 171
   sponsorships 49–55, 63–4, 67 n.1
Schulpflicht (compulsory schooling) 25
scientific knowledge 23, 61
Scott, James 125
secularism 145, 155, 159, 162–7, 172
self-esteem 80, 84–5
sexism 118
Shawcross CVO, William 143, 153–4 n.2
Sikhism 139
South Dakota 105
Spanish flu 14
Spanish law 89 n.7
standards 54, 76, 104–5, 116, 118, 125–6, 128, 179–80

STEM education 59, 61
stereotypes 85, 135, 137, 141, 182
students
   activism 98–9, 103
   engagement 34, 95–6, 100
   Muslim 140, 156–7, 160–3, 166, 168–9, 172, 185
   non-Muslim 158, 164
   rights 7–8, 10, 15, 24, 40, 76, 83, 96–7

teachers
   citizenship 41
   French 154 n.3, 158
   values 80
technology 1, 5–6, 22, 40, 50, 58, 61, 78, 82, 172
Ter Info (FYI) 38
terrorism 135, 137, 143, 153–4 n.2
Texas 91, 104–5, 113 n.22, 123
Trump, Donald 13, 115

vaccines 14–16
victimization 84
violence 18, 40, 71, 99, 112 n.14
vocational education 31
vulnerability 34–5, 170

Wisconsin 105

Zoom 32, 36, 136